PASTORAL IDENTITY AS SOCIAL CONSTRUCTION

PASTORAL IDENTITY AS SOCIAL CONSTRUCTION

Pastoral Identity in Postmodern, Intercultural, and Multifaith Contexts

Samuel Park

Foreword by Christie Cozad Neuger

◆PICKWICK *Publications* • Eugene, Oregon

PASTORAL IDENTITY AS SOCIAL CONSTRUCTION
Pastoral Identity in Postmodern, Intercultural, and Multifaith Contexts

Copyright © 2017 Samuel Park. All rights reserved. Except for brief quotations in critical publications or reviews, no part of this book may be reproduced in any manner without prior written permission from the publisher. Write: Permissions, Wipf and Stock Publishers, 199 W. 8th Ave., Suite 3, Eugene, OR 97401.

Pickwick Publications
An Imprint of Wipf and Stock Publishers
199 W. 8th Ave., Suite 3
Eugene, OR 97401

www.wipfandstock.com

PAPERBACK ISBN: 978-1-61097-507-0
HARDCOVER ISBN: 978-1-4982-8743-2
EBOOK ISBN: 978-1-5326-3116-0

Cataloging-in-Publication data:

Names: Park, Samuel

Title: Pastoral identity as social construction: pastoral identity in postmodern, intercultural, and multifaith contexts / by Samuel Park.

Description: Eugene, OR : Pickwick Publications, 2017 | Includes bibliographical references.

Identifiers: ISBN 978-1-61097-507-0 (paperback) | ISBN 978-1-4982-8743-2 (hardcover) | ISBN 978-1-5326-3116-0 (ebook)

Subjects: LCSH: Pastoral Theology. | Vocation, Ecclesistical. | Clergy—Psychology. | Identity (Psychology)—Religious aspects—Christianity. | Identity (Psychology)—Social aspects. | Self-perception—Religious aspects—Christianity. | Self-perception—Social aspects.

Classification: LCC BV4392 P22 2017 (print) | LCC BV4392 (ebook)

Manufactured in the U.S.A.   09/14/17

To my parents, Sangmin Park and Gumnam Lee,
wise counselors who urge me to listen to God's wisdom
while listening to care-seekers' stories

Contents

Figures and Tables | ix
Permissions | xi
Acknowledgments | xiii
Foreword by Christie Cozad Neuger | xv

1 Pastoral Identity in a New Paradigm | 1

2 Grounded Theory of Pastoral Identity | 30

3 Pastoral Identity in Care-Giving Relationships | 55

4 Pastoral Identity in Postmodern Contexts | 99

5 Pastoral Identity in Theological Perspectives | 132

6 Perichoretic Pastoral Identity in Caregiving Practices | 171

Bibliography | 195

Figures and Tables

Figure 1. Historical and Contextual Locations of Pastoral Identity Studies | 18
Figure 2. Pastoral Theological Methodology | 20
Figure 3. Situations in Which to Think of Pastoral Identity | 39
Figure 4. Axial Coding: Structural Context of Pastoral Identity | 50
Figure 5. Process of Presumed Pastoral Identity as Spiritual Representative | 62
Figure 6. Process of Humbled Pastoral Identity as Human Fellow | 75
Figure 7. Process of Requested Pastoral Identity as Compassionate Pastor | 85
Figure 8. Process of Care-Giving and Constructing Pastoral Identity | 96

Table 1. James Côté's Table of Identity Studies Approaches | 25
Table 2. Helping Sources/Strategies for Pastoral Identity | 40
Table 3. Responses to the Who Am I Question | 41
Table 4. Open Coding of Pastoral Identity in Practice | 44

Permissions

Revised Standard Version of the Bible, copyright 1952 [2nd edition, 1971] by the Division of Christian Education of the National Council of the Churches of Christ in the United States of America. Used by permission. All rights reserved.

A summary version of the empirical research findings in this book was published as "Pastoral Identity Constructed in Caregiving Relationships," in *Journal of Pastoral Care and Counseling* 66 (June 2012) 1–13, and is reused with permission.

The following table and figure are used with permission to reuse for this book: With kind permission from Psychology Press Taylor & Francis Group: "Identity Studies: How Close Are We to Developing a Social Science of Identity?—An Appraisal of the Field," in *Journal of Identity* 6/1 (2006) 9, James Côté, Table 1, Copyright 2006 © Psychology Press

With kind permission from Routledge Taylor & Francis Group: "An Evolving History and Methodology of Pastoral Theology, Care, and Counseling," in *Journal of Spirituality in Mental Health* 9/1 (2007) 28, Samuel Park, Figure 6, Copyright 2007 © Routledge

Acknowledgments

THIS BOOK I PRESENT is more than a product of my personal academic struggles. This work has not come to light without countless debts to and interactions with many supportive and stimulative "partners."

Without God's grace and wisdom, I would not have completed the challenging project. God has helped me go through this task by giving hope, courage, and wisdom, as I have planned this project, have researched and conducted empirical studies, and have composed the drafts. God has changed my sighs into "Aha" exclamations and has filled my puzzled mind with insightful ideas.

I am deeply thankful to Christie Neuger who has guided my research throughout the project and has faithfully accompanied me in my writing process. Also special thanks go to Joretta Marshall, Tim Lee, Nancy Ramsay, and Loren Townsend who provided helpful and sometimes challenging comments on my drafts and helped me improve my thoughts.

I cannot ignore contributions of my empirical research participants in a survey and/or interview. Their lived stories shared from their real experiences often sparked my thoughts and sometimes moved my heart. Many of the voices I quoted or cited in the book made contributions beyond their statements. Many other practitioners who could not participate in the research expressed their interest and support.

My special thanks also go to the officers and administrators of the American Association of Pastoral Counselors (AAPC) and the Association of Clinical Pastoral Education (ACPE) who helped in the process of contacting the research population—especially Douglas Ronsheim and Teresa Snorton. And I am thankful for helpful responses to my presentation of the empirical research in the Theological Anthropology Group of the Society for Pastoral Theology.

In particular, I acknowledge that Nancy Gorsuch's seminar class, "History and Methods of Pastoral Theology," sparked my interest in pastoral identity and helped me develop my career in publication. In addition, I am grateful to my supervisors, colleagues, and care-recipients in my pastoral clinical experiences in Jackson Memorial Hospital in Miami, FL and the Pastoral Care and Training Center of the Brite Divinity School, TCU—especially Howard Stone, Andrew Lester, Duane Bidwell, Ward Knight, and, Patricia Wilson-Cone.

Finally, I greatly appreciate all the support Central Seminary has provided throughout my writing.

Samuel Park

Shawnee, Kansas

Foreword

Pastoral identity, as Park notes, is a central yet under developed theme in the ministries associated with pastoral care. In the training of clergy, especially for the work of pastoral care, identity is at the heart of the curriculum. Yet, pastoral identity in a postmodern age is a complex undertaking, especially in multi-cultural, multi-religious settings like chaplaincies and pastoral counseling centers. In our earlier history as a field, pastoral identity was primarily located in the person of the caregiver. The caregiver carried a relatively unwavering sense of identity formed in their theological training, their ministry practice, and their own cultural community. These sources of pastoral identity tended to be more uni-cultural. Whether or not this was ever legitimate, it certainly is no longer a reflection of the realities in which we live and minister.

Park, a pastoral theologian who has committed himself to multi-cultural, multi-religious reflection and practice, has taken on this issue of pastoral identity in a postmodern age. In the exploration reflected in this text, Park has examined how chaplains and specialized pastoral counselors both form and maintain their pastoral identities as they minister to people with diverse theological and cultural traditions. Using both surveys and in-depth interviews of chaplains and pastoral counselors, he has discovered that their pastoral identities were developed, and continually transformed, interactively within the care relationships that they engaged. This is a very important finding for the field of pastoral theology and for the training programs we develop.

Park doesn't stop his exploration with this conclusion about the contextual, relational, and dynamic nature of pastoral identity in contemporary pastoral care but continues to develop their implications through both psychological and theological channels. His work with symbolic interactionism expands the notion of the dynamic and dialogical nature of pastoral identity as it focuses on the meanings both caregiver and care receiver bring to the ministry experience. The caregiver's experience and interpretation of that shared meaning-making reflect directly back into the pastoral identity suitable to and emerging in the midst of the pastoral encounter.

Park further engages these insights theologically, focusing particularly on a theological anthropology based on Trinitarian and incarnational notions of *perichoresis*. This rich theological conversation suggests that God's own communal interaction provides a model for pastoral identity that is both one and multiple. As Park has stated, "pastoral caregivers construct their identities interactionally with care-seekers by interweaving God's providential calling and clients' specific callings for help. Such constructions result in an embrace of multiple pastoral identities."

This book offers the field of pastoral theology generally, and pastoral care practitioners specifically, a way to think about pastoral identity as pastoral care contexts become increasingly diverse. As such, it is a creative and substantive contribution to the field.

> Christie Cozad Neuger, PhD
> Professor Emerita of Pastoral Theology, Counseling, and Care
> Brite Divinity School

1

Pastoral Identity in a New Paradigm

TOWARD A TURNING POINT IN THE STUDY OF PASTORAL IDENTITY

PASTORAL IDENTITY IS A prevailing yet underdeveloped theme in Christian scholarship and ministry. In Christian ministry, and in pastoral literature and practices, the identity of the person who ministers in the name of God and the faith community has been rightly "a central theme" (J. L. Marshall 2004; Thornton 2005). In any seminary education program and any pastoral care and counseling pedagogy and training program, educators and supervisors emphasize the significance of pastoral identity, as in clinical pastoral education and pastoral counseling and supervisory programs (Aleshire 1995; Yim 2001). Pastoral theologian John Patton states the importance of pastoral identity thus: "The acquisition of the practical knowledge of ministry, particularly the ministry of pastoral care and counseling[,] cannot be adequately discussed without examination of the concept of pastoral identity" (1983, 49).

Since the 1960s, scholars and practitioners in the field of pastoral care and counseling have struggled with pastoral identity, and many writings have explicitly and implicitly dealt with it (Everett et al. 1983; Gerkin 1966, 1967; Greenwald et al. 2004; Jackson 1964; Jernigan 1961; Kae-Je 1993; J. L. Marshall 1994; McGrath-Merkle 2011; Nauta 1993, 1996; O'Brien 2007; Oden 1980, 1988; Wittwer 2006). Ironically, however, few published volumes intensively and exclusively examine the essential theme of pastoral identity. A previous study found in 2008 that only 28 hits for the keyword *pastoral identity* were found in the American Theological Library Association's database (Park 2012). As of August 11, 2016, the keyword shows 90 hits in the ATLA database. Some scholars and theologians may have addressed this topic implicitly in their writings by using some other keywords, such as *theological, professional, ministerial, and role identity*. Nonetheless, less than 100 entries seem quite meager given the importance of the concept of pastoral identity in Christian ministry and pastoral disciplines. More astonishingly, few, if any, authors have used the term *pastoral identity* in the title of their book publications.

The concept of pastoral identity remains a significant theme in the pastoral scholarship and ministry, prompting one to ask why pastoral scholars have not written major works about it. Is the term *pastoral identity* such an unusual concept to us? Are we ignoring the importance of pastoral identity? Or is the notion too difficult to deal with? It seems to me that our field has taken a defensive posture to prevent any dilution of our proper roles and authorities but has not proactively researched the subject. We may be afraid that without addressing the importance of pastoral identity and making it our tenet, the practitioners might lose their proper roles, authorities, and boundaries *and* the discipline of pastoral care and counseling would be at great risk of dying out in a contemporary interdisciplinary environment. In the past, pastoral practitioners and theologians expressed such concerns:

> Pastoral counseling is a specialized form of ministry, and there is an ever-present threat that it will leave home, become an alien in another land, and thereby lose its identity, surrender its own implicit values (both intrinsic and instrumental), and become a confusion both to its own parents and to cognate helping services. (Jackson 1964, 250; cf. Gerkin 1966)

However, in a time of "redefining the paradigms" of pastoral care-giving (Ramsay 2004), our field needs to overcome such a passive posture and to take a progressive action of research on pastoral identity. Presently, pastoral care professionals will benefit by attention to pastoral identity from a renewed perspective.

Studying pastoral identity itself is, indeed, a challenging task in several ways. First of all, there is no commonly accepted definition of *pastoral identity*, as there is of the concept of identity in the larger circle of identity studies (Côté 2006). For this reason, pastoral literature, to a certain degree, interchangeably uses the terms *personal, pastoral, theological, professional, ministerial*, and *role identity* of the person offering religious ministry, which causes confusion. Moreover, professionals in the field have regarded pastoral identity as a (natural) product of pastoral formation, which gives the impression that caregivers have achieved pastoral identity adequately in the process of theological education and/or clinical training. Lastly but more importantly, few attempts have made to bring into dialogue a new perspective of pastoral identity, even though a large body of pastoral literature has continuously pointed to the importance of pastoral identity. We will come back to the third point later.

With regard to the second approach to pastoral identity, the field has had a keen interest in pastoral formation. Several conferences, articles, and published books discuss this topic (e.g., *Journal of Supervision and Training in Ministry* 15, 1994; and 24, 2004). In their book, Duane Bidwell and Joretta Marshall (2006) also articulate, with fellow contributors, pastoral formation and discuss its content, context, models, and practices. They make "the turn to [pastoral] formation" (2) from pastoral identity, an identity that is one of the three layers of formation (personal, professional, and pastoral). By doing so, they define pastoral identity as something that is "rooted and grounded in the faith experience and ecclesial connection" of the pastoral caregiver (4). Based on the importance of pastoral formation in Christian ministry, this book tries to construct a refreshed view of pastoral identity that consists not only in pastoral formation but also in pastoral transformation, which will be discussed later.

The current pool of literature dealing with the identity of pastoral care and counseling professionals has a fourfold character. One way of approaching pastoral identity is mainly anecdotal, describing and reflecting on personal experiences of pastoral care and counseling (Childs 1993; Gerkin 1966). Some of the authors who take this classic approach observed well what was going on in their contemporary milieu of pastoral practices and articulated, from their experiences, problems and future directions. Another approach to the study of pastoral identity is often empirically quantitative, describing the current status of pastoral clinicians' perceptions of their ministries (Everett et al. 1983) or developing a measurement scale or profile (Shostrom 1985; Praamsma 1989). The third approach often uses qualitative methods in order to understand pastoral identity on a theoretical or clinical training basis (Hardwick 1995; Moore 1982; Rollins 1987). Other methods try either to suggest a training model for developing pastoral identity based in a specialized context of care-giving along with some experiential and theoretical discussion (Burton et al. 1990) or to discuss pastoral identity in light of theological discourses (Davis 2012; McGrath-Merkle 2011) or in a form of story-telling (Wittwer 2006). In addition to the fourfold approach, more recent literature shows a postmodern shape of pastoral identity studies, discussing the subject from a queer theory (Coble 2014) or bicultural perspective (Huh 2011), for example.

A number of the scant previous studies on pastoral identity share the following characteristics. First, the studies defined or assumed pastoral identity to be an individual interiority in the inner depth of pastoral practitioners (e.g., J. L. Marshall 1994). Moreover, the studies focused on pastoral identity in relation to a theological and ecclesial commitment (e.g., Jernigan 1961). The existing studies, furthermore, discussed pastoral identity in a conceptual and abstract way in the sense that pastoral identity remains in the minds of pastoral caregivers or in the background of pastoral practices, instead of becoming an actual component of pastoral care-giving (e.g., Young 1997). Finally, many studies focused pastoral identity from a developmental or formational perspective (e.g., G. I. Hunter 1982).

Being complementary to these previous studies, this book brings a renewed perspective of symbolic interaction, postmodernity, and social construction into discussion and approaches the concept of pastoral identity in the following ways. Instead of discussing the topic in a broad sense, I approach it with a particular population and its context. Surveying 63 pastoral counselors and chaplains and interviewing 20 among them, I have found, first of all, that care-giving—rather than training or educational supervision—situations are the most frequent context in which pastoral caregivers reflect on their pastoral identity. Second, pastoral caregivers build a pastoral identity interactively with their care-seekers rather than conceptually forming it alone in relation to a theological and ecclesial commitment and more than in training and supervision settings. Finally, pastoral identity, therefore, is not merely developmental but also socially constructed between care partners (among them God is in their midst) (see chapter 3 of the book) and between the human partners and cultural structure (see chapter 4). Keeping these three points in mind, in this book I depict pastoral identity as deriving from social construction created through interactions and relationships between pastoral caregivers and care-seekers, and also constructed through interplays between agency of the care partners and the cultural structure. By shifting the paradigm, this book aims to offer an alternative framework and perspective, namely interactional, intersubjective, and constructive.

A CONSTRUCTIVE HISTORY OF RESEARCH ON PASTORAL IDENTITY

In the twentieth century, studies on pastoral identity have evolved *from* viewing it as individual interiority of the pastoral person *to* seeing it as an interpersonal construction. Historically, pastoral theologians and scholars have claimed pastoral identity in the following four motifs: the faith community and ecclesial tradition, deep engagement in lived experience, critical integration of theological and cultural perspectives, and a mutual construction of pastoral relationship.

First of all, one's self-awareness of a pastoral identity is an important element of pastoral practices, and this awareness is deeply rooted in the faith tradition and community to which the person belongs (J. L. Marshall 1992). Pastoral caregivers placed their identities within the sense of belonging and commitment to the faith community and tradition and identified themselves as representatives of God and the faith community (e.g., Jackson 1964). They struggled with their pastoral identities in the context of working within an interdisciplinary healing team or in a setting where secular therapeutic theories heavily influenced pastoral counseling. In such an interdisciplinary context, they wondered about how they perceived themselves in caring for others and whom they represent to care-seekers. In the process of struggling with their pastoral identities, several Christian pastoral theologians and care practitioners found an answer in the self-awareness that they are God's representatives and belong to the faith community (see Gerkin 1967; Oates 1982). This awareness of themselves as representatives of their faith community and tradition and as a divine healing power gave pastoral care practitioners a deep sense of pastoral identity and authority.

In addition, pastoral theologian Charles Gerkin's understanding of pastoral identity is especially insightful. In *Widening the Horizons* (1986), he articulates another meaning of pastoral identity. For Gerkin, pastoral identity connotes a pastoral response to a particular person and community in a particular situation. In other words, by participating in and responding to the particularity of immediate lived experience and human needs, Gerkin articulates, caregivers gain a pastoral identity. Thus, if a caregiver does not attend to immediate human needs and experiences, his or her identity may not be pastoral (Park 2005b).

Historical discussions of pastoral identity also suggest an interdisciplinary nature of pastoral care and counseling, which entails a relationship between theological and scientific perspectives. Historically, when an adequate balance between theological and psychological perspectives has broken down, caregivers also struggled for a pastoral identity. Due to our discipline's heavy dependency on psychology, several pastoral theologians contended that the field should recover a lost pastoral and theological identity (Oden 1980, 1988; Patton 1981). This point of view implies that pastoral caregivers should form their pastoral identity by critically and skillfully integrating Christian wisdom and cultural perspectives into their practices.

In addition, some pastoral theologians claim that the integration should maintain an asymmetrical balance, giving conceptual primacy to theology over cultural perspectives (Hunsinger 1995).

In a new millennium, new perspectives on pastoral identity seem to emerge along the line of redefining the paradigm of the field. Even though they did not explicitly discuss pastoral identity, two pastoral theologians, in my estimation, put an emphasis on the mutuality of pastoral care-giving between caregiver and receiver. From his teaching and supervision experiences, pastoral theologian Loren Townsend (2002), for instance, emphasizes the importance of theological reflection in pastoral counseling. For him, theological reflection is at the core of pastoral identity in maintaining integrity with care-seekers' differences, claiming pastoral caregivers' own religious life in therapy, relating to theological sources of knowledge, and still managing effective care-giving. He points out that pastoral counselors have only limited success in their practices when they abandon theological dimensions of the ministry to daily clinical pressures and methodological frustration.

Townsend sees a pastoral counselor as a "theologically reflective therapist" and contends that pastoral counseling needs to integrate theological reflection into clinical practices. Thus, he places theological reflection at the center of pastoral counseling training and regards the reflective method as a central value of pastoral counseling. He names three motifs of theological reflection: correlation, formation, and liberation. He criticizes correlation and formation motifs of theological reflection for making an epistemic boundary between counselor and client and for becoming "harmful through objectification and reductionistic intervention" (2002, 66).

Instead, Townsend proposes the liberation motif of theological reflection, which represents his best approach toward a pastoral method that embodies pastoral identity. The reflection begins by attending fully to social location and embodied experience. This type of theological reflection does not objectify clients but invites them to full partnership in the reflective motion of meaning-making and transformation, which leads not only the oppressed toward their own empowerment but also the counselor toward a more challenging and renewed knowledge and awareness of God and new directions for empowering others. Thus, such a liberative action-reflection motif pursues "mutually transforming relationships of love" (70).

Thus, Townsend explicates pastoral identity as being embedded in the theologically reflective praxis of both caregiver and client. Through such liberative transformation of the unheard and marginalized, Townsend argues, pastoral counselors establish a pastoral identity. For him, pastoral identity does not come from the caregiver's own theological reflection but from a mutually constructed theological reflection between caregiver and care-seeker to facilitate the liberation of the unheard and marginalized.

Likewise, in *In Living Color*, another pastoral theologian Emmanuel Lartey (2003) defines pastoral care as helping activities in which caregivers acknowledge a transcendent aspect of life to assure, relieve, or facilitate persons coping with anxieties and to foster care-seekers' growth as full human beings in a context of the development of holistic communities. In such environment, all people may live humane lives ecologically and sociopolitically. Hence, his definition of pastoral care-giving consists of holistic, liberative, and intercultural approaches to pastoral care.

Lartey explores the meanings of the term *pastoral* and describes the values that the term may have in qualifying care and counseling. He describes five usages of pastoral counseling, in addition to pastoral care in an educational setting in Britain that signifies teachers' concern for students' personal well-being. He finds that people have seen pastoral counseling as counseling that the ordained offer, counseling which takes place within and around the religious context, counseling offered within and by a faith community, Christian counseling, and counseling for the whole person.

Lartey argues that such understandings of pastoral counseling fall into psychological reductionism, sociopolitical apathy, theological weakness, and individualism. From perspectives of liberation theology, intercultural relations, and spirituality, he develops intercultural pastoral counseling, which consists of concrete experience, social and hermeneutical analyses, and the pastoral praxis of liberation. This approach emphasizes critical self-awareness and mutual transformation between caregiver and care-seeker.

In summary, pastoral theologians have historically recognize pastoral identity from different perspectives. From romanticist and modern points of view, pastoral identity has connoted (1) attending to immediate lived experience of a particular person and community in a particular situation, (2) being a representative of the faith community and theological tradition, (3) critically integrating theological and scientific perspectives of lived experience and human needs. In the new millennium, postmodern thinking seems to have changed the view of pastoral identity as (4) an emerging sense of identity in the process of, or as a result of, mutual construction of theological reflection and mutual transformation between caregiver and care-seeker. Hence, perspectives of pastoral identity have evolved *from* an identity that a pastoral caregiver forms as a representative of God and derives from his or her own theological reflection alone *to* a sense of identity constructed from a care-giving relationship in which caregiver and seeker work mutually on theological reflection and transformation toward liberation. This book is part of this evolving history of pastoral identity studies.

SHIFTING A PARADIGM: FROM SELF-IDENTIFICATION TO SOCIAL CONSTRUCTION

As is the case with the definition of *identity*, defining *pastoral identity* is no easy task. Even though most writers do not articulate the definition of pastoral identity in discussing it, a few pastoral theologians have attempted to define pastoral identity. In the *Dictionary of Pastoral Care and Counseling*, Edward Thornton (2005) defines "pastoral identity" as "the relatively enduring pattern of attachments, behaviors, and values characteristic of persons providing religious ministries, usually but not necessarily referring to seminarians and ordained clergypersons" (567). Patton (1993) also refers to pastoral identity as "something that can be discerned as an inner awareness of being a duly authorized representative of a Christian community of faith" (75). Moreover, recognizing the dynamic nature of identity, feminist pastoral theologian Joretta Marshall (1994) defines preliminarily pastoral identity as "the internal integration of the 'pastoral' dimension into one's total identity, and implies [the] ability to articulate core theological values, perceptions, and beliefs" (18).

Although these pastoral theologians define pastoral identity in different terms and voices, one can see some commonalities in these definitions that reflect a broadly recognized way of seeing pastoral identity in our field. First of all, the scholars see pastoral identity as one's own faculty or property. It could be one's theological ability, cognitive awareness, or distinctive habits. Such a conception of pastoral identity further gives us an impression that it belongs to the care-*giving* person—regardless of care-receivers—who is God's representative, has pastoral and theological dimensions in his or her whole identity, and ministers to people. Furthermore, such definitions of pastoral identity lead us to think that it should be relatively enduring, stable, and constant. The definitions rarely reflect how social and cultural contexts, especially a pastoral relational context, can influence pastoral identity.

In an effort to define and assess professional identity in clergy, Franz Shostrom (1985), in his research project, formulates a definition of pastoral identity based on his empirical research concerning the perceptions of academic and clinical educators. His efforts also remain within the parameters that I have described above. He summarizes his definition of the professional identity of Christian clergy:

> It [the identity] addressed issues of the faith of the person, a sense of call to the profession of ministry, his or her relation to the Church, educational preparation, development of pastoral skills, self-awareness and an ability to use oneself as a pastoral

tool. In pastoral professional identity these are integrated into the personality of the minister and are a natural, comfortable part of the person['s] make-up. (98)

Thus, our field has often depicted pastoral identity as a matter of a pastoral person's own constant faculty. In particular, Patton's definition underscores a folk-understanding of pastoral identity in our field; that is, pastoral identity is a pastoral person's self-conscious identification as God's representative.

There are some characteristics of such a traditional definition of pastoral identity as a self-identification by the pastoral person. First, the conventional approach to pastoral identity confines pastoral identity within individual property and rarely interprets it in the scope of a social function or role in a (faith) community. Pastoral identity is not only a faculty of the person but also a "property of interaction" (Côté 2006, 9). Second, depicting pastoral identity as the pastoral person's own stable faculty, the traditional approach does not amount to much in terms of an intersubjective nature of pastoral identity between care-giving and receiving partners. Furthermore, the definition does not reflect a social contextual interaction between identity and culture (for an in-depth analysis of the relation between identity and society, see Côté 1996; Burke 2003).

Preliminarily speaking about the evolution of identity studies, Erikson's work on identity consists of "three interrelated dimensions" or "three forms of continuity," according to social psychologists James Côté and Charles Levine (2002). The first one is the subjective or psychological dimension called ego identity, and it focuses on the continuity of a sense of self-sameness and constancy over time. The second type is the personal manifestation, in which one displays a "behavioral and character repertoire" (15), and it focuses on the continuity of interrelationships between the self and the other. The last one is the social dimension, in which one plays a role in a community, and this dimension emphasizes the stability of functional integrations in a particular group. When one does not integrate these components of identity, the individual suffers an identity crisis. The crisis is "characterized by a subjective sense of identity confusion, a behavioral and characterological disarray, and a lack of commitment to recognized roles in a community" (ibid.).

In the early periods of identity studies, people focused on the subjective and experiential dimension of identity from a psychological-developmental perspective, especially attending to Erikson's eight identity stages. According to social-cognitive developmental psychologist Michael Berzonsky (1993), such psychologically oriented researchers have looked at identity formation as a product of "discover[ing] a preexistent intrinsic essence" (169).

In contrast, looking at identity formation as a process of "construct[ing] a sense of self" (ibid.), sociologically oriented scholars have later emphasized the interpersonal and social manifestation of identity. Scholars in identity studies refer to the former as "psychological approaches" to identity, which focus on the subjective-experiential dimension of identity, and to the latter as "sociological approaches" to identity, which emphasize sociological characterization of identity (Côté 1996; also see Weigert et al. 2005; Côté et al. 2002). In other words, using Côté's language, a psychological approach sees identity as one's property, such as psyche or "inner workings," whereas a sociological approach understands identity as "something that is 'realized strategically and circumstantially' through one's interaction with others" (Côté et al. 2002, 49).

Existing approaches to pastoral identity in our field, as it is now evident, have often looked at the concept from the psychological-developmental perspective. Scholars employing this approach regard pastoral identity as part of ego or personal identity and treat it as an intrinsic essence of self. Thus, many pastoral theologians and practitioners have asserted that pastoral caregivers should form a pastoral identity by becoming aware of who they are in their sense of vocation and calling (Gerkin 1967; Oates 1982) or developing a capacity for theological reflection (O'Brien 2007; O'Connor 2008; Townsend 2006). I agree with these authors that theological reflection is essential to pastoral identity, but "private" theological reflection (O'Connor 2008) is likely to result in the establishment of a personal level of identity. Some theologians, thereby, have seen pastoral supervision and training as "formation for ministry" (G. I. Hunter 1982) and have focused on *developing* a sense of pastoral identity as an inbuilt property endowed by God and the faith community (Jackson 1964).

Contemporary identity studies have found that identity develops through social experiences and interactions and by taking on others' perspectives. Identity, like mind and self, emerges from the social process of interaction and communication by way of symbols and meanings (Blumer 1969; Mead et al. 1934). Hence, current identity studies agree that identity is not a fixed conceptual abstraction but a product of ongoing processes of interactions with everyday life in a specific culture (Howard 2000; Schilling-Estes 2004). These scholars claim that people construct identity through a dynamic interplay of daily life experiences in specific social contexts in which "pre-existing linguistic and social structures also come into play" (Schilling-Estes, 163).

Thus, current studies of identity have changed their direction and perspective from studying ego identity to examining interpersonal and social identities, which creates a space for a social constructionist perspective of identity. From social psychological and social constructionist perspectives, contemporary identity studies focus on relationship and interaction between persons and between identity and society. Drawing on social psychology in general and social constructionism in particular, this book, in part, attempts to depict pastoral identity as "a property of interaction" and as relational in the sense that pastoral identity is "embedded in interpersonal relationships" (Côté 2006, 9). This evolving perspective helps us shift a paradigm of the study of pastoral identity from the pastoral caregiver's self-identification to a social construction between care-giving and receiving partners and between them and their cultural contexts in which the care partners interact with each other toward the accomplishment of a shared goal of care and counseling.

In this sense, one can view pastoral identity as a social and relational construction mutually created by pastoral caregivers and seekers through a dynamic interaction of lived experience and care-giving activities within specific social contexts. A few researchers and scholars have considered pastoral identity in relation to its social contexts on a precursory level. For example, Zina Jacque (2006) explores how integrative therapy, in which clinicians and clients openly discuss faith issues, has affected clinicians' identities. To integrate faith and psychology, Jacque developed an 18-week training program for local clinicians in the greater Boston area. Through her interviews with the 21 clinicians who finished training and worked with religiously-oriented clients, she found that their work affected identity formation as they developed an enhanced relationship with God, became confident with their religious identity, transformed their clinical work into a clinical vocation, lived a more integrated life, and came to better understand the power of spiritual community.

Moremore, Dutch pastoral theologian Reinard Nauta provides a good example of studying pastoral identity in relation to its social contexts. His enduring interest in pastoral identity has led him to publish several articles on the topic (1993, 1996, 2003). His early research on "Pastoral Identity and Communication" (1993) features an intriguing aspect of this study. He formulated 43 items to measure a pastor's concept of self, parishioners' complementary role model of pastoral conversation, and the function of communication. In his study with 270 Dutch Catholic and Protestant ministers and 310 parishioners, he delineated some of the qualities of pastoral identity by comparing the pastors' and parishioners' perception of one another and by relating pastors' self-concept to relationship style and communication patterns. He envisions pastoral identity as something developed in pastoral communication. Even though he did not fully explore the relational and interactional construction of pastoral identity, his work acknowledges that "selfconcept is . . . a social construction reflecting the opinions and attitudes communicated by significant others" based on American pragmatist George Herbert Mead's idea (6).

Adjusting our frame of reference, we thus need to construct pastoral identity from a progressive perspective that supplements the previous one. From a contemporary social constructionist perspective, one can see pastoral identity as something realized in a process of care-giving that is interactional, relational, and constructive. Throughout the book, therefore, I examine whether pastoral identity is a social construction as the identity becomes something socially narrated, realized, and constructed in the pastoral relationship between caregiver and care-seeker. I do not mean to separate psychological and sociological dimensions of pastoral identity, which accompany each other. Scholars need to integrate the two into the study of pastoral identity. In this study, however, I focus on the intersubjective and social dimensions of pastoral identity in order to adjust a tilt to the psychological weight in the discussion of pastoral identity.

Recognizing that cultural and societal structures influence and shape human life and identity is not new in our field, as the field of pastoral care, counseling, and theology has redefined its paradigm and reformed its perspective on, and approach to, focus and method (Ramsay 2004). We have already evolved to such a level that we are ready to embrace the communal-contextual and intercultural approaches to our ministries (Lartey 2003; Miller-McLemore 1996; Patton 1993). The transition from the "living human document" to the "living human web" and now to the "living document within the web" (Miller-McLemore 2008) indicates how the field has tried to appreciate carefully the value of the relation between human agency and communal context. In this regard, exploring pastoral identity in the contemporary stream is an important step to take and is at the core of redefining a paradigm of pastoral care, counseling, and theology.

TWO PASTORAL THEOLOGICAL DILEMMAS

What influence do one's social and cultural context and one's psychological development have on identity formation? This question is important in the study of identity, according to Côté, who approaches identity from a multidimensional perspective. From social psychological and sociological perspectives in identity studies, the link between self and relation, between identity and society, between individual and culture, or between agency and structure is inseparable. For this reason, understanding how social context affects human development and how human agency influences identity formation in that social context is an intriguing, yet formidable, task.

One of the influential contexts in our contemporary time is the postmodern, since the "incredulity toward metanarratives" is growing as the world becomes a global, intercultural, and multifaith village (Lyotard 1984). People need to know, and humbly realize, that they live in a limited time and space, in general terms, and in the historicality and locality of an "aftertime" world (Lartey 2002), in particular terms. It is not so difficult to look at contemporary changes in our daily lives and their impacts on our selves and identities. Describing a postmodern impact on self, Gergen (1991) depicts the postmodern self as a "saturated self"; after all, the postmodern world is so full of relations and meanings that it risks flooding the self. Likewise, sociologist Norman Denzin describes the self as a "cinematic self," arguing that we know ourselves through the images of cinema and television (Holstein et al. 2000).

Moreover, the postmodern epistemology has influenced secular academic disciplines, and this impact also seems to take place in the field of pastoral care, counseling, and theology. Describing the postmodern impact on religious belief and theological education, narrative feminist pastoral theologian Christie Neuger (1998) articulates the challenges we face:

> For one, it [coming to terms with postmodernism] means allowing ourselves to face the void which postmodernism and the work of deconstruction [have] revealed. It means, I think, listening carefully to perspectives which challenge some of our most dearly loved symbols, recognizing them as symbols rather than as the ultimate object of devotion, and allowing new symbols which represent diverse voices to surface. (7)

As the postmodern perspective has also influenced theological education, several authors and theologians have described how postmodernity impacts the discipline of pastoral care, counseling, and theology (H. Anderson 1998; Couture 2003; Goodliff 1998; R. J. Hunter 1998; Lartey 2002; Neuger 1998; Wimberly 2003). As pastoral theologian Nancy Ramsay (2004) rightly observes, the contemporary changes in our field have effected a paradigm shift, including those of "the scope of care; the authority for care; the identity, role, and accountabilities of those who care; the fact and significance of asymmetries of power in care; and the significance of difference for the practice and conceptual foundation of care" (1).

Despite the postmodern impact, pastoral scholars and researchers have done little work aimed at empirically describing and analyzing these phenomena of change in our clinical and practical arena. Some scholars see that modernity is obvious in our practical and clinical field, as many pastoral specialists still operate under the influence of modern psychotherapeutic models such as those of Freudian, Jungian, and gestalt therapies (Couture 2003; Doehring 2006; Neuger 1998). Reporting his provisional findings of interviews on theological reflection and pastoral formation, Townsend (2006) mentions pastoral counselors' struggles to describe the process and model of their own theological reflection. From his research experience and other observations, he contends that postmodern influences "may only exist on the margins of the field at this point," are limited to teachers in an academic setting, and "have been very slow to impact" pastoral practitioners in clinical settings (L. Townsend, personal communication).

Thus, the postmodern impacts our everyday life, the academic arena, and the practical experiences of Christian ministry, each to different degrees. If gaps exist in the contemporary parish life, in academic settings, and in practical settings of pastoral theology and care-giving, then pastoral practitioners may well experience a confusion concerning their pastoral identities because identity has a significant relationship to practice and community (Wenger 1998). Thus, it is a significant task to observe and describe how and to what degree, if any, the contemporary milieu in the field of pastoral care, counseling, and theology affects pastoral practitioners in their clinical and practical settings. Based upon that assessment, we need to explore whether and how these contextual changes affect their pastoral formation, especially identity construction, and their care-giving (see chapter 4). As a way of participating in this task, pastoral theologians in their current practices have to deal with two pivotal dilemmas interwoven between self and relation and between theological groundedness and cultural inclusiveness.

A Paradoxical Relationship between Self and Relation

A relational understanding of personhood is widespread in contemporary philosophy, social psychology, and theology. According to psychologist Kenneth Gergen (1991), humans' sense of self has changed over time. In pre-modern and modern societies, people located the self in an inner deep center of their being, such as soul, passion, or rationality. As centered selves, they could construct and control their world by their own will and intention. However, such centered and willful selves no longer have power in a postmodern society. Social relationships connected through communication technologies in a highly industrial society often are momentary, fragmented, and evaporable. In particular, people try to trace others' patterns and imitate celebrity in a consumerist and image-oriented society, "gardening" themselves like one of their "idols." Such self-images and superficial relationships often inundate one's sense of a centered self and identity. Thus, a postmodern self exists in and by social relationships. In a postmodern context, social relationships now construct and shape the self contextually. People discover and create their identities within a maelstrom of political, economic, and cultural forces. Thus, as the self loses its center in social relationships, a centered core self disappears, and a relational self is revived.

One may see the revived relational self as celebrating (Gergen 1991); however, one may view such a relational self as losing agency (Côté et al. 2002; Thiselton 1995). On the one hand, social relationships construct a relational self, but on the other hand, the self can be trapped in these relationships. People live in a world of multiple "truths" and are confused by pluralistic and fluid sets of values, norms, and principles. People have their identities constructed by social relationships, which may not reflect their inner being and reality. The self in a postmodern society is always subject to relationships. Individuals constitute their shifting selves according to the various relationships, conversations, and language. Numerous social relationships often saturate people's sense of a core self or identity. One may feel de-centered, fragmented, and lost in numerous relationships. Being saturated by superficial social relationships, the self loses its inner identifiable center and situates itself in multiple and fluid identities. Thus, a postmodern relational self may be passively situated in the social structure. Postmodern social relationships seem to damage individuals' self-agency, trapping the self in the social structure.

Accordingly, the self often has a contradictory relationship with a social structure of which the self is part. The first dilemma is that a postmodern relational self may take place at the expense of losing its core self. In other words, one may have a social, relational, and communal self by being part of the social network and losing one's self in that relationship. To resolve the dilemma, the question we have to ask is what force(s) help social saturation deconstruct an essential self and also construct a relational self. In other words, to what extent does the postmodern saturation affect a sense of self-agency? Moreover, we have to ask how to build life-giving relationships without losing a sense of agency, authenticity, and coherence.

Interestingly, in my empirical study, pastoral caregivers seem to construct a pastoral identity that is relational and interactional but do not lose their sense of a stable self. They, surely, adapt to postmodern cultural characteristics of identity that are multiple, emergent, other-directed, and inclusive. They also, however, maintain the coherency and agency of pastoral identities in the course of their everyday practices. Contemporary pastoral clinicians seem to adapt to and resist postmodern cultural structure in some way by utilizing their agency under that structural power. In other words, they hold some form of integrity, coherence, and authenticity in their identities in spite of their postmodern culture of social saturation.

Accordingly, one must answer the questions above by addressing a paradoxical relationship between self-agency and social structure. Searching for an answer to these questions, this book emphasizes pastoral practitioners' personal agency for directing their practices and constructing pastoral identities within their fluid but still reliable relationships with care-seekers. In this book, I will also determine a theological framework for resolving the dilemma by attending to a contemporary trinitarian theology (see chapter 5). One can apply the same framework to the second dilemma of the pastoral theological issue, that is, the dilemma between theological groundedness and cultural inclusiveness.

A Paradoxical Relationship between Groundedness and Inclusiveness

In today's postmodern, intercultural, and multifaith milieu, pastoral practitioners face challenges to their pastoral identity. In these challenging contexts, pastoral caregivers are supposed to consider the multiple meanings and values of their work with care-seekers whose cultural and faith meanings and symbols differ from those of the caregivers. Pastoral care in healthcare settings, for example, becomes independent of the faith community and turns into a part of the health care system which asks chaplains to work toward promoting the generic spirituality of care-seekers. In this contemporary pluralistic and inclusive milieu, some caregivers may be rather reluctant to deal with religious or spiritual issues and afraid that they might impose their religious values on care-seekers.

Pastoral theological perspectives on such phenomena seem split into two contradictory parties. One party that is mostly on the pastoral frontline claims that pastoral care and counseling should attempt to help people as much as possible by modifying the traditional Christian mode of caregiving (Lartey 2003; Schmidt & Egler 1998). To provide people from different cultures and religions with approachable care, this party says, chaplains and pastoral counselors should be culturally and religiously inclusive and deal with religious faith in a generic sense of spirituality. Inclusiveness and spirituality are core notions for this party. On the contrary, the other party harbors suspicions toward this current frontline approach and has concerns about becoming generically spiritual in pastoral care-giving and losing theological groundedness. The party has emphasized the importance of the theology and identity of pastoral care-giving and caregivers (Hughes 1998; R. J. Hunter 1997; Joseph 1998). Thus, pastoral practitioners and theologians fall in a position on this spectrum and have not yet elaborated a good solution to reconcile the frontline claims and the mainline suspicions (for detailed debates over the issue of generic chaplaincy, see *Christian Bioethics* 4 (3) 1998 & 9 (1) 2003).

On the one hand, the inclusive and generically spiritual approach to pastoral care-giving has stimulated the field to honor diversity and dismantle the privileged power position. The faith grounded approach, on the other hand, has challenged the field to adequately present the theological wisdom in postmodern, pluralistic contexts. Thus, pastoral theologians need to propose a new framework to resolve the contradiction between the emphasis on theological groundedness and the request for cultural and religious diversity. With regard to this contemporary challenge, the current dilemma and core question in our field is "How can we honor religious pluralism and adequately represent the wisdom of particular traditions?" (Ramsay 2004, 42). In other words, "How ... could pastoral [caregivers] maintain integrity with the otherness of clients, claim their own life of faith in therapy, relate to the theological sources of knowledge, and still manage to be effective therapists?" (Townsend 2002, 63). Such struggles are not only within our field but also in other academic and practical disciplines which fall under the power of postmodernity. Concerning the "hyperreality of identity," sociologists James Holstein and Jaber Gubrium (2000) have raised a question regarding a self in postmodern society:

> Is there a way in which an empirical self can be grounded in everyday life, yet retain the postmodern characteristics of decenteredness and diversity of meaning? Can the self's location in lived experience be conceptualized to coincide in some fashion with postmodern sensibilities? (68)

Hence, in such postmodern milieu, an important issue is that one is grounded in the concrete reality and at the same time effectively flexible and inclusive.

Within the larger framework of such questions, this study investigates how pastoral caregivers form their pastoral identities in a context of providing pastoral care and counseling in a generic and inclusive sense. In other words, how do pastoral counselors and chaplains describe and construct their pastoral identity in culturally and religiously diverse contexts? One can further rephrase the question in the following manner: How can one find one's groundedness in a pluralistic and inclusive "marshmallow" (in the terms of one of the interviewees of the empirical study)?

As we have seen so far, a historical scale indicates that pastoral identity studies have not yet fully blossomed in Christian education and ministry in general and in the field of pastoral care, counseling, and theology in particular. Contextually, moreover, the theme is at the core of resolving the dilemma we face in postmodern, intercultural, and multifaith contexts—tensions between self and relation, between unity and diversity, between integrity and multiplicity, between authenticity and ambiguity, between personal agency and cultural structure, and between groundedness and inclusiveness (see fig. 1). Throughout the study, we will try to find out a way of balancing the paradoxical dilemmas. We need a new pastoral theological framework to handle the still under-investigated and unbalanced status of pastoral identity studies.

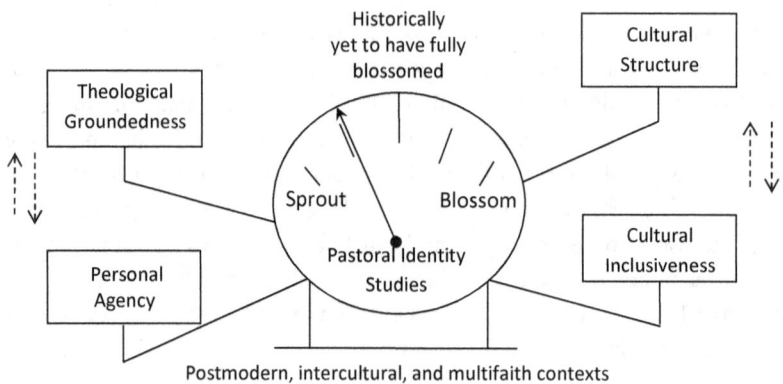

Figure 1. Historical and Contextual Locations of Pastoral Identity Studies.

METHODOLOGY FOR HERMENEUTIC ARCHITECTURE AND ORCHESTRATION

Pastoral theology is an art of constructing a theological perspective and anthropology of human experiences, often for care and counseling, by integrating theological wisdom and cultural discourses in order to develop a "hermeneutical action-theory" or a "hermeneutical-empirical approach to human action" (Hermans et al. 2002, vii). In examining pastoral identity in the book, we will hold such a perspective and employ a methodology for a pastoral theology. I start by giving a "thick" description of lived experience of the pastoral caregivers involved in this study and their experiences with identity construction. I describe pastoral caregivers' care-giving experiences with the help of a grounded theory method. I further discuss a process and dynamic of pastoral care-giving and identity-construction by drawing insights from a social psychological perspective of identity and a theological interpretation of identity.

I do pastoral reflection on the lived experience of pastoral caregivers through these perspectives of grounded theory, social psychological discourse, and theological wisdom. This process of pastoral reflection helps us perform a "third-order reflection" that relates to a second order theology explicating basic meanings of everyday religious language (Jennings 2005; J. L. Marshall 2004). In other words, I perform a mutual dialogue and critical integration (third order) of interpretations from each of the three theoretical perspectives (second order) concerning meanings of the raw data of the surveys and interviews (first order). I draw on these integrated discourses to develop a theological framework or principles for pastoral care and counseling (see fig. 2). For this particular project, I have adopted and slightly modified the diagram below from my original version of the methodology for constructing pastoral theology.

Even though I use several clinical and theoretical sources from lived experience, theology, and the social sciences, hermeneutics offers an overarching perspective from which to integrate these different sources. Gerkin (1984) was a pastoral theologian and practitioner who used hermeneutics as his overarching tool for bridging theology and psychology. By utilizing several lenses (empirical study, theology, and the social sciences) in examining pastoral identity, I aim to facilitate a "hermeneutic circle," a kind of partly comparative and partly divinatory understanding that moves back and forth between the parts and the whole of the text that is under scrutiny (Gadamer 1975; Palmer 1969). Each interpreted second order theory derived from the three hermeneutic lenses leads to a partial understanding of pastoral identity that hinges on looking at the larger whole, which, in turn, can help one better understand the parts.

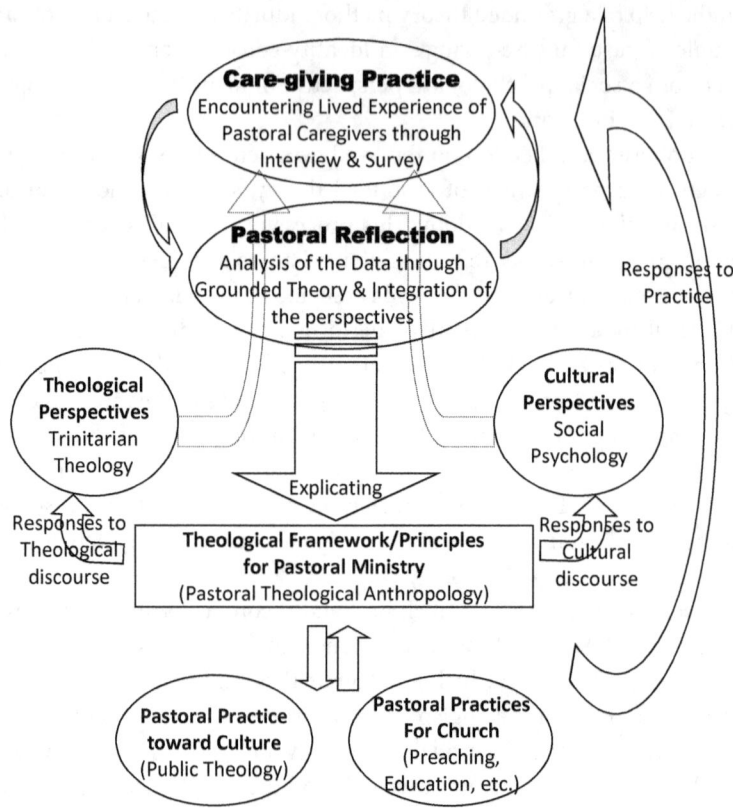

Figure 2. Pastoral Theological Methodology
Adapted from Park (2007, fig. 6)

Text and its reader "co-determine" meanings of the text, leaping into a hermeneutic circle. The lived experience of pastoral caregivers collected in surveys and interviews consists of a text of "human living documents" which I read and interpret along with the participants' storylines. Interviews are "windows on the world" to generate empirical information on human lived experience by asking the participants about their perceptions and experiences. Interviewing is highly interactional and provokes meanings of lived experience by socially encountering between the conversational partners (Holstein et al. 2003). In this regard, my interview partners and I socially produce and construct narratives. These empirical research data are "the archaeologically recoverable information about human thought and human behavior" (Ryan et al. 2000, 769), as the reader and "text" co-determine meanings of the lived experiences the participants narrated. Nonetheless, my interpretation of the data is perspectival in that I still interpret data from only one part of the social constructive matrix.

MAIN QUESTIONS AND RESPONSES

Aiming for such methodological integration of various resources and perspectives, the book comprises empirical research and theory-building along with theological and cultural perspectives. The main questions of the study as a whole have a threefold nature:

(1) In postmodern, intercultural, and multifaith contexts, how do contemporary pastoral caregivers establish pastoral identity within their daily care-giving practices?

(2) How do postmodern cultures and contexts influence and shape pastoral care-giving practices and identity construction? How do caregivers respond to such contemporary environments?

(3) How do these empirical and social scientific discourses inform a theological discourse of identity, and how can theology respond to them? What theological metaphor can provide pastoral caregivers with a framework for constructing their identities in postmodern, intercultural, and multifaith contexts?

As the field has widened its horizon to embrace cultural discourses and contextual influences, the contemporary intercultural and multifaith milieu requires dynamic and dialogical views of pastoral identity in relation to the care-giving context. In this regard, exploring pastoral identity in terms of dynamic care-giving interactions in a contemporary context is an important step in envisaging a renewed paradigm of pastoral care, counseling, and theology. For this reason, this book will analyze micro-level everyday interactions and a macro-level social structure. First, from a micro-level perspective, the book describes, through an empirical study, how pastoral caregivers construct a pastoral identity in the midst of daily interactions with their care-seekers. The study pays a special attention to the pastoral care-giving context and process in and by which caregivers and seekers interact with each other and make a constructive relationship that shapes both partners' identities. Moreover, in a macro-level view, this volume also discusses how institutional structures and postmodern powers influence the everyday interactions within culturally and religiously diverse care-giving contexts.

To examine the first question, I have conducted empirical research with chaplains and pastoral counselors and examined, from a micro-level interactionist perspective, how they form their pastoral identities (see chapters 2 and 3). According to the empirical research, one can draw three conclusions:

(a) Care-giving situations, in which pastoral caregivers encounter lived experiences of people who seek help, influence identity construction.

(b) Pastoral caregivers construct pastoral identity through care-giving interactions and pastoral relationships with care-seekers.

(c) Pastoral identity in postmodern, multicultural, and interfaith contexts consists of a social construction mutually created between care partners who bring with them their stories and histories into each new encounter.

In regard to the second question about postmodern influences on pastoral identity, I draw on contemporary social psychological discourses of identity and discuss a postmodern influence on identities and its limitations from a macro-level perspective (see chapter 4). As our field has evolved in (post)modern cultures of psychology, inter-disciplines, secular-institutionalization, and plurality *and* as cultures of fragmenting and de-centering the self spread postmodern tints on identity formation, pastoral caregivers tend to adapt to postmodern characteristics of identity in their identity construction. Even though these postmodern impacts on identity are enormous, pastoral caregivers still maintain integrity, coherency, and authenticity in their pastoral identities. By returning to everyday care-giving practices, pastoral practitioners not only adapt to but also work to change the postmodern conditions in efforts to reach a shared goal of care-giving with care-seekers.

In regard to the third inquiry about how these empirical and social psychological discussions inform a theology of identity and how theology sheds light on identity construction of pastoral practitioners, social scientific discourses of identity challenge theology to resolve conflicting forces of identity construction, that is, the duality between self and relationships and between agency and structure. I turn to contemporary theological discussions of *perichoresis*, which means coinherence or interpenetration, in order to overcome the limitation of a relational approach to identity (see chapter 5). A renewed perspective of the triune God in the last century has changed the traditional view of persons and has profound implications for constructing identities in contemporary pluralistic contexts. A trinitarian concept of interpenetration and reciprocal co-dwelling will help us dynamically integrate self with relation, agency with structure, and groundedness with openness to diversity.

A ROAD MAP TO THE BOOK

I interweave several theoretical threads in order to find a constructive way through this somewhat complicated project. The first thread is Grounded Theory, which I will follow in order to describe a way of collecting and analyzing data concerning the lived experience of the participants in my research. Grounded theory, originated by two sociologists, Barney Glaser and Anselm Strauss (1967), is "a systematic, qualitative procedure used to generate a theory that explains, at a broad conceptual level, a process, an action, or interaction about a substantive topic" (Creswell 2002, 439). In Chapter Two, I will delineate detailed information regarding my empirical research design and findings along the line of open, axial, and selective codings (Strauss et al. 1990, 1998).

The second thread of this project is a social psychological view of identity. This project utilizes two major social psychological views of identity: a view of symbolic interactionism at the micro-level of analysis and a view of postmodernism at the macro-level. In particular, my empirical findings concerning pastoral identity fit into a symbolic interactionist approach to identity (see chapter 3). This approach is theoretically grounded in the work of American pragmatic philosopher and social theorist George Herbert Mead (1934) and his follower Herbert Blumer who originated Symbolic Interactionism (SI). SI is "widely regarded as the most sociological of all social psychological theories" (Reynolds et al. 2003, 7), and a symbolic interactionist approach to identity is regarded as "sociology's dominant theoretical approach" (Callero 2003, 115). SI rests on three "simple premises": (1) people "act toward things on the basis of the meanings that the things have for them"; (2) these meanings are "derived from, or arise out of the social interaction that one has with one's fellows"; and (3) "these meanings are handled in, and modified through, an interpretive process used by the person in dealing with the things [one] encounters" (Blumer 1969, 2).

Even though the empirical data fit into SI, one can recognize that it is naïve to look at pastoral identity only at the interactional level because this approach can be blind to a large structural power that affects individuals' everyday interactions and relationships. Thus, I also employ a postmodern approach to identity in order to see how a postmodern structure affects pastoral identity construction and how pastoral care partners, nevertheless, use human agency to construct their identities by conforming to and resisting the structural power (see chapter 4).

At first glance, these two social psychological approaches seem to conflict each other since a postmodernist perspective may dismiss as the residue of modernist thinking the Meadian approach to identity that is based on the pragmatist tradition. However, SI has some affinity to social constructionism in the sense that they both recognize that the social actors define the situations and (re-)produce social actions (Schwandt 2007, 39). Accordingly, postmodernist and symbolic interactionist theories share some central commonalities concerning "the centrality of language and communication, a common problematizing of symbols and objectivity, and recognition of the socially contingent nature of identity" (Callero 2003, 116).

Sociologist Peter Callero points out that an emerging social psychological approach to self and identity puts emphases on power, reflexivity, and social construction, moving toward mutual elaboration of postmodernist and symbolic interactionist thoughts. On the one hand, drawing mainly on Foucault's view of self as constituted within relations of power imposed by discourse systems and disciplinary practices, Callero sees Foucault's perspective as a postmodern corrective to the Meadian approach to identity. On the other hand, Callero views SI's reflexive process of social interaction—"the uniquely human capacity to become an object to one's self, to be both subject and object" (2003, 119)—as a resource for providing an important foundation for understanding agency, which is what the Foucault tradition misses by reducing "consciousness and identity formation to coercive socialization" (118). Furthermore, Callero argues for identity as a social construction that is common to symbolic interactionist and postmodernist approaches to identity. Indeed, Callero shows how an emerging social psychological view connects postmodernist and symbolic interactionist approaches with a social constructionist view of identity (cf. Sandstrom et al. 2003; Weigert et al. 2005).

Grounded theory and symbolic interactionism are theoretically compatible with each other since the Meadian interactionist and pragmatic traditions strongly influenced one of the founders of grounded theory, Anselm Strauss (Strauss et al. 1998). Comparing objective and revised methods of grounded theory, sociologist Kathy Charmaz has proposed a constructivist model of grounded theory which is less objective than the traditional one and focuses on the subjective meanings of participants in the study. Based on a symbolic interactionist perspective that recognizes human agency and reflexivity, in chapter 3, I will describe a process and dynamics of the interactional construction of pastoral identity as a theory of constructing pastoral identity.

Côté (2006) sorts out eight positions of identity studies with a helpful table (see table 1). The first criterion of sorting the positions is an emphasis on individual or social focus. While psychological approaches focus on individuals and see identity as a property of individuals, sociological approaches emphasize the social and view identity as a property of interactions. The second criterion is researchers' assumptions about the social order, whether the existing social structure "is accepted as is, and therefore inevitable, or whether the existing order is viewed critically or as one of many potential contexts for different types of identity formation" (10). The third dimension of sorting the positions represents epistemological division, whether one can understand reality as fixed (objectivism) or as indeterminate (subjectivism).

Table 1. James Côté's Table of Identity Studies Approaches

Identity Studies Approaches: Fundamental Assumptions Regarding the Nature of Social Reality, Social Order, and Psychosocial Focus

Epistemology	Individual Focus		Social Focus	
	Status Quo	Critical/ Contextual	Status Quo	Critical/ Contextual
Objectivist	Identity status paradigm Self-psychology	"Critical and cultural psychologies" (e.g.,Cushman, Baumeister, Kurtines)	Structural symbolic interactionism (e.g., Stryker, Burke)	Late-modernism (e.g., Beck) Critical social psychology (e.g., Wexler)
Subjectivist	Life history and narrative approaches (e.g., McAdams, Chandler)	Postmodernism (psychological variant; e.g., Gergen)	Symbolic interactionism (interpretive approach— e.g., Goffman, Weigert)	Postmodernism (sociological variant; Bauman; Rattansi & Phoenix)

Note. Adapted from Côté (2006, 9)

As we can see, (interpretive) symbolic interactionism has a social focus with a subjectivist approach and is based more on the *status quo* of identity than on the contextual. My perspective of identity in this book combines the symbolic interactionist and late-modern approaches to identity that recognize both the power of domination and control over self and the human agency that is "on the horizon of the possible" against oppression (Callero 2003, 120). Thus, my approach values human agency and supports "the potential for individuals to direct their own development" (Côté 2006, 13). Sociologists Andrew Weigert and Viktor Gecas (2005), working from a symbolic interactionist perspective, also argue that selves are "embodied agents struggling for meaningful identities by adapting to their social and physical environments and sometimes working to change these environments through individual and collective action" (161).

As these theoretical backgrounds indicate, I see identity as interpreted and constructed in specific linguistic, socio-cultural, and historical contexts along with the human agency of interpreting meanings. The relation between personal agency and social structure has a long history in the social sciences and is at the core of the social psychological debate of identity (Sandstrom et al. 2003). In this vein, integrating the social psychological perspective into the empirical research findings, chapter 4 will explore how pastoral practitioners balance contradictory tensions between agency and structure, between fluidity and stability and between inclusiveness and groundedness in constructing pastoral identity in postmodern, intercultural, and multifaith contexts.

The third thread is a theological one. In chapter 5, I will discuss a theological perspective of identity that arises out of contemporary trinitarian theology. Drawing on contemporary trinitarian theologians like Jürgen Moltmann, Colin Gunton, Catherine LaCugna, and Stanley Grenz, I mainly focus on a paradoxical nature of the identity of the triune God—God's threeness in unity, Jesus Christ's two-natures-in-one person, and God's relation to creatures. In this discussion, the notion of *perichoresis* is a key theological concept that scholars have recently revived in order to articulate the paradoxical integrations of unity and multiplicity in these theological issues. These theological discourses will help us understand a communal identity constructed in social relationships and find a possible way of integrating personal agency into structural power and also inclusiveness into groundedness. The discussion will further help us lay a foundation for building a theological framework for pastoral practices. The final chapter will provide a renewed perspective on pastoral practices, redefine pastoral identity, and conclude with implications for pastoral theology, care, and counseling.

To sum up, this study argues that pastoral identity in postmodern, multicultural, and interfaith contexts consists of a social and relational construction mutually created between pastoral caregivers and care-seekers in continued efforts to find an answer to the seekers' predicaments in spite of the postmodern bombardment of fragmenting and eroding an agentic self. To argue the thesis, I use human experience as a resource for setting off the context by analyzing empirical data in light of grounded theory. The study further employs a social scientific discourse to explore my key questions. Biblical and theological discourses based on a trinitarian theology will help us search for an answer to the two pastoral theological dilemmas. Finally,

I draw on a theological anthropology, or principle, for pastoral care and counseling.

BOUNDARIES AND LIMITATIONS TO THE PROJECT

I have three major limitations to this volume: my theoretical lens, my ability to manage the empirical research, and my social location. First of all, the lens through which I look at pastoral identity not only helps me do an in-depth examination of the subject but also limits my scope. Coming from the theoretical background that I have for this project, I may be biased toward socio-contextual aspects of pastoral identity. To delineate a complete picture of pastoral identity construction, one inescapably needs to integrate a psychological-developmental approach into a sociological-cultural approach to identity (Côté 1996). This book does not aim to take on such a huge project but rather focuses more on sociological and cultural analyses of pastoral identity—the area the study of pastoral identity has so far neglected the most. Thus, I would be satisfied with this project if it could contribute—in Christian ministry and in the field of pastoral care, counseling, and theology—to the stimulation of the study of pastoral identity from a renewed perspective and within a new framework.

In a related vein, since my study focuses on pastoral care partners' social interactions, it does not fully address some other aspects that can affect the construction of pastoral identity. For instance, in this study, I do not deal directly with the dynamic of the faith or denominational tradition upon the pastoral caregiver's identity construction (for more on this issue, see J. L. Marshall 1992). The project, however, handles this issue by looking at how pastoral caregivers' theological groundedness can affect their pastoral identity construction along the line of dealing with dynamics of institutional powers upon their identity formation (see chapter 4). Moreover, although the book at times employs postmodern feminist views and process and liberation theological resources, I yield to future studies an in-depth critical analysis of pastoral identity, which is another huge area to explore. Hopefully, this research will become a stepping stone toward that task.

In the second place, I have set a boundary to manage my empirical research. First, my research population consists mainly of Christian pastoral caregivers, and I discuss this topic from a great deal of Christian theological perspectives. Since pastoral identity is not exclusively for Christian ministers, my study might also apply to a religious or spiritual identity of other religious ministers/workers (e.g., imams, rabbis, or interfaith ministers).

However, this application may be restricted depending upon their religious views and commitments to their traditions.

In a related vein, my study population consists mainly of pastoral care and counseling practitioners. Such population limits my ability to define and construct pastoral identity within clinical settings exclusively. Hence, the finding of this research may not accurately describe pastoral identity of those who serve as ministers or religious persons in parish settings or other relevant settings. However, the framework and principles this study utilizes could apply to the analysis and description of parish pastors' experiences.

Moreover, the book would be much more persuasive if I could have included in my empirical research project people who have received pastoral care and counseling. Care-receivers' perceptions of pastoral caregivers and their care-giving ministries would surely add valuable insights to my findings. However, conducting field observations and/or interviews with care-seekers in addition to interviewing and surveying caregivers is beyond my time and energy capabilities. Hence, this project may construct one side of the full story of pastoral identity construction. I also defer the other side of the story to the next research project.

Finally, my social location is another limitation of this study. I am a male Asian having grown up in Korea, and I teacth in a seminary in a North American academic context. I am also an ordained pastor from a conservative Presbyterian background and have studied pastoral theology, care, and counseling in progressive theological institutes. Such blended social locations and cultural dynamics perhaps help me make a unique contribution to the study of pastoral identity by giving me an alternative perspective. My social contexts and my pre-understanding and previous experiences influenced by those contexts limit my own "horizons of understanding" of the "texts," in hermeneutic philosopher Hans-Georg Gadamer's (1975) terms. The texts include lived experiences of the living human document (in this case, pastoral caregivers mainly) and sociological and theological discourses in which I have involved myself. Despite my attempts at the self-awareness of and critical reflection on this bias and prejudice, my clinical experiences as chaplain and pastoral counselor and my interpretation of those experiences may affect my understanding of the "texts." Power differentials between me and my texts could "merge" or "empower" my vantage points (Doehring 1995), depending on how my horizon of understanding fuses multiple horizons of understandings of the texts. I hope the positive side of the power dynamics will succeed in this project.

2

Grounded Theory of Pastoral Identity

THIS CHAPTER AND ITS subsequent two chapters (chapters 2–4) depict pastoral identity by analyzing empirical data and discussing them in light of grounded theory and sociological and social psychological perspectives. In chapter 2, I offer details of my empirical study methodology, including the process of collecting and analyzing data, along with the grounded theory coding method. The chapter helps us set an overall structure that embeds the phenomenon of pastoral identity construction. I further describe, in chapter 3, how pastoral caregivers interact with their care-seekers, whereby both of the care partners construct their identities. A symbolic interactionist perspective facilitates this analysis. Looking through multiple social scientific lenses, including social constructionism and post/late-modernism, chapter 4 further deals with the postmodern and social constructional nature of pastoral identity. The chapter, then, discusses some remaining issues, such as balancing paradoxical features of the identity construction between self and relation and mitigating the tension between groundedness and inclusiveness.

In this chapter, I describe the empirical study that has explored how contemporary pastoral caregivers form their pastoral identities in their daily practice. The purpose of this chapter is to analyze and delineate a contextual structure within which pastoral caregivers construct their identities in the course of their daily clinical practices. The context will be a setting for further discussion of the process of pastoral identity construction in subsequent chapters. In the contextual structure, chapter 3 looks at the interactional nature of pastoral identity, whereas chapter 4 discusses the cultural nature of pastoral identity. As is indicated in the previous chapter, this analytic description lies within the horizon of my perspectival understanding, which may be only a part of the many possible interpretive matrixes, even if I follow the principles of grounded theory to analyze systematically the empirical data that I collected of lived experiences of pastoral practitioners.

To make a "thick" description of lived experience, I designed and conducted an empirical study based on grounded theory (Strauss et al. 1990, 1997, 1998). The purpose of the empirical research was to understand the process of constructing pastoral identity and to generate a theoretical model of the ways in which chaplains and pastoral counselors identified and constructed their identities in practice. In the collection and analysis of the narratives of chaplains and pastoral counselors, grounded theory was a helpful tool for investigating how these caregivers perceive and experience pastoral identities in the course of their daily care-giving practices.

AN INTRODUCTORY DESCRIPTION OF GROUNDED THEORY

The Discovery of Grounded Theory, coauthored by Barney Glaser and Anselm Strauss (1967), established grounded theory with their conviction that people need to "discover theory from data" rather than testing hypotheses generated from preexisting theories (1). These authors, and others, have continued to develop different perspectives on grounded theory. For example, Strauss and Corbin have built up a "systematic design," which motivated Glaser's critical responses that emphasize a more bendable and less prescribed design of grounded theory. Charmaz has added to the theory a "constructivist" view, which opens up the possibility for a more subjective interpretation of the data.

According to Strauss and Corbin (1998), grounded theory refers to a "theory that [is] derived from data, systematically gathered and analyzed through the research process" (12). To help people generate a theory that emerges inductively from empirical data, the scholars have offered a step-by-step procedure for collecting and analyzing data. Thus, the grounded theory method is a useful "means for developing theory in which theories are inadequate or non-existent" (Creswell 2002, 447).

The grounded theory method begins by developing codes, concepts, and categories derived inductively from gathered raw data and ends by developing a theoretical model that is "grounded" in the empirical data (Creswell 2002). In this process, the collection and analysis of data are concurrent and continual actions, as grounded theory views asking questions as one of the analytic methods used to "open up the line of inquiry and direct theoretical sampling" (Strauss et al. 1998, 73). Thus, grounded theorists analyze data as they are collecting data. They often find important concepts and categories as they conduct a first (set of) interview(s), for example. From the data, the researcher defines preliminary categories and conducts the next (set of) interview(s) with the categories, which the new data will, in turn, refine. This process of collecting and analyzing data continues until "theoretical saturation" occurs, which means the point at which new information or concepts are no longer emerging from the data. Data in grounded theory can include interviews, field notes, memos, journals, and other forms of written or visual materials in addition to quantitative data.

Systematic grounded theorists analyze data through three analytic stages of open, axial, and selective coding along with a constant comparative method. "Open coding" starts by reading transcripts line by line and naming and labeling words, phrases, or concepts significant to the study topic. The researcher groups certain concepts under a higher order concept, discovers categories (and subcategories) derived from the concepts, and organizes the categories with their properties and dimensions. According to Strauss and Corbin (1998), properties are "the general or specific characteristics or attributes of a category" while dimensions "represent the location of a property along a continuum or range" (117). During the analytic process, the theorists constantly compare categories, concepts, and raw empirical data from which they inductively construct a theory.

In the second place (axial coding), the analyst looks for possible relationships between categories and selects one category as the core phenomenon of the problem being examined. Then, the researcher relates the phenomenon to other categories (and subcategories) along the lines of their properties and dimensions. Depending on their relationship with the core phenomenon, other categories will refer to "causal," "intervening," or "contextual" conditions, "action/interaction strategies," or "consequences" of the key phenomenon. Causal conditions refer to events or happenings that give rise to the occurrence or development of the phenomenon, and intervening conditions are broader structural conditions that facilitate or constrain the action/interaction strategies. Also, contextual conditions are a certain set of conditions that influence the circumstances of actions/interactions by which the actors handle the phenomenon (Strauss et al. 1990 & 1998). According to Strauss and Corbin (1990), the researcher can propose hypotheses or propositions through the constant interplay *between* proposing relationships between the key phenomenon and categories *and* checking the relationships against the actual data. Propositions (or hypotheses) "permit deductions, which in turn guide data collection that leads to further induction and provisional testing of propositions" (62).

Selective coding as the final place of analysis in grounded theory integrates and refines the theory. This process first explicates a story line within the categories of the axial coding by connecting and integrating their interrelationships. The story line systematically integrates categories around the key phenomenon. The procedure validates the relationships of categories against data and fills in any missing details that may need further refinement. Oftentimes, grounded theorists make use of diagrams. Strauss and Corbin (1998) encourage using diagrams to visualize "the architecture of the written manuscript" (251). Diagrams help the researchers sort out the relationships among categories by displaying their visual connections. Once data become a theoretical scheme, the researcher refines the theory by "reviewing the scheme for internal consistency and for gaps in logic, filling in poorly developed categories and trimming excess ones, and validating the scheme" (156).

Glaser (1992) criticizes this systematic design for overly focusing on specific procedures and preset frameworks instead of letting a theory emerge from the data. Charmaz also emphasizes subjective views, meanings, and assumptions of research participants and the researcher's roles in interviewing and analyzing data. Using "active codes," she tries to capture each participant's experiences along with the researcher's perspectives, experiences, and beliefs. As a result, Charmaz's narrative discussion is "more exploratory, more discursive, and more probing of the assumptions and meanings for individuals in the study" (Creswell 2002, 446). In my current empirical study, being aware of the shortcoming of Strauss and Corbin's view, I will combine their systematic procedures for analysis with Charmaz's constructivist approach for a better narrative construction. In other words, while the systematic design leads us to a specific step-by-step procedure for analyzing the data, the constructivist view helps us to generate a narrative form of theory with the constructive flexibility.

DESIGN AND PROCEDURE OF THE EMPIRICAL STUDY

Based on the grounded theory method, this empirical study aimed to explore the following two questions:

In postmodern, intercultural, and multifaith contexts,

(1) How do pastoral caregivers perceive and establish their pastoral identities?

(2) What relationship does pastoral identity have with pastoral practice?

To answer those questions, I employed a grounded theory design that offers an overall guideline for conducting the empirical study and generating a theory of pastoral identity. The qualitative study followed a two-step procedure of data collection: online surveys and telephone interviews. Even though the interview was a major method for collecting data, I employed the survey method to get preliminary information from a larger population. The surveys consisted of short, open-ended questions which were designed to identify important concepts and themes described by a greater population than interviewees. In addition, I used the surveys, to some degree, as a way of recruiting interview participants, at the end of the survey questionnaire asking them if they were willing to participate in the interview.

In the first place, I created an online survey, which included a cover letter, three main questions, demographic questions, and an optional question, which asks whether the respondent would like to participate in a follow-up interview. I posted the survey questionnaires on the surveymonkey.com website. The online survey was a useful tool, both time and money-effective. Web-based surveys have become an "indispensable research tool" that contemporary research commonly uses (Mann et al 2003, 250). The online survey was open first to the chaplain group (the Association for Clinical Pastoral Education (ACPE) clinical members) and then to the pastoral counselor groups (American Association of Pastoral Counselors (AAPC) certified pastoral counselors and fellows). The survey remained open to participation by members of these groups for about one month.

With approvals from both organizations for using their mailing lists, I sent initial letters via emails (with an opt-out option from further contacts) to the AAPC and ACPE members in order to introduce to them my research project and invite them to participate. Among the final 158 AAPC members and the 284 ACPE members who did not opt out, 58 pastoral caregivers participated in the survey (a 13% participation rate). Later, I expanded an invitation to 178 AAPC fellow members in an effort to recruit more interviewees from the pastoral counselors group. Among them, six more pastoral counselors participated in the survey, and two more interviewees participated in the follow-up study. Of the total 600 recipients of the invitation, 64 participated in the surveys and/or interviews. Therefore, the total participation rate is approximately ten percent (64 participants / 600 recipients).

Even though the participation rate was low, the survey was successful in collecting enough data to find important concepts, in recruiting sufficient interviewees, and in supplementing interview data. This survey design helped me collect simple clear data of pastoral identity from a larger sample. The design also served well at the recruitment process, and 18 of the 20 interviewees (90%) were from the survey participants. Nineteen pastoral caregivers participated in both surveys and interviews, which means 44 participated in the survey alone and one participated in the interview only.

The survey questions are simple but nonetheless central to the project. The questions consist of a set of three open-ended inquiries about (1) a situation that sparked the participant to reflect on his or her pastoral identity, (2) what helped the person construct a pastoral identity in that situation, and (3) who the participant is as a pastoral caregiver (chaplain or pastoral counselor). These survey questions aim to generate a general idea of some contexts, strategies, and images that the participants describe for pastoral identity. In particular, the research adopted the third question, "Who am I as a pastoral caregiver?" from symbolic interactionist Manford Kuhn and his colleague's (1954) "Twenty Statements Test" (TST), which many scholars recognize as a "useful instrument for monitoring so-called postmodern trends in identity formation" and for capturing the multiplicity of identity (Côté 1996, 138; cf. Vryan et al. 2003).

While gathering and analyzing web-based survey responses, I also conducted interviews with the participants who were available. The interviews follow what Strauss and Corbin (1998) called "theoretical sampling," sampling that collects data necessary to fill theoretical gaps for a further development of the emerging theory based on the theoretical comparison. I supplemented some interviews by conducting written communications via emails, if needed. I recorded all interview conversations digitally, which a professional transcriber transcribed into texts. I analyzed all survey and interview data using Weft QDA, a free computer software application for qualitative data analysis (available from http://www.pressure.to/qda/). However, I used the computer software on a limited basis in order to enhance my analytic rigor since the computer program conducted a more careful reading of the data (Seale, 2003).

As potential participants either emailed me or left their email addresses at the end of the surveys, I emailed them back, made certain about their qualifications for the interview, and requested that they fill out and sign a statement of informed consent. I set the following specific criteria for interviewees:

1. The participants are pastoral counselors or chaplains as AAPC or ACPE members, for example.
2. They are full-time caregivers. However, if they have retired or moved to different ministries, such as a parish ministry or an administrative

position, but still deliver part-time pastoral care/counseling services directly (not through supervision) to clients/patients as a counselor or chaplain, then they qualify.

If they have retired, no longer deliver pastoral care-giving (even though they have long careers in pastoral care-giving), and/or do only supervise and train others, then they do not qualify for this study.

3. Their experience in full-time care-giving ministry can range from one year to more than 20 years.
4. The location of their ministry can vary as well, even though most cases may be in North America.

I scheduled interview dates with the volunteers at a mutually convenient time and conducted 20 telephone interviews, ranging from around 45 minutes to 90 minutes each. Interview questions were semi-structured but open enough to allow me to follow emerging concepts during the interviews. The interviews revolved around the following major inquiries:

(1) How do contemporary pastoral caregivers perceive pastoral identity?

    a. "In the daily practices you've just described, what gives you a strong sense of pastoral identity?"

    b. "What springs up in your mind when you hear the term *pastoral identity*?"

(2) What are the contexts in which pastoral practitioners reflect on pastoral identity?

    a. "Please try to recall a typical moment in recent weeks or months when you were able to reflect on your pastoral identity. What situations prompted you to think of your pastoral identity?"

    b. "As a result of the reflection you've just described, what did you learn about your pastoral identity? How would you describe what pastoral identity means for you?"

(3) What helps caregivers shape and construct pastoral identity?

    a. "What do you, as a pastoral counselor (or chaplain), think shapes your pastoral identity the most?"

    b. "What kinds of experiences or relationships have been most important in shaping your pastoral identity?"

(4) How do pastoral caregivers interact with care-seekers in the course of their daily practices? How do care-seekers contribute to caregivers' pastoral identity?

    a. "What practices do you think make your care receivers realize that you are a 'pastoral' person?"

    b. "How do care-seekers contribute to your pastoral identity?" "What role does the care-seeker play in helping you construct your pastoral identity?"

    c. "What relationship do you have with your care-seekers in constructing your identity?"

(5) How do they describe the development of pastoral identity over time?

    a. "How would you describe your pastoral identity over time?" "How has your pastoral identity evolved throughout your career as a pastoral caregiver?"

    b. "Is your pastoral identity relatively stable or flexible throughout your ministry?"

(6) How does a larger context impact their pastoral identity?

    a. "What do you see as contemporary changes in your care-giving environment, as compared to your past practices?" "How do these changes you've just described affect your pastoral identity and practices?"

    b. "Reflecting on your contemporary contexts, how do you see these contexts militating for or against your pastoral identity?"

    c. "How would you accommodate your religious call and institutional expectations in these contexts?"

The main focus of the interview was on how pastoral caregivers establish their pastoral identity in everyday practices and how pastoral relationships between caregiver and care-seeker contribute to the identity. I was also interested in how pastoral caregivers find a way to maintain their pastoral identity and at the same time provide effective care and counseling in postmodern, intercultural, and multifaith contexts.

The interview partners co-constructed pastoral practitioners' experiences through the interviews. While asking questions, I was especially interested in actions and interactions that the care partners do in their relationships. Of course, talk is also an important action in human interactions. I tried to get their actions and interactions in an active, behavioral form as postmodern counseling questions do (e.g., O'Hanlon et al. 1999).

In this report, I labeled all research participants and used pseudonymous names for interviewees (as in chapter 3). I called survey participants S1, S2, and S3 up to S63 in the order of their participation in the survey. I also labeled interviewees from I1 through I20 in the order of conducting interviews. As for the transcribed interview data, I numbered each turn of interview conversations as I1, I2, I3, etc. for the *Interviewer* and P1, P2, P3, etc., in turn, for the *Participant*. The following is an example of transcribed interview data:

> I35: So, it's not [that] you are the giver and they are the receivers, but it's [equal and collegial.]
>
> P35: No, it's much more of a giving and receiving, but from the both sides I give and receive as much as they do.
>
> I36: Right, it's not monologue, but it's . . .
>
> P36: Oh no, no, no, no. Definitely not. Definitely not.

For validation and reliability, I contacted the interview participants via email, asking them to respond if they would be able to read my preliminary draft of the findings and give me their feedback. Ten of them replied back, and nine participants reviewed my report of findings and made comments. The respondents affirmed the finding, and I reflected their comments in my final writings.

RESEARCH PARTICIPANTS

Sixty-three pastoral practitioners participated in the survey study. Among them, 54 participants (86%) were ordained, six (9%) were laity, and three (5%) gave no response. Thirty-one pastoral counselors (48%) and 30 chaplains (47%) (two with no response) answered the surveys. In terms of gender, there were 31 males (48%) and 30 females (47%) (two with no response) participated. Years of ministry as a pastoral caregiver varied. Twenty participants (32%) has served more than 20 years in the ministry, eleven (17%) 10–20 years, nine (14%) 5–10 years, ten (16%) less than five years full-time, eight (13%) more than five years part-time, and three (5%) less than five years part-time (two (3%) with no response).

Twenty participants in the interview study consisted of ten chaplains and ten pastoral counselors, with clinical experiences ranging from two years to more than 20 years. Ten of the twenty were female, and seventeen were ordained. Five listed their religious affiliations as Baptist, four as Presbyterian, three as Roman Catholic, and two as interfaith (adherents of new religious movements). The remaining participants included an Episcopalian, a Methodist, and a Lutheran, a Mennonite, a Seventh Day Adventist, and one non-denominationalist with a Methodist background. Almost all participants were located in North America except one from a European country.

Types of pastoral care-giving in which the participants engaged included parish-based pastoral counseling (three participants), center-based pastoral counseling (three participants), and private pastoral counseling (three participants), counseling in hospital as a spiritual advisor (one participant), hospital chaplaincy (seven participants), hospice chaplaincy (two participants), and prison chaplaincy (one participant). Some of the caregivers were full-time pastoral counselors (three interviewees) or chaplains (seven interviewees), others half-/part-time pastoral caregivers (seven interviewees) with church ministry (three of the seven interviewees), and still others were doing both chaplaincy and pastoral counseling (two interviewees). One interview participant had just started serving a local parish after nine years chaplaincy experiences. The participants' professional affiliations also vary depending on their preference for AAPC, ACPE, ACCCA (American Catholic Correctional Chaplains Association), APC (Association of Professional Chaplains), CPSP (College of Pastoral Supervision and Psychotherapy), or mixed affiliation within these organizations.

DATA ANALYSIS

There were two major steps of analyzing the empirical data collected from the surveys and interviews. I analyzed the survey data first to find an overall impression of pastoral identity and then analyzed both survey and interview data based upon the coding procedures of grounded theory. Overall, both findings from the first and second-step analyses are compatible and fit each other in the sense that the second set of findings gives detailed descriptions of the first findings while the first set of findings delineates a preliminary sketch of the second results. These findings are helpful for generating a theory of pastoral identity.

A Brief Description of the Survey Analysis

To get an overall outline of the survey data, I used a form of content analysis and frequency test for all three questions: (1) In a recent week or month, what situation sparked you to reflect on your pastoral identity? (2) What helped you construct pastoral identity in that situation? and (3) "As a pastoral caregiver, I am . . ." In regard to the first survey question, the participants described care-giving situations as prompting them to reflect on pastoral identity. Thirty-eight participants (60.3%) illustrated care-giving situations in which they encountered care-seekers who were patients, counselees, families, staff at worksites, or spirituality groups. In particular, of the 38 respondents, eleven illuminated the end-of-life situations in which chaplains offered care for dying patients in terminal illness or their families in decision-making. Also, eleven participants described care-giving situations in which they conversed with care-seekers about religious issues and God-talks. Thus, care-giving situations were the main circumstances in which survey participants thought of their pastoral identities.

Besides care-giving situations, other situations included those in which respondents were in certification process as counselors or chaplains or discussed theological issues with an individual or in a group (S12, S40, S42, S20). In particular, five survey participants pointed out some role-confusing situations in which they were wondering about their appropriate roles as caregiver and staff (S8, S30) or as pastor and psychotherapist (S25, S38). Five other respondents mentioned job-related issues such as things being in transition (S2, S4, S15). The rest of the responses were not easy to categorize. Accordingly, the majority of the situations the participants described were care-giving situations in which they encounter care-seekers and provide them with care and counseling (see fig. 3).

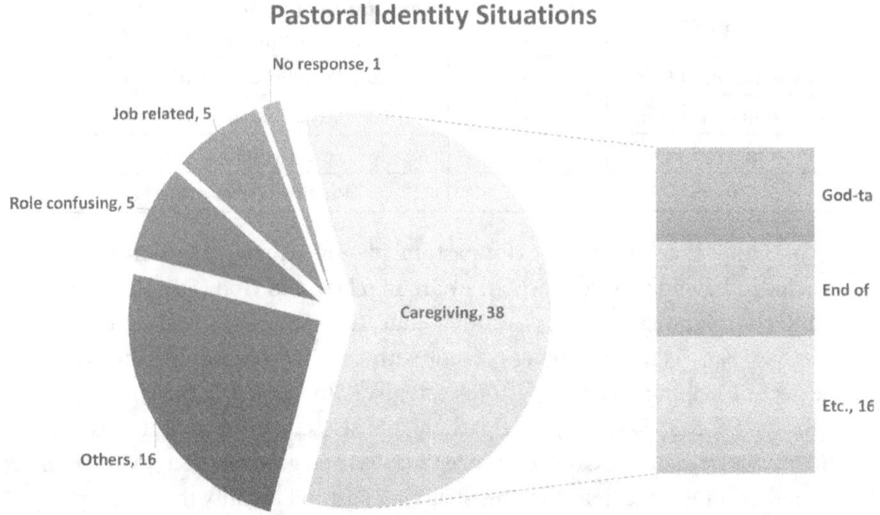

Pastoral Identity Situations

- No response, 1
- Job related, 5
- Role confusing, 5
- Caregiving, 38
- Others, 16
- God-ta
- End of
- Etc., 16

Figure 3. Situations in Which to Think of Pastoral Identity.

As for the second survey question, what helped pastoral caregivers construct their identities in situations that sparked them to think of pastoral identity, survey participants expressed various opinions that show some strategies for pastoral identity. Among them, (theological) reflection got the most attention from the respondents. Seventeen instances pointed out that reflecting on biblical and theological themes, images, and stories helped them to construct their pastoral identities in those situations. Five other instances also talked about reflection on something that is not religious or theological (see table 2).

Table 2. Helping Sources/Strategies for Pastoral Identity

Helping Sources/ Strategies for Pastoral Identity	Numbers of Instance that were Mentioned	Examples of the Sources/Strategies
Reflection	22	On the biblical and theological (17), On general issues (5)
Remembering Who They Are	10	In relations to God (3), Faith community (2), and Education, trainings, & skills (5)
Interaction with Care-seekers	10	Their requests (2), Appreciations (3), Acceptance (1), Life-stories (1), Others (3)
Presence	8	Being present (5), Accepting (1), Listening (1), Providing a safe space(1)
Realization of God	6	God's presence (3), Guidance (3)
Personal Devotion	3	Prayer and Bible reading
Supervision	3	Individual, Group
Others	8	Previous experiences (3)

Other shaping strategies for pastoral identity expressed by participants included having a sense of who they are in relation to God (S24, S58), their faith communities (S54, S55), or their educations, trainings, and experiences (S39, S46, S51, S26). Being present with care-seekers was another good aspect of helping some of pastoral caregivers to construct their identities (S1, S5, S6, S11, S21, S59). The participants also constructed their pastoral identities by realizing God's presence (S9, S64) and guidance (S24, S32, S63). Another important source for constructing pastoral identity that many pastoral caregivers mentioned was their care-partners. Care-seekers' requests (S3, S10), acceptance (S50), sharing stories (S57), appreciations (S7, S30), and "word of mouth referrals" (S15) all helped participants' identity construction, according to the respondents. They also mentioned individual/peer supervision (S9, S37, S47) and prayer and bible reading (S8, S27, S33). If we count caregivers' being present with care-receivers as an interaction with them, then the interrelationship with them contributes to pastoral identity construction the second most (18 instances).

In regard to the ten-statements test as to "Who am I as a pastoral caregiver?," the survey respondents offered many ways of identifying themselves. Since the question qualified themselves as pastoral caregivers, the respondents, rather than listing socially "consensual" statuses (e.g., "Presbyterian," "psychotherapist"), were likely to describe and interpret themselves in terms of relationships, belongings, images, beliefs, social roles, inner qualities, professional traits, pastoral attitudes, and existential statements. These qualities require "interpretation by the respondent to be precise," which Kuhn and McPartland (1954) called "subconsensual" (69). Nonetheless, obviously repeated concepts and themes emerged from the respondents' interpretations of themselves as pastoral caregivers.

As shown in Table 3, the most obvious self-concepts by which the respondents described themselves are relational and inter-subjective. The most frequent concepts the participants identified were listening, compassion, and presence. These qualities most clearly define who pastoral caregivers are and what they do, according to this research. Besides these three self-concepts, qualities such as encourager, supporter, guide, companion, and fellow human also characterize relational identities of pastoral caregivers. These relational qualities of pastoral identity include relationships with God, as they define themselves as God's representatives and partakers.

Table 3. Responses to the Who Am I Question

Identity	Variables	Number of Instance/Respondent	Examples
Listener	Hearer, Listening ear	32/31	"called to listen as a form of service" (S14) "hearer of stories" (31) "I am an ear so I can hear" (S32)
Compassion	Empathy, Caring	25/23	"compassionate friend" (S40) "called to the ministry of compassion and healing" (S58)
Presence	Humanly, God's	26/21	"someone who just is with the patient and family" (S39) "God's visible presence" (S18)

Theologian	Theological, Integration	21/18	"able to think theologically and bring that dimension to the therapeutic experience" (S62) "knowledgeable in theological reflection" (S45)
Encourager	Support, Nurture, Comfort, Empower	21/17	"empathic encourager of positive transformation" (S10) "supporter of emotional health, relational success, and spiritual growth" (S58) "hugger for those who need hugs" (S32)
Teacher	Guide, Coach Educator, Shepherd	20/15	"a guide along a journey" (S47) "mentor," "guru" (S59) "provider of information/assistance" (S50)
Therapist	Counselor, Clinician	17/15	"a crafter of helpful questions" (S15) "able to find patterns in a patient's narrative to find the underlying problem if it is different from the presenting problem" (S46)
(Pastoral) Caregiver	Helper, Servant	22/14	"available to serve God's people" (S41) "wanting to be helpful" (S46)
Companion	Walking-with, Friend, Partner	19/14	"a companion in health, illness or grief journey" (S47) "mourning/celebrating with the patient" (S50) "will to walk that walk with those I care for" (S56)
God's representative	God's vessel, Instrument, Witness	17/13	"to channel the healing power of the Spirit" (S14) "extension of God to hurting people" (S32) "symbol of the comforting love of God" (S33)
Fellow human	Human being, Sinner	15/12	"hurting brother" (S1) "humbled by the task that I can only complete with God's help" (S10)

Pastoral counselor	Spiritual Director	16/11	"listen to God's presence and power to unfold in my work as a pastoral counselor" (S58) "to help others sort through their spiritual struggles" (S63)
Divine partaker	Working with God, Co-creator	14/11	"co-creator with God in growth and change" (S9), "sees God working incarnationally via human encounter with fellow humans" (S38)
Healer	Healing	11/11	"a balm for those who are suffering" (S16), "able to bring a healing process for broken lives" (S62).
Pastor	Minister, Clergy, Priest, Preacher	13/10	"a universal priest: leading the patient in worship in the midst of their own Christian or Jewish tradition" (S49), "the only minister many of my unchurched clients have" (S58)

In addition to being persons who listen to care-seekers and are empathic and present with them, the participants identified themselves most often as theologians. They recognized the importance, as pastoral caregivers, of having a theological perspective and integrating with theological perspectives the psychological, behavioral, and spiritual resources for healing. Thus, the respondents described themselves as theologians, encouragers, teachers, caregivers, and pastors who have a more holistic approach to their care-seekers than therapists who focus on a psychological dimension of life. The participants cared for care-seekers' physical, emotional, and spiritual distresses and concerned themselves with the individual and social issues of the helped (see chapter 3 for detailed descriptions of these qualities).

Open Coding of the Whole Research Data

Based on the analytic procedure of grounded theory (Strauss et al. 1998), I analyzed interview transcriptions as well as survey data. From open coding, which is an analytic process of capturing categories and their properties and dimensions, I found seven major categories: (1) contexts in which care-giving takes place, (2) perceptions of caregivers on pastoral identity, (3) strategies for shaping pastoral identity, (4) styles of relational, therapeutic, theological, constructional, and developmental stances, (5) social acts between caregivers and seekers, (6) care-giving phases, and (7) constructed pastoral identities. These categories were refined and saturated with their proper properties and dimensions (see table 4).

Table 4. Open Coding of Pastoral Identity in Practice

Categories	Subcategories	Properties	Dimensionalized Examples	
Contexts		Care-giving	Routine visits	End-of-life
		Faith community	Deeply engaged	Loosely connected
		Institutional	Team ministry	Generic spiritual care
		Contemporary	Inter-culture	Multi-faith
Perceptions		Sense of vocation	God's calling	Care-seeker's calling
		Goal of ministry	Meeting needs	Traditional care goals
		Meaning of PI	Representative	Presence
		Who I am	Listener	Prophet
Shaping strategies		Self-care	Daily devotion	Retreat
		Supervision & consultation	Within the department (e.g. Supervisor)	Outside the department (e.g. Spiritual director)
		Reflection	Theological	General
		Presence	Sitting with care-seekers	Listening deeply to them
		Interactions	Introduction	Appreciation/ rejection
Styles		Pastoral relationship	Authoritarian	Collaborative
		Therapeutic stance	Compassionate	Neutral
		Theological stance	"Grounded"	"Fluffy"
		Identity construction	Self-construction	Social-construction
		Professional development	"Theologically unaware"	"Pastorally competent"

Social acts	Interactions (in)visible	Caregivers	Approaching people	Maeeting needs
		Care-seekers	Open deeply	Reject
	Talks	Both partners	Social talk	God-talk
	Emotions	Caregivers	Frustrations	Joys
		Care-seekers	Grief	Appreciation
Care-giving phases		Introduction	Education	Accepting/rejecting
		Development	Presence	"Entering"
		Turn	"Calling"	Meeting needs
		Conclusion	Affirmation	Realization
Pastoral identity construction		Spiritual figure	Representative	Interfaith caregiver
		Fellow human	Presence	Companion
		Pastoral caregiver	Theological reflection	Meeting needs
		Divine partaker	Realization of God's presence	Collaboration with God

The first category, "contexts," refers to cultural circumstances in which pastoral caregivers work and reflect on their identity. Among many possible properties, this study focused primarily on four properties: care-giving, faith community, institutional, and contemporary contexts. The "care-giving" context is an immediate circumstance that stimulates a person to reflect on pastoral identity. In that context, pastoral practitioners encounter care-seekers and their sufferings, which often make caregivers mull over the human condition and their roles and identities. Care-giving situations include routine visits by chaplains or counselees and pastoral care and counseling in prison or hospice ministries (e.g., end-of-life situations).

In addition to care-giving contexts, the relation to the faith community sets an important context for pastoral care and counseling. Some of the care-giving ministries are deeply engaged in the faith community in terms of locations (where the care-giving takes place) and resources that support ministry (I10, I14, I17, I20). By contrast, other ministries are loosely connected with, and often located outside, the faith community, as they provide generic spiritual supports (I13, I16). In general, pastoral caregivers perceive care-giving outside the faith community as more challenging than the care-giving in a close relationship with the faith community (I11, I14).

The phenomenon of losing a connection with the faith community results, in part, from an institutional context. This context refers to a structural influence of the health care institution whose philosophy, missions, and policies impact the caregivers' pastoral practices. Some secular psychotherapeutic supervisions or health care institutions were insensitive to faith traditions and perspectives of pastoral caregivers, which made it difficult for them to provide pastoral care and counseling (I14, I20). Some institutions approached pastoral care and counseling as one small component of the large machine called health care systems that focus on the outcome (I1). On the other spectrum of the institutional context, some institutions recognized the importance of pastoral care-giving and work as part of an interdisciplinary team that can deliver both health care and spiritual care at the same time. The following is a description of such cooperative team work in a health care institution:

> P13: [I]t is also very common when I am introduced to [patients] then I will stand there at their bedside and hold their hand while they are being asked medical questions by the team and they feel that strong connection with me; that I am there for them to help support them. And I may or may not have said very much to them at all yet. But there will be a connection made that they feel comfortable. And then we can talk as we need to through that process. And I may be able to ask a question and reflect on it spiritually, a medical question or a medical situation in a way that is comforting or helpful for them.
>
> [Ellipsis]
>
> I15: So the team seems like very cooperative with each other.
>
> P15: Yeah.
>
> I16: Okay.
>
> P16: And if the patient gets very emotional, say it is someone who has just gotten a new cancer diagnosis, and they are very tearful and very upset and it becomes obvious that faith is a very important thing to them. It is not unusual for one of the physicians even to say, "Would it be helpful if we stopped and we asked [chaplain name] to say a prayer now to help us through this so that we can do what we need to from all of these disciplines to help take care of you?"
>
> I17: Then the pastoral care-giving would be more powerful than just doing alone.
>
> P17: Yes. It is very soothing to patients that physicians would be open to suggest, to participate in that, [and] to be present.
>
> I18: So, when you visit patients you usually go as a team?

P18: That is correct. [Most days I return alone to see 2–3 patients later in the day.] (I8)

While such an institutional context shapes pastoral care-giving in many influential ways, contemporary cultures spray a postmodern, intercultural, and multifaith color on pastoral care-giving. These contextual colors take shape not only in the caregivers' perceptions but also in their approaches and responses to needs of the helped and to the institution's expectations (I1, I13, I16). The study found some noticeable influences of postmodernity on the participants' perceptions and experiences of pastoral identity. The postmodern characteristics of pastoral identity are perceptible. They are more immediate than ultimate in terms of goals, more inclusive than focused in terms of approaches, sensitive to care-seekers' needs, more flexible than stable in terms of identity, collaborative in terms of relationships, and intercultural and multifaith in terms of contexts, as chapter 4 will discuss.

The second category, "perceptions," reflects the caregivers' understanding of several issues related to pastoral identity. The participants perceived two distinguished senses of vocations: one related to vertical dimensions of pastoral identity and the other its horizontal aspects. In addition to seeing the pastoral vocation as a product of their psychological and educational development, the respondents saw their vocations not only as God's calls but also as calls from the care-seekers. Some respondents contended that they felt a sense of God's call to their current ministry. Other participants articulated a horizontal call, which for some was a confirmation for their divine calls and for others was a specific call from their care-giving ministries. Thus, the horizontal dimension has two distinguishing callings: one from the environments in which to become pastoral caregivers and the other from care-seekers they encounter. Moreover, goals in their ministries range *from* providing traditional goals of pastoral care such as healing, reconciling, guiding, sustaining, "celebrating" (I1), and "reminding" (I15) experiences *to* serving "in whatever way" they can do to meet needs of care-seekers (I13, I16). Meanings of pastoral identity the respondents described vary from the embodiment and representation of God to being present with care-seekers. Moreover, the participants see their pastoral identities as listener, theologian, encourager, helper, prophet, and so on, as noted above.

The third category, shaping strategies, connotes tactics of how the pastoral helping professionals shape their pastoral identities. These strategies include personal self-care, supervision and consultation, theological reflection, and interactions with care-seekers. Self-care ranges from daily devotions, such as Bible readings and prayers, to a weekend retreat. The respondents have consultations not only with a supervisor or in peer groups but also with someone outside of their care team like their regional denominational friend, spiritual director, or social work friend. In response to a question such as what shapes pastoral identity the most, the pastoral clinicians often refer to reflection upon theological, biblical, and religious issues, as well as on incidents and encounters. Presence is another important strategy by which the respondents just sit with their care-seekers or deeply attend to their stories. Moreover, interestingly, the respondents also claim that care-seekers help them construct their pastoral identities through various relationships and interactions, such as rejecting, accepting, and/or appreciating pastoral services.

Participants take different approaches to such issues as pastoral relationships, therapeutic relationships, theological stances, identity constructions, and professional developments. Some respondents start with an authoritarian relationship with care-seekers (like a relationship between a doctor/surgeon and patients) at the beginning of their pastoral care careers, but many participants articulate their pastoral relationships as a collaborative companionship. Therapeutic stances are neutral or without agenda on the one hand and compassionate on the other hand. Theological stances differ between those of denomination-oriented pastoral caregivers and interfaith clinicians, one group trying to ground care-giving practices on theological perspectives and the other being more inclusive in meeting needs of care-seekers. Some participants are less aware of the care-seekers' contribution to their pastoral identity, but others understand the importance of interactions with care-partners in constructing their identities. In regard to the professional development, one interviewee (I20) articulates her development of pastoral identity by using the "four stages of the competence" learning model in which one learns a new skill from a stage of "unconscious incompetence" to a stage of "unconscious competence" through stages of "conscious incompetence" and "conscious competence." Likewise, another interviewee (I5) describes his development from a stage of "theological unawareness" to a stage of "pastoral competence."

Social acts, the fifth category in Mead's terms, consist of "joint activity directed, explicitly or implicitly, toward an objective or end" and occur readily "in the form of purposeful cooperative behavior wherein participants are engaging in the accomplishment of a common task" (Blumer et al. 2004, 96). In this sense, pastoral care and counseling is a social act in which the care partners jointly interact in order to handle care-seekers' lived experiences and stories. Social acts in pastoral care-giving include actions, talks, and emotions as subcategories in this open coding. Interactions between caregivers and seekers vary from visible activities, such as visiting, rejecting, and having a conversation, to invisible actions, like internal projection, opening the heart, and inner reflection. Talks are also an important social act in pastoral care-giving. They revolve around life-stories in which care-seekers confront their predicaments, and they can go deeper into existential, spiritual, and theological issues the stories contain. Moreover, emotions are a socially shaped embodiment of the social actor and crucial to facilitating cognitive processes (Franks, 2003). Depending on their interactions, both care partners can get frustrated, upset, or joyful.

The study also found that as the care-giving progresses, the relationships and interactions between the care partners take different shapes. The sixth category, care-giving phases, refers to developmental phases of the care-giving process in which pastoral encounters start, develop, turn, and end. These phases are not sequential building blocks that happen always one after another but are various dynamic processes of care-giving and receiving interactions. Nonetheless, one can construct the collected data to look at how a care-giving process develops a pattern from its introduction to the conclusion. In these care-giving phases, pastoral practitioners construct their identities in the midst of interacting with care-seekers, as will be described in chapter 4.

The last category, pastoral identity construction, reflects how the respondents can, collectively, construct their pastoral identities in the course of daily care-giving practices. According to the study's findings, four significant properties of this category are noticeable in the phases of care-giving interactions between the social act partners. These properties are "spiritual figure," "fellow human," "pastor," and "divine partaker," as the next chapter will describe in detail.

Axial Coding for a Structural Context of Pastoral Identity

Once major themes and categories are identified, the procedure of axial coding looks for relationships between the categories along with the central phenomenon (see fig. 4). The most notable key phenomenon in this study lies in pastoral caregivers' encounters with care-seekers, through which the helpers construct their identities. The study indicates that pastoral identity is not primarily a personal awareness; rather, it is a social construction of the social actors in a care-giving context. After identifying this central phenomenon, I look for its connection with other categories. First, pastoral caregivers construct their identities by "symbolically" interacting in the care-giving and receiving process. The interactions are symbolic in that both social actors act toward a common goal to handle the care-seeker's issues, interpreting the meanings of language and symbols they communicate. The main phenomenon and its (inter-)action strategies shape a process for and the dynamics of constructing pastoral identity, as Chapter Three will describe. Depending on how care partners interact and interpret the meanings of their communications, the consequences of constructing pastoral identity will vary.

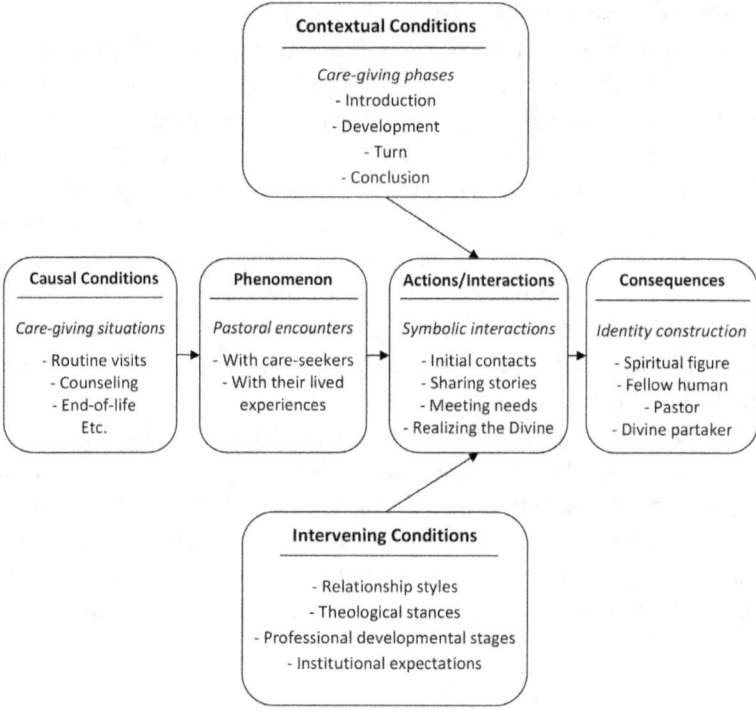

Figure 4. Axial Coding: Structural Context of Pastoral Identity

Furthermore, some variable conditions influence this process and dynamic. Strauss and Corbin (1990) call these conditions "causal," "intervening," and "contextual" conditions depending on their functions. "Causal" conditions, or events that lead to the development of pastoral encounters, are care-giving situations. In various pastoral care-giving situations, pastoral caregivers encounter care-seekers and their lived experiences, which cause caregivers to think of their identity and to engage in identity construction. "Intervening" conditions such as pastoral professional development, relationship styles, theological stances, and institutional expectations can facilitate or constrain the actions/interactions strategies for identity construction. Moreover, identity construction takes place under the specific conditions at each care-giving phase of introduction, development, turn, and conclusion. At each care-giving phase, the care partners interact with different strategies to construct their identities in that particular situation. As Figure 4 shows, the axial coding diagram presents a good structural context of pastoral care-giving and identity construction.

Selective Coding for a Story of the Pastoral Identity Construction

From the open and axial coding, we can deductively propose, by constantly interplaying "between proposing and checking," provisional statements of relationships between categories. Throughout the coding procedure in general and through the constant interplay between provisional statements and actual data in particular, this study proposes the following provisional propositions:

(1) Various care-giving situations give rise to the occurrence of pastoral encounters between caregivers and seekers (and their lived experiences), which provides an ample space for the caregivers to think of their identities.

(2) In such pastoral encounters, the care partners interact in mutual efforts to find an answer to the seeker's predicaments and, in this course of care-giving, construct their identities.

(3) Accordingly, pastoral identity is, indeed, a social construction co-created by the care partners who bring with them lived experiences into the encounter and interact toward their shared goals.

(4) Thus, pastoral caregivers construct a pastoral identity in the midst of their care-giving practices, and the pastoral identity, in turn, guides and informs their practices.

Like axial coding, the selective coding procedure also relates the core category to other categories, but in a more abstract and narrative mode, by integrating these categories to generate a grounded theory of the topic being examined. This selective coding is like facilitating a hermeneutic circle as this procedure moves back and forth between the categories and a higher conceptualized story in order to generate a theory. The selective coding procedure also validates the relationships of categories and fills in any missing details. By taking into consideration all of these codings, the study generates a grounded theory of pastoral identity construction, as will be described in Chapter Three. Before turning to the full story of a process and dynamics of the pastoral identity construction, I provide here a story line of this phenomenon:

> The main story in the narratives of the respondents seems to be about how pastoral caregivers form their identities in their everyday practices. When pastoral caregivers try to provide care and counseling to people (causal conditions), they encounter the care-seekers and their lived experiences (phenomenon) by interacting each other to obtain a common goal of caring (action strategies) along with their relationships and/or theological stances (intervening conditions) at each different phase of the interactions (contextual conditions), which leads to a socially constructed pastoral identity (consequences). Each care-giving encounter gives rise to the need to think about who pastoral caregivers are in relationship to their care-seekers. In the course of the daily care-giving process, the care partners interact with each other to handle the issues the care-seekers have brought up by interpreting meanings of the social acts they communicate.
>
> In the introductory phase, chaplains' and pastoral counselors' care-giving approaches to people at times means representing a spiritual figure. In turn, people welcome or reject the pastoral approach, depending on their interpretation of the meaning. As the care-giving process goes on, care-seekers share their stories while caregivers are present with them and listen to their stories. As a fellow human, the caregiver learns from care-seekers and walks with them into their sufferings. Such companionship makes the caregiver deeply compassionate and attentive to care-seekers' calls for help and, thereby, allows him or her to enter their world. By theologically reflecting on the issues and making meaning with the seekers, pastoral caregivers become their "pastors." In these whole processes, the care partners at times realize that God is present and acts with them and that the caregiver has been a partaker in the divine presence and work.

SUMMARY

In this chapter, I have delineated my empirical study based on grounded theory. I collected data from 63 survey participants and 20 interviewees and analyzed them by using open, axial, and selective coding methods. The data show a contextual structure in which pastoral caregivers offer care-giving to care-seekers in everyday practices and construct identities with the seekers.

Pastoral identity is a social and relational construction mutually created by pastoral care partners through dynamic care-giving interactions within a specific cultural context. This relational, interactional construction will be the target of the next chapter. Moreover, the cultural context as a shaping force often influences identity construction of pastoral care partners. The care partners adapt to the cultural forces and sometimes work to change them. Chapter 4 will focus on the interaction between cultural structure and human agency.

3

Pastoral Identity in Care-Giving Relationships

PASTORAL IDENTITY FROM A MICRO-LEVEL PERSPECTIVE

IN THIS CHAPTER, I will describe the core phenomena that comprise experiences of a pastoral care-giving process and of a pastoral identity construction in that process, as narrated by the chaplains and pastoral counselors who participated in the empirical study. The identity formation in this study reveals the dynamics of pastoral identity construction, which result from the process of offering pastoral care and counseling and the interactions between the caregiver and care-seeker. In reality, the process of a pastoral caregiver's construction of pastoral identity is not linearly organizable but rather dynamically interactive. Nonetheless, guided by a grounded theory design for a theory-building purpose, I try to follow, through the data analysis, some obvious themes in this interactive process that surface throughout the narratives of the research participants. This analytic description derives from fusing two horizons of understanding: one of the textualized data narrated by the participants and the other of my perspectival interpretation of the data, which may be biased from my epistemological and theological point of view.

The data analysis in this study reveals several key themes of the identity construction in the course of pastoral care-giving: (a) encountering care-seekers as a spiritual representative, (b) being present with and listening to care-seekers as a compassionate fellow human, (c) becoming a theologically and spiritually sensitive pastor in responding to their stories and needs, and (d) discovering a divine presence and power as a partaker of God's ministry. Here is a brief description of these four phases of pastoral identity construction, according to the participants in this project. Before entering into a caregiving situation, pastoral caregivers often keep in mind an identity as spiritual figures. Encountering human lived experiences, however, the caregivers humble themselves like care-seekers in suffering and listen to their stories. As the care-giving relationship proceeds, the helpers hear care-seekers' requests for a pastoral presence and support, and the care partners may realize at some point that God has been within the pastoral relationship. Within these thematic procedures, many unique and various dynamics of interactions between the pastoral caregiver and care-seeker take place, depending on the nature of pastoral relationships.[1]

1. ENCOUNTERING CARE-SEEKERS AS A SPIRITUAL REPRESENTATIVE

[Pastoral identity is] being able to understand who I am, how I am particularly wired from God in my calling to be able to help other people. I have to have an understanding of who I am before I can help others.

—CHAPLAIN GEORGE

As Chaplain George suggests in the quotation above, before entering into a care-giving situation, pastoral caregivers have a certain perception of who they are. One of the dominant ideas the respondents articulated is that they represent God or something spiritual and divine. This idea has a long history in the contemporary discipline of pastoral care and counseling. In his 1961 article, Jernigan said that the pastoral caregiver is a "representative of God" to others and has "authority which is both uniquely his [or hers] as

---

1. One precautionary remark: I mean that these four phases are by no means sequential building blocks, in which one always follows another. In reality, care-giving processes can be suddenly stopped and discontinued at any time (even at the offset) or in many ways (by clients or emergent situations). Rather, the process is dynamic and flux movement depending on the care-giving situations and relationships between the social actors. Hence, my construction of the four-phase care-giving process is a heuristic, dramaturgical description to illustrate how a care-giving process develops a pattern from its introduction to the conclusion. As a result of the research finding, the description does not suggest an ideal of care-giving practices to follow all the way or any criterion to judge them.

an individual and commonly his [or hers] as a chosen representative and leader of the Christian community" (196–97).

With this presumed identity, intentional or unintentional, pastoral caregivers approach people in immediate or potential need. In this initial contact period, people also have a pre-understanding of chaplains or pastoral counselors and their work and, thereby, are likely to act upon this understanding. People can reject or respect the pastoral caregivers depending on their needs, religious orientations, previous experiences, and so on. Accordingly, pastoral caregivers need to introduce themselves and explain who they are and what they do in order to help people accept their pastoral services. Thus, in such an introductory phase, care-giving encounters consist of five processes respectively: (a) approaching with a presumed identity as a spiritual representative, (b) briefly introducing pastoral care-giving and its provider, (c) people's projection onto the caregivers, (d) educating people, and (e) people's responses to the caregivers.

Approaching People with a Presumed Identity

A presumed pastoral identity means a pastoral caregiver's self-understanding as a spiritual figure that he or she constructs through a religious, vocational, educational, and communal sense of calling, as well as previous care-giving experiences of who he or she is, before entering into an encounter with a care-seeker. This presumed pastoral identity consists of who they believe they are as caregivers based on their engagement in (a) a personal relationship with God, (b) a vocational relationship, and (c) a relationship with the faith community. Needless to say, educational training to be a pastoral caregiver and previous experiences as a pastoral counselor and chaplain also contribute to his or her presumed identity (I14, I20).

Several pastoral caregivers in the study identify themselves (a) as children of God (S1, S7, S45, S63, cf. S14, S20), (b) as persons called by God to care for others (S10, S14, S42), and (c) as ministers endorsed or authorized by the church to serve as pastoral caregivers (S55, I4, I12, I19). Such personal, vocational, and communal commitments to the faith and God play a central role in the conception of pastoral caregivers as spiritual figures. Such grounds of the presumed pastoral identity are important resources for doing pastoral ministry so that they do not have to wonder who they are every day when they help other people (I2).

Especially, the presumed pastoral identity is strongly interconnected with the divine calling to the ministry. Of the 20 interview participants, 14 described their pastoral identity in a vertical dimension, and eight of them had a strong pastoral identity as being called by the divine to their ministry. Chaplain Shelly explains this vertical sense of pastoral identity: "Through reflection and prayer and through the opportunities that have come up, I have a strong sense that God has led me to this place even though I didn't know where I was going . . . I have a very definite sense that God has called me to this place" (I6). Moreover, pastoral counselor Cale describes this vertical dimension of call in relation with his faith community, saying "first and foremost I am ordained to a ministry of the Church and of Jesus Christ as a pastor. And that is central to it" (I4).

This dimension later clearly relates to the idea of God's representative or embodiment. In this regard, Chaplain Gloria contends, "I'm a cleric. I'm a chaplain. I represent God in my role" (I13). In the same respect, chaplain Bill further articulates, "as a pastoral caregiver I have a very strong sense that [in] each encounter I have with a patient or family, whether the family would identify this in these words or not, my presence is in some ways the embodiment or the representation of the presence of God" (I3). This vertical sense of pastoral identity fueled chaplain Debra to start her prison ministry and helped her see care-seekers as "the people God has given [her] to love" (I7).

From these grounds, the interviewees and survey participants state explicitly or implicitly that they represent God to certain degrees. Thirteen of sixty-three survey participants identify themselves as representing, witnessing, and/or embodying God's presence, healing power, and love. The expressions vary depending on the survey/interview participants' perspectives: a "minister of Christ or person of God" (I5), a "representative of God" (S3, S43, I3), an "embodiment of God" (I3), "often God enfleshed for clients" (S62), a "vessel of God" (S62), a "quiet witness of the presence of God" (S1), a "partner with God" (I6), a "means of connection with God (S1), a "conduit of God's love and grace" (S58, I6), an "instrument of God's love and healing grace" (S58, S24), and a channel of "healing power of the Spirit" (S14). Such presumed recognitions as a divine or spiritual figure are a strong essence of pastoral identity when pastoral practitioners approach people.

Introducing Pastoral Care-Giving and Its Provider

The presumed self-understanding as a spiritual authoritative figure helps pastoral practitioners engage in difficult situations into which people fall. As persons who represent faith and God, they believe that they have a calling from God to care for people and an expertise to deal with spiritual issues and emotional and psychological concerns. Thus, pastoral practitioners bring a pastoral identity pre-constructed within their faith community and enter into the care-giving space with a spiritual authority.

Approaching a care-giving situation as figures of divine or spiritual authority, explicit or implicit, however, pastoral caretakers recognize that their clinical ministry settings are different from those of a parish ministry. Interview participants are aware of their care-giving ministry settings in which they minister to hurting and suffering people who might not automatically accept the pastoral authority the caregivers bring. Compared to parish pastors who minister to their parishioners with an authority of word and sacrament, clinical pastoral professionals experience different responses from care-seekers (I10). Pastoral counselors and chaplains in this study take different steps toward being accepted as pastoral care providers, a process of constructing pastoral identity.

From the first moment of entering into a care-giving situation, pastoral clinicians experience the dynamics of constructing pastoral identity in their interaction with care-partners. People often contribute to the construction of pastoral identity by accepting or challenging the authority that pastoral practitioners voluntarily or unintentionally bring into the care-giving encounter. There are several scenarios in this interaction, but each encounter helps pastoral representatives to rethink their identities. In any case, pastoral practitioners realize the importance of introducing themselves and explaining their work to those who seek help or are in potential need of seeking care.

In their introductions to people, pastoral clinicians try to convey to them an idea of who they are as pastoral counselors or chaplains and what pastoral care or counseling is about. These attempts help pastoral caregivers set a context for pastoral care-giving and give potential care-seekers a better idea of how they benefit from the service (I13). Pastoral caregivers usually keep these introductions brief.

The context and settings of pastoral counseling are important in conveying an identity of pastoral counselors. Pastoral counselor Sage, who practices in a local church, says, "When the clients come in, they see the steeple and stained glass windows and hear the carillon playing, and those icons by themselves communicate a sense of the religious and the pastoral. They create the context. That reminds the client that this isn't secular counseling" (I11). In addition, the church and denominational organizations that sponsor pastoral counseling are also important settings for indicating the caregivers' identity (I11, I14). Some pastoral counselors unashamedly called themselves "Reverend" or "Pastor" when they introduced themselves to counselees or on their business card or in the yellow pages (I2, I18).

As for chaplains, they usually introduce themselves with their badges or at the door when they make rounds. A usual pattern of introducing themselves is "Hi, I'm [name]. I'm a chaplain. I was wondering if I might be able to visit with you for a few minutes" (I13, cf. I15). But some chaplains, like Bill, never assume that people know what the word *chaplain* means and offer a word of explanation, saying, "I am a minister or a pastor who also has some training in being able to provide care and counseling for you while you are here" (I3). Thus, an introduction from the very beginning defines who the pastoral caregivers are.

In the introduction, chaplains get permission. Some chaplains (I13, I16) mention the importance of getting permission, saying that doctors, nurses, and housekeepers come in whenever they want, but pastoral care is the only service that asks the patient's permission. After getting permission, chaplains set a context for their visits, establishing why they are there. Chaplain Gloria says, "We can talk about anything you'd like, anything at all. I know that being a patient is often not a fun experience. It is often stressful and even boring, you know. How are things going so far?" (I13). Thus, chaplains introduce themselves broadly and inclusively so that they can approach anybody in providing care.

Sometimes when chaplains walk in and introduce themselves, the patients and families burst into tears. Such cases of emotional expression already imply permission to intervene. However, some patients and families upon the introduction reject any service from chaplains with their internal projections. Chaplain Bill describes this sort of interaction in detail. When he introduces himself and the idea of pastoral care, people respond in two ways. People who are religious quickly "latch on to" spiritually, religiously oriented concerns. Others "erect a barrier" by saying, "I'm not very religious" or "I am not sure I believe in God" (I3). Thus, when pastoral practitioners identify who they are, people also respond to them by clarifying who they are spiritually.

Projection On the Part of Care-seekers

Some interviewees suggest that there is a psychological representation behind these visible phenomena of accepting or rejecting pastoral care-giving. Some caregivers call it "projection" (I12, I13, I16), "putting on" (I12), "immediate[] connect[ion] with" (I8), "association" (I4), or "transference" (I2). They report that patients project "what a chaplain might do or is doing" (I16) and put on the chaplain "any image they want of what that looks like" (I12). Chaplain Julia says, "I would guess probably seventy-five percent of my patients don't have a clue ... [T]hey put on me what they need me to be for them in order to receive me ... but I think what I come in with is a sense of God, a sense of where is God in this" (I12).

When chaplains approach people in need and suffering, some religious people may welcome them, thinking that they are God's people or representatives of God. The image the patient projects onto the chaplain gives him or her access (or denies access) to parts of the patient's life that other helping professionals would not receive (I12). Thus, people who are religious or have spiritually oriented concerns would pick right up and "latch on to" the pastoral visit.

On the other hand, some other people reject pastoral care services or pastoral caregivers. When chaplains introduce themselves, some people immediately make that mean "something," which sometimes is not positive (I13). From their projections, they may think that chaplains will try to convert them or that they are not sick enough to need pastoral support. They may have had negative experiences with a religion and church in the past (I16).

The rejection is one of the major issues about which several chaplains expressed their frustrations. For instance, Chaplain Sam illustrates how he was frustrated with some patients who were grappling with some existential issues or some issues related to physical or sexual abuse but resisted pastoral care. Even if nurses recommended that these patients see the chaplain who could help them relieve their suffering through spiritual support, they refused a pastoral service. Sam remarks that a patient threw a negative projection onto him, saying, "I don't want to see a stinking chaplain" (I16, cf. "angel of death" (S36)). In this case of resistance, the pastoral clinician had to be a "witness for [the patient's] suffering," and that was frustrating to him (I16).

Educating People

A couple of pastoral counselors and chaplains use a strategy for avoiding this rejection or for dealing with it. This strategy involves educating people about pastoral care and counseling. Some pastoral counselors briefly explain their roles and educate people when they receive paperwork in the first session, sometimes giving them a brochure (I20). Pastoral counselor Cale points to the introduction as an important process of letting people know who he is. He speaks about how he introduces himself:

> Well ... one of the first [practices] would be disclosure of the fact that I am. I even have a disclosure statement that I give

to every client, a written one. That sets forth the nature of my practice; it also gives them an understanding of what they can expect by way of introduction to the process of counseling. It talks about my training and certification and what not; but it also talks about the fact that I am a pastor and a teacher of the church and have served [in] pastoral positions. (I4)

Thus, for Cale, educating people at the beginning of pastoral counseling is an important step toward identifying who pastoral counselors are.

Since chaplains sometimes meet patients and families who are unwilling to accept pastoral services, the caregivers take some steps to educate people. Chaplain Bill's typical response to patients' rejection is that "being pastoral and being a pastor in this setting means being able to work with all people" and that the fact that they are not religious or do not believe in God is not an issue for him (I3). When patients and families are not clear about what a chaplain's role is, pastoral caregivers re-articulate what the purpose is for a visit in a brief manner (I13) and educate them about the nature of spiritual support (I10). Chaplain Keri explains that pastoral care provides emotional and spiritual support for people. And by *spirituality*, she means "what is important to you [patient], what's meaningful in your life, what gets you up in the morning?" (I10). Keri continues to say that educating people is her important role:

> I see my role as giving pastoral care but along the way educating them [patients and families] about what pastoral care is. One of the things I found [is that] when they used to come to our hospital, the admissions people would ask them "Do you want a visit from Pastoral Care?" and people would say "No." And we were ignoring that. We would go in anyway when making our rounds, but obviously if they would ask us to leave we would . . . I think part of it is the patients don't understand what pastoral care is. Or they may think, "Oh no no no, I don't want to bother the chaplain" or they may think, "Oh, my gosh, I'm not that sick. I don't need a chaplain." So I just encourage all of our chaplains to go in to rounds to make the initial visit and offer emotional support to them. (I10)

Some pastoral practitioners describe their ministry as a choice for people (I13, I16). Chaplain Sam says to a patient who does not like his first visit, "Hey look, I'm a member of the hospice team. Like a buffet you get to see all the different kinds of foods you could have, and I'm one of them" (I16).

Despite attempts to educate people about accepting pastoral services, some do not necessarily accept the caregiver as a pastoral figure. One of the important points here is that when a care-seeker accepts pastoral care or counseling, he or she might accept the chaplain or counselor only as a general caretaker, like a secular doctor, social worker, or nurse, not necessarily as a "pastoral" figure. For instance, when counselees come to a pastoral counselor for help, they may choose intentionally to come to pastoral counseling and already accept the counselor's pastoral authority. In many other cases, however, counselees come to pastoral counseling for help but do not want to talk about any spiritual and theological issues. For this reason, pastoral counselor Linda explains to her counselees what it means to her to be a pastoral counselor and assures them that her training has given her "the ability to integrate spirituality as one of their healing resources along with their cognition and their emotion and their behavior" (I20). By doing so, pastoral caregivers construct their identity with their clients by negotiating what role the clients need from the pastoral caregivers.

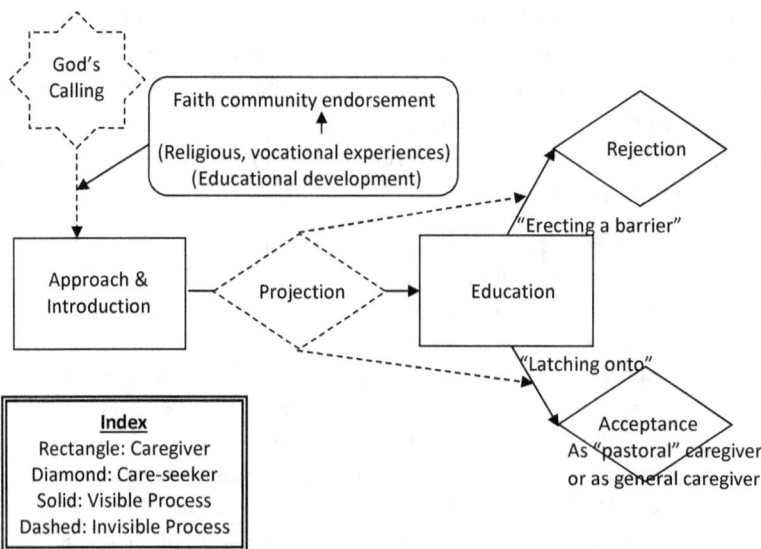

Figure 5. Process of Presumed Pastoral Identity as Spiritual Representative

As Figure 5 shows, before entering into an encounter with care-seekers, pastoral caregivers have an idea of who they are, as constructed by religious and educational experiences. A vocational sense or sense of God's calling defines this presumed identity, which is also endorsed by the faith community and evolved through a religious, vocational, educational development of the calling. When approaching an individual who is in potential or immediate need of seeking care and counseling, pastoral care and counseling professionals may need to introduce themselves and educate people about who they are as helpers and what they do to be their "pastoral" caregivers. In turn, the person may accept them as their pastoral care or counseling providers or just as secular clinicians like nurses or social workers depending on their projection, religious identities and orientations, and needs.

Thus, ways of identifying the nature of relationships between pastoral caregivers and care-seekers are one of the significant dynamics shaping identity construction. Experiences of being accepted or rejected as a pastoral caregiver reinforce or reshape the existing presumed identity. The helper brings the reinforced or reshaped identity to the next encounter with a client. Therefore, one of the accountabilities the caregivers have is to clarify who they need to be to the person they are serving and what it means to be pastoral caregivers to their counterparts. The responsibility further shapes the construction of pastoral identity, as both care/counseling parties interact in their pastoral relationships.

2. BEING PRESENT AND LISTENING AS A COMPASSIONATE FELLOW HUMAN

My role was really to be present, to be her companion in that moment that I shared with her and to deeply hear her spiritual pain. I mean I was with her, with where she was at, with what she was feeling and what she was expressing, to bring God's presence, to bring divine love.

—CHAPLAIN GLORIA

Even though clinical pastoral professionals may have a spiritual authority primarily given by God and the faith community, they cannot fully exert the authority until care-seekers accept or request them as their own spiritual care-providers. The practitioners may say a prayer with a patient and deliver a religious message with spiritual authority. This study, however, found that a real spiritual impact on the person is possible only when the care-receiver opens his or her world. And entering into the world is possible when the spiritual representatives themselves first disarm their authority and humbly become companions for those who need care and counseling.

In *Pastoral Counseling: The Basics*, pastoral theologian James Dittes (1999) describes such a humbled identity within his concept of pastoral counselor as "ascetic witness." For this concept, Brita Gill-Austern (2003) summarizes Dittes' first of the four ascetic renunciations thus: when entering into a pastoral relationship, "one needs to surrender any fixed identity that comes with being a pastor. One begins with no assurance of what it means to be a pastor so that one is totally free to meet others where they most need to be met" (94). In her personal reflection article, Karen Webb (1990) also describes a "humbling awareness" by saying that she does not fully agree with the idea of being a "living symbol of the presence of God" because she is acutely aware of her own humanity (78).

Dittes' and Webb's remarks seem to capture what the interviewees are trying to describe in the second phase of constructing pastoral identity, the humbled identity. This phase consists of five processes: (a) humbling him or herself as a fellow human and being present with care-seekers, (b) listening to their stories and needs as a safe-space creator, (c) learning from them as an emphatic participator, (d) walking with them as a companion and (e) caregivers' projection and learning through failure. As a fellow human being, a pastoral caregiver is fully available to care-seekers, empathically listens to their stories, learns human lived experiences from them, and humbly accompanies them in their life journey of suffering and hope.

In this phase, pastoral caregivers are "being" rather than "doing," as Chaplain Julia articulates so well:

> I10: Can we talk a little bit detailed description? For example, coming from your patient or family's perspective, what practices do you think make them realize that you are a pastoral person?
>
> P10: What practices? I would say in a word, "None."
>
> I11: None.
>
> P11: I don't think I can come in and do, perform practices. I mean, you know, "Hey, let me do a prayer here." I think that's what they [patients and families] get from their ministers . . . I want to hear their story and to make that into a bigger story if they are able to hold it . . . So, if a practice is active listening and presence, then that's a practice. You know, it's not a doing activity; it's a being activity." (I12)

This "being activity" allows the caregivers to "humble" (S10, I7) themselves to serve as needed. Thus, from this "being" phase, pastoral caregivers further see a potential for a "doing activity" in the next phase, in which they find a requested pastoral identity.

Being Present Humbly As a Fellow Human

One of the meaningful findings from the research data is that pastoral practitioners are aware of their own humanness and fragility. They remind themselves that they are fellow human beings as well as divine representatives. When seeing people in trouble and crisis, the pastoral professionals do not see themselves as apart from the situations or the persons in need. They see themselves as one of the troubled people and the crises as situations in which they could be. Such a pastoral attachment leads them toward a care-giving relationship. From this perspective, people are not objects that receive care and chaplains and counselors are not subjects who provide care. Rather, they are "(fellow) human being[s]" (S7, S18, S23, S52), "fellow seeker[s]" (S15), "fellow wounded traveler[s]" (S30), and "fellow pilgrim[s]" in life and in the world (S18, I15). Each caregiver and seeker is a "hurting brother [and sister]" and "brother [and sister] of many different persons that come from so [many] different walk[s] in life" (S1).

Such humbled recognition not only comes because of a difficult situation in which pastoral practitioners encounter overwhelming issues, but it also derives from a theological awareness that the pastoral caregiver is also a "sinner, fully capable of doing bad things" and a "fellow human lacking the grace of God" (S1). Because of this awareness, the pastoral helpers are willing "to say 'I don't know the answer'" (S56) and "willing to be wrong" (S46), "praying that God will sustain [them] to [do] a little good where they are" (S1).

With this spirit, pastoral helping professionals humbly present themselves to people in need and are fully present with them. They are willing to be open to the life of the care-seeker (S21) and available to one who is suffering in order to serve them (S41, S56). The helpers feel "called to center [themselves] daily to be fully present for people in their struggle" (S10). Thus, the ministry of presence has a power to meet people's needs and build a close relationship.

Chaplain Sam shares a story about a "difficult patient." The staff at the hospice home where Sam was working asked him to see a patient who had been really difficult with the staff. The patient even refused to see a chaplain in the beginning. The patient seemed to make a lot of projections onto what a chaplain might do and could easily throw him or her out of the room. However, Sam was able to build a rapport with the patient and handle the situation.

What the chaplain did was to be fully present with the difficult patient. He "centered" himself before he walked in the room. He put his spiritual authority aside by not identifying himself as a chaplain and encountered the patient with an open heart. He started ministering to the patient by saying, "The administrator had told me that you were not happy with some of the things that have been happening and I'm wondering if I could just talk to you about those." As the patient talked, Sam reflected back to him some of the things he heard. Sam found a rapport that started happening between the two of them. He described this care-giving as such: "I was practicing a ministry of presence... a ministry of being calm, and... a ministry of being interested in him and concerned about him... I was just open, and that allowed some rapport to happen" (I16). Like other pastoral caregivers who were present to their care-seekers, Sam identified the core of his pastoral identity as pastoral presence, "being open and receptive to what's needed" by being present with care-seekers (I16). Chaplain Gloria also sees her job as "to stand in this neutral place with [her] heart open and to deeply listen to what is being called for" (I13).

When pastoral caregivers are present with care-seekers, the helpers try to convey unconditional positive regard and love. Pastoral counselor Cale believes that in counseling he provides counselees with a sense of "the unconditional grace of God" to help them change their sense of unworthiness (I4). As the sun sheds light, according to Chaplain Gloria, the helpers shed unconditional positive regard for those seeking help while being present with them. Pastoral counselor Linda speaks her experience:

> And I dare say that most of my clients would tell you that I love them. And I believe that I don't do that in my own power, that I am a conduit of the love of God to the folks with whom I work. And some of them have never experienced that in an overt way and I am able to offer that to them. (I20)

By being fully present with people and available to them, pastoral caregivers convey a sense of love and respect. Especially in the case of caring for dying people, being present with them and showing unconditional love has a tremendous impact on them.

Chaplain Gloria shared her stories about being present with a dying man through her unconditional love. Gloria got paged three times while she was with other emergencies. When she finally showed up in the Emergency Department, the nurse literally pushed her into the room with an elderly man who was facing death. The doctor and nurse wanted the chaplain not to leave the patient alone. They felt that "he needed someone to bring some spiritual presence to him at the moment of dying." He was totally unresponsive. Gloria was there and went into a prayer with God, "So, what's being called for in this one?" She continued to narrate her experience:

> I'm standing with him [the dying patient] and I felt that what I needed to do was open my heart and just give as much as love, unconditional, divine love to this man as my heart could give him . . . part of the task as a chaplain is to create an environment as loving and comfortable an environment as possible when someone is making that transition towards death. So I looked at him and . . . said, "I'm [name], I'm the hospital chaplain. I don't know what religion you are or if you even have a religion, but I want you to know that I am here to give you as much love and blessings as I can." (I13)

By practicing the ministry of presence and offering an unconditional love, she was able to provide the dying patient with some spiritual, emotional support.

Humbly identifying themselves as fellow humans and being present with people in need, the caregivers connect and engage with care-seekers (S11) and "meet people where they are—meet them in their world" (S5). By being present with care-seekers and "being open and receptive to what's needed," pastoral caregivers also provide an unconditional love. Furthermore, such a "human presence, as a child of God with another one" (S1) embodies a divine presence, as we will see later.

Listening As a Safe-Space Creator in Relationship

Being present with others embodies listening deeply and being fully available to them. Thus listening is part of presence, and silence is a "listening openness" (Lashley et al. 1994, 194). Chaplain Julia says, "I am present to them listening. So, it's my presence I bring to them and in the time I am with them. I hear what their issues are, what they are struggling with and hold that struggle with them" (I12). Being present and connected with people in the process that evolves, pastoral practitioners open a space to listen to their stories. By listening, pastoral caregivers create a safe space that will become filled with hope, healing, and divine mystery, as pastoral care-giving proceeds.

One of the most obvious pastoral identities that many participants mentioned in the survey and interview signifies listening. Many pastoral caregivers articulate the importance and power of listening. For the participants, listening is a way of relating to their patients or counselees and being a companion to them. Listening is "a willful engagement" of the self with others (Lashley et al. 190). Through the process of listening, the pastoral caregivers have a fuller understanding of who the care-seekers are and establish a deeper relationship with them. When pastoral caregivers are not present by way of empathic listening, they can sometimes experience disconnection from and rejection by their care-seekers (I5, I7).

According to the ten statements test survey questionnaire, which asks, "As a pastoral caregiver, I am . . . ," thirty-one of sixty-three survey participants identify themselves as listeners with variants such as "(very) good listener[s]" (S8, S34, S46, S49), "prime listener[s]" (S44), "careful listen[ers] (S43), reflective listen[ers] (S36), "empathic and curious listener[s]" (S15), "hearer[s] of stories" (S31), and "(listening) ears" (S10, S32). This study found three kinds of listening: listening to care-seekers, listening to oneself as a caregiver (I4, I7), and listening to "the third voice," God (I4, I16, cf. I2), which will be discussed later.

The interview participants witness to the significance of listening. Thirty-six passages from 16 of 20 participants speak about the importance of listening in their care-giving practices. First of all, listening is at the hub of pastoral care-giving. Listening allows pastoral caregivers to hear care-seekers' needs as a calling. Through deep listening, pastoral caregivers (I2, I6, I13) feel a sense of calling from people who need to be heard. Pastoral counselor Neil says, "[I provide] very, very much a listening ear, and people hunger for someone to listen to what they have to say. That's the sense of calling I have as I approach this form of ministry" (I2). Thus, listening is a way of finding care-seekers' needs (I6), and "patiently waiting and listening" is what makes pastoral care-giving pastoral (I1).

Secondly, listening is "the heart of the relationship" between the caregiver and care-seeker (I4). Supportive, reflective listening communicates to people in suffering a sense of empathy and understanding so the care-giving relationship goes deeper. By listening, the caregiver offers a safety net to the seekers, who thereby open their worlds. Chaplain Julia finds that what leads her into a deep relationship with her care-seekers is listening. "I think the reason I am able to enter so deeply into their [patients'] lives," she says, "is that I offer them a safe enough space to do so." She wants to hear their stories and is curious to know who they are. Such attentive listening allowed her to have a deep care-giving relationship.

Furthermore, listening is a way of helping. By listening and reflecting what he or she hears back to the talkers, the listener helps them realize what is going on within them, what values are important to them, and how well they may be living those values (I7). Thus, many participants in the study appreciate listening as a key and primary skill for accomplishing the goal of care-giving. They appraise listening as helping care-receivers "promote self-understanding for them" (I11) and "facilitate their meaning-making" (12) and healing (I1, I15). Pastoral counselor Cale asserts that "It [listening] is so central to the whole enterprise that I do not see how effective pastoral care and counseling can be rendered to anyone apart from very deep listening" (I4). Listening renders the helper an effective pastoral caregiver.

In regard to the stance of listening, the participants uniformly emphasized "neutrality" (S5, I2, I10, I13). Neutrality in pastoral listening includes the posture of being "non-judgmental," "without agenda," "not-knowing," and "not-fixing." When pastoral listeners make a "willful engagement of the mind" with the story-teller, they try to avoid judgments concerning the person (I13). They attend to what is important to the care-seeker rather than what is important to themselves (S5). They try to leave their "own agenda at the door" (S56), curiously sitting "in the gap of not-knowing" (S6). Thus, they find their role in listening as supporting and understanding the talker instead of fixing the problem from their perspectives (S5, S18, S46). Such a posture of listening reveals "greater truths of what is being called," whereas inattentive listening prevents the listener from hearing something critically important and makes the caregiver "least helpful at all and may even be dangerous" (I4).

Chaplain Bill illustrates how important listening is in his pastoral ministry through the following story. In his hospital chapel one day he met a grandmother of a patient. When he introduced himself, she said, "I don't even know why I came to the chapel except that I've forgotten how to pray and I felt like I need to." Reflecting on the encounter and his pastoral care for her, Bill said that what she said might be "on the edge of blasphemy" in her church tradition and that she might be afraid to mention her frustrations to her pastor. By providing non-judgmental listening and care to her, Bill was able to help her to be "heard and respected and accepted." Bill reflects on this encounter:

> I find that for me, that [listening] really gets at what is really crucial in my pastoral identity that I can give people permission and empowerment to take their deepest and most primal feelings and experiences to God and know God can hear and accept those experiences and those feelings. (I3)

As a natural flow, moreover, listening creates a space for those in need. Several research participants (S9, S12, S19, S31, S43, I12) contend that they offer a "safe enough space" for care-seekers to share their stories. Metaphorically speaking, a pastoral listener sets up a stage on which the story-teller shares a story of pain and predicament. By listening, the hearer is able to enter deeply into the story-teller's worlds shown on the stage. Thereby, the stage created by listening becomes a space for potential healing and meaning-making. Listening creates "a healing environment that nurtures hope" (S12, 19), and the listener provides a safe space for the teller to share and unburden his or her pain (S43). Pastoral listeners offer a container in which the patient can make meaning (S31), create a space for the mystery to unfold (S6), and manage a safe holding environment (S9).

Learning as a Virtual, Emphatic Participator

By being present with and listening to people in a quandary, pastoral professionals expose themselves to new learning. Many research participants identify themselves as learners. They are "willing to learn" (S56) and "open to new learning" (S59). They "constantly" learn (S30) and "always" learn from every "teachable moment" (I5). They learn as a student with a "beginner's mind, bracketing assumptions, [and] disciplined naiveté" (S26). From any situations and moments they encounter, they learn something (S5). They learn to grow to be able to help others (I5) and learn "new ways to minister better" (S10). They learn what their anger tells them about limitations and possibilities (S26). Thus, from care-giving experiences, pastoral caregivers learn some lessons.

They learn "from" and "with" care-seekers so-called "living human documents." Chaplain James describes his experiences with the human documents that became "open books" to him:

> When people give you permission to really be with you, they really become open books and you learn a lot of things from them that books don't teach you because it's their own life experiences; it's their own wisdom; and it's their own insight. It's their own ways [of] how they struggle and cope with life. (I1)

Thus, pastoral care and counseling professionals learn what the human condition looks like, how sufferers struggle with the condition, and how pastoral caregivers can help them, thereby coming to know more clearly who they are and who their care-seekers are. Facing people's troubled life stories or existential human conditions, they learn what they have never thought or experienced.

In this listening and learning process, pastoral caregivers go into human lived experiences as "virtual and empathic participators" (Park 2005b, 64). Even though they have never experienced the human condition that a care-seeker describes, as virtual, empathic participators they can participate in his or her lived experiences by empathically listening to his or her stories and co-constructing a world narrated by the care-seeker. Such participation becomes an ample ground for theological reflection. By listening to life stories, pastoral caregivers learn about various human experiences that they have not suffered, which often challenge them with surprise and shock. The existential issues and theological questions people bring into a care-giving conversation puzzle and perplex the pastoral listeners, which expands their existing knowledge and beliefs and asks them to reflect on several issues theologically (I2, I4, I17, I18, I19).

By not only listening to the stories but also by facing an existential human limitation where a person may be dying, pastoral caregivers learn human powerlessness and the power of divine presence, which makes them humble learners of the human condition. Thus, pastoral learners gain knowledge of something with each patient that makes them a better caregiver. The caregivers are often amazed anew at the real power of God involved in these care-giving situations (I3).

"Walking-With" As a Companion

With compassion and empathy, pastoral care and counseling specialists are willing to serve as a companion to their care partners. The pastoral caregivers are "interested in the journey of the people with them, finding reward in walking with the cared" (S21). The pastoral helpers "stand alongside" (S33) and "walk the walk with those they care for" (S56). As companions (S59), partners (S52), and "compassionate friend[s]" (S40), the caregivers take a journey with care-seekers (S18, S42) in any situations like health, illness, or grief (S47). As co-sufferers (S9), they "laugh, weep, mourn, and celebrate" with those in suffering and grief (S50, S56). They work through the end-of-life issues with patients and families and even dare to walk with their patients through the process of dying (S19). In the whole process of companionship with them, the pastoral caregivers feel "honored to walk with people who experience brokenness and are seeking wholeness" (S58).

A few interview participants (I7, I10) mentioned a metaphor of Mary at the foot of the Cross. Similar to Mary, in their ministry the pastoral caregivers try to serve as companions to their care-seekers in their hopeless, terrible suffering. Chaplain Keri says that even when the doctor gives up and the family avoids the patient, the chaplains would not leave or abandon the dying patient in the gravest hour. "My pastoral theology," Keri claims from a feminist Lutheran theological perspective, "informs my pastoral identity as someone who companions and walks with, someone who stays the course no matter how horrible or terrible it gets" (I10).

Thus, several interviewees mention a friendship and companionship with their care-seekers, as the relationship gets deeper. Pastoral counselor

Cale portrayed his relationship with counselees as a process of becoming friends from strangers (I4). Chaplain Chris also identifies himself as a companion:

> I learned that I am someone when I listen, when I walk as a friend, you know, as a friend walking together in the valley of pain or fear or anxiety. So as someone walking together in their grieving journey . . . being a friend with someone suffering, grieving with tremendous anxiety, I am there to help [and support] them. I would say that [I am] a fellow supporter, a pilgrim in life. (I15)

In such a friendship and companionship, pastoral caregivers walk through the journey as faithful companions to the end. This companionship makes their care-giving pastoral.

Projection on Caregivers' Part and Learning through Failure

Just as people project their associations or needs onto pastoral caregivers, the care-providers also put something on their care-seekers, while attending to them. Some caregivers want to help others from their own perspective on what the patients and families need. The helpers project their own needs onto those seeking help, even when the caregivers try to put themselves in the care-seekers' shoes. Chaplain Gloria is keenly aware of this issue and says that

> people have different values and worldviews so what would be important to us if we were in their shoes may not be important to them at all. So we project our needs or what our needs would be if we were them onto them . . . People always . . . want to help so they go into helping mode in what they feel would make a difference, not what's being called for or what's really needed. [When] people will go into tears a lot, the tendency sometimes is to want to get up and get them a tissue. But, whose need is that? Is that their need to have a tissue or is it your need to have a tissue because that is what you would want if you were in their shoes or you don't like the way their snot is coming out of their nose. And it's hard for you to be with so you want to get them a tissue. You know, what is your driving motivation to want to get them a tissue? (I13)

Thus, caregivers should discern their driving motivation by deeply listening to and learning from the care-seekers. Caregivers need to distinguish what their own needs are and what is being called for.

To discern those needs and find clarity of meanings, caregivers need to listen to themselves as an important quality of care-giving. Chaplain Debra in prison ministry says that she and her inmates come to a better understanding of what is going on by hearing herself talk and helping them hear themselves talk (I7). By examining one's own inner perceptions of others' experiences and reflecting on these, a pastoral care-provider can better tune into the needs of others. Pastoral caregivers need to make sure their needs are fulfilled so they do not project their issues onto others (S10). Not projecting their own agenda, pastoral caregivers need to discern "where the listening is to and what is being called for" (I13).

In this regard, several research participants emphasized the importance of a thoughtful use of power. Not only do they not project their own needs and leave their own agenda "at the door," but they also put the care-seeker's struggle before their own (S10). These pastoral professionals are careful in using their power (S12) and "reticent to normalize [their] own faith experience" (S17). They are even "willing to walk away if the patient is not ready" (S19). Especially, pastoral counselors are careful not to impose their faith perspectives on their counselees, even though the counselors are willing to share their theological perspectives when the counselees request them to do so explicitly or implicitly.

When pastoral caregivers use their power inappropriately, however, it impacts their ministry and identity as well as care-receivers' experiences. The pastoral professionals can grow within that situation as they learn from their "bad experiences" and failures. When things go bad, those experiences raise questions to a pastoral identity and offer the caregivers an opportunity to reshape their identity (I5, I12). Sometimes these bad experiences have a huge influence on their pastoral identity, transforming them theologically and pastorally. These bad experiences take place especially when pastoral caregivers minister to people not listening to or learning from them but acting from their presumed identity and biased idea of pastoral care-giving. Often performing a "doing activity" without a "being activity" causes a problem. Here is an illustration.

In the beginning chaplain George seemed a little bit nervous to share his early memory of a "very bad experience." When he first started chaplaincy as a volunteer chaplain, he did not have enough training or the sense of pastoral care he has now. When he went in a room and worked with a family, he had a preset mind of what to do in that situation and did "pastoral work." However, the family was upset and went out to ask a nurse, "Is there any way you can get rid of this chaplain? We don't want him here. He is making us very anxious." George remembers that experience as "crushing." He likens this experience to "the Titanic" story in which he had to move his "ship" theologically and professionally to avoid a "potential iceberg." He reflects on this experience thus:

> I thought that this is what I was going to do in this situation. I was thinking pastoral work. . . . it really was my pastoral identity that was coming out . . . I go into a room and do to somebody, like a doctor would say, "I'm going to come and I'm going to give you a shot" or "We are going to put you to sleep and cut off your leg." . . . [The bad experience] helped me to move in my pastoral identity that this is really about the patients and about what they want. I need to go in there and listen instead of going and doing something to them . . . my pastoral identity has been shaped more by the bad things that have happened to me than the good. (I5)

As he echoes in this description, Chaplain George realizes that he "moved" in his pastoral identity. This experience made him change his identity and attitudes toward pastoral care. He now sees himself as a listener who shows concern for patients and learns what they need, not as a doctor who prescribes what to do. The "bad" experience was a transformative moment for George's chaplaincy.

As fellow humans, pastoral caregivers put aside their spiritual authority for a while to be present with sufferers, listen to their needs, learn from them, and companion with them. By doing so, pastoral caregivers incarnate themselves as fellow sufferers in the world of human sufferings and predicaments the care-seekers construct in language. As Figure 6 shows, as the caregiving goes on, the pastoral caregivers humble themselves more to the point of becoming fellow suffers and life companions in listening and learning. On the other hand, holding onto a presumed authority, a pastoral caregiver may do one-way "pastoral work" like preaching or "prescribing" instead of listening. Some who are religiously ready to accept the work would appreciate his or her ministering; others may be upset about the caregiver's insensitive care-giving. Nonetheless, the caregiver will learn something from that.

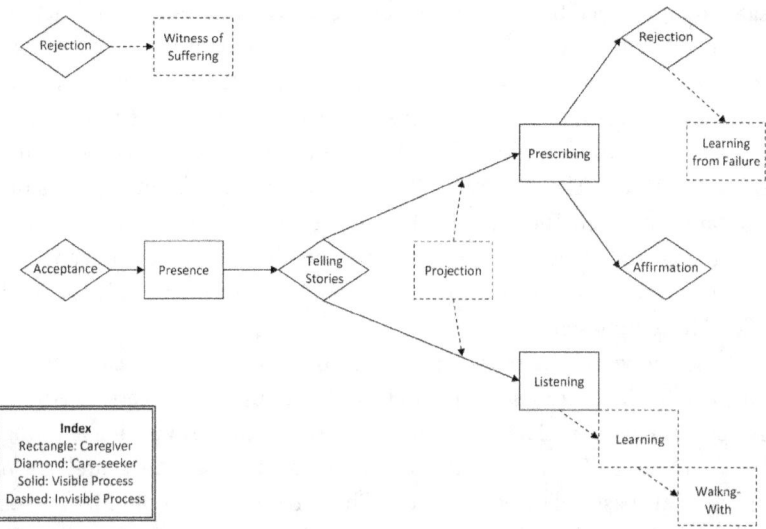

Figure 6. Process of Humbled Pastoral Identity as Human Fellow

3. BECOMING A THEOLOGICALLY AND SPIRITUALLY SENSITIVE PASTOR

I was truly caring about this man [patient]. I was truly empathic and truly wanting to hear his story as part of giving his pastoral care, and I think he felt all that and believed all that and was able to see me as a pastoral caregiver and express his needs and his hurts.

—Chaplain Shelly

I believe that a great deal of my pastoral identity has developed in the crucible of walking with my clients . . . especially those clients who struggle spiritually. That has called out my pastoral identity; their struggles have called out my pastoral identity and strength in that and shaped it.

—Pastoral Counselor Linda

Once pastoral care and counseling professionals have fully presented themselves as fellow listeners, learners, and companions, the care-seeker exposes little by little his or her world of suffering and predicament in the safe enough space that the helpers create for their care-partner. The more deeply the teller opens his or her inner worlds, the stronger the compassion emerges from deep within the listener and the greater the privilege the caregiver has to access the world. In this interaction between the care partners, the caregiver empathically attends to the life of the partner and hears his or her call for help. The call invites the fellow human to operate as a pastor to the care-requester. Thus, lay chaplain Julia says, "my ordination or vocation into this [chaplaincy] is, yes, bestowed on me by the grace of God and *given to me by those with whom I walk, who bless me in my work*" (I12, italics added for emphasis).

As shown in one of the block quotations above, European-American chaplain Shelly becomes a true caregiver for a mid thirty-year-old African-American cancer patient. At their very first meeting in which she thought he would not fully trust her, he expressed his needs and hurts and saw her as his "real" pastoral caregiver. When Shelly truly cared about him and empathically listened to his story, the patient shared his deep pains in his life, including the death of his father when the patient was eighteen, the loss of his two-year-old son, and the loss of two jobs. He let his defenses down enough to be honest and to share how he felt, crying. Attending truly to him, Shelly heard the call to be his caregiver and "pastor" (I6).

The ways care-seekers request pastoral caregivers to be their "pastors" vary depending on the nature of their religious orientations, their crisis situations, and the pastoral relationships. Some would explicitly request pastoral services by asking for prayer (I7, I10, I20) or religious rituals like a funeral (I2, I8, I12, I16) or just bursting into tears upon or during the encounter with a pastoral caregiver (I2, I6, I8, I13). Others would call for pastoral responses by raising a theological and existential question or statement or sharing stories that involve theological themes such as guilt, forgiveness, or low self-esteem (I3, I4, I8, I10, I14, I17, I18, I19, I20). Still others would trust the pastoral caregiver, open their world of wounds and suffering, and thereby invite the helper to provide pastoral support and presence with compassion (I6, I20).

Steps the pastoral practitioners take to become requested pastors in this phase of the identity construction include three themes: (a) using the self as a compassionate responder in helping others, (b) reflecting theologically on their issues as a theologian, and (c) meeting needs by making meanings in life as a pastoral facilitator. These steps take place in a dialogical, conversational field where pastoral clinicians engage themselves in dealing with the problems care-seekers present. In responding to care-seekers' requests for help, the care-providers use their inner emotional reactions in care-giving, think about the issues theologically, construct meaning-making with the clients, and thereby fill their needs.

Using the Self as a Compassionate Responder

One of the most common emotional reactions that pastoral caregivers feel toward the helped is compassion and empathy. Twenty-three of sixty-three survey participants reported that they are "compassionate." Sixteen participants answered that they are "empathic" (9 participants), "empathetic" (6), and "sympathetic" (1) in addition to "considerate" (2) and "caring" (7). Thus, pastoral caregivers' core virtues the respondents describe include compassion and empathy. Being compassionate means caring with an open heart, being dedicated to, and "embodying in living out compassion in its deepest sense" (I10). Compassion and "genuine caring" are what make the care-giving pastoral (I5, I10, I11, I14, I18). The respondents indicate that they are "compassionate agent[s] for God" (I20) and that compassion is what distinguishes pastoral care-giving from other secular helping professions. As such agents, pastoral caregivers try "to reflect God's love with compassion" (S43).

According to the research, the respondents not only feel compassion and empathy toward their care-seekers, but they also use their feelings and experiences as a resource for care-giving. They use the self as an important instrument in recognizing the needs of care-seekers. Pastoral caregivers seem comfortable with using their own feelings and wounds in helping others (I15). Thus, the helpers are well aware of their own struggles and "use them as a rich resource for empathy" (S21). They are aware of their "own wounds as best [they] can be at the moment" (S31). They also recognize that they are "perhaps too compassionate if [their] pastoral side obscures [their] therapeutic commitment to be forthright" (S54). Pastoral counselor Sage, as he has matured, feels counselees evoking more compassion from him, which reminds him that he helps them find a "safe mooring, a foundation in life, a foundation that will endure" (I11). Compassion and empathy convey to the care receiver a sense of presence and care, and that in turn shapes the caregiver's pastoral identity.

As a compassionate and empathic caregiver enters into the inner world of care-seekers, the caregiver becomes clear about what is being called for. The care-seekers call on the caregiver for help. This call often provides the care-provider with an opportunity to be a theologian, to be a meaning-maker, and to be a "pastor" to them. This kind of request to be their pastor is often implicit for many "general" care-seekers who do not use religious or theological language. Often unspoken in this request is their acceptance of the caregiver into their world and their agreement to reveal more of who they are (I6). For many "un-churched clients," the pastoral caregiver is the only minister they have (S57). Such a summons calls for a significant moment of the identity construction, making the pastoral relationship a transformative turning point. The request for pastoral presence and comfort plays a significant role in building a caregiver's pastoral identity (I8).

Research participants articulate the roles of pastoral caregivers mainly into two major components: one a supportive role and the other a guiding role. First of all, survey participants see themselves as those who support (8 participants), nurture (4 participants), comfort (6 participants), encourage (6 participants), and empower (2 participants) their care-seekers. As requested pastors, pastoral caregivers nurture hope for those who are hopeless (S12, S16), comfort the afflicted (S43) and encourage those who are discouraged (S16). They support "emotional health, relational success, and spiritual growth" (S58). Pastoral caregivers maintain that they are "cup[s] that hurting people can pour their stuff into" (S32) and "mirroring and validating as well as empathic encourager[s] of positive transformation" (S44). Thus, as "a wholesome nurturer" (S49) and "nurturing encourager" (S58), a pastoral caregiver is able to listen and respond to the patient's calling for spiritual needs and nurture his or her spiritual well-being.

Being pastors to care-requesters, however, means not only comforting and nurturing them but also challenging and confronting them at times. The caregivers not only comfort the afflicted but also "confront the comfortable as spiritually appropriate given the circumstances" (S43). By confronting the helped, pastoral professionals challenge "the view someone has of who they are" (S21). Chaplains and pastoral counselors are "not afraid to confront" (S25) because they challenge care-seekers to "grow spiritually" (S43) and "challenge towards a vision of a more fruitful life" (S45). On some rare occasions pastoral caregivers become "admonisher[s]" (S50). Thus, pastoral caregivers are flexible enough to provide spiritual care and counseling as appropriate.

Reflecting Theologically as a Theologian

When pastoral caregivers comfort and confront their care-seekers, the pastoral practitioners clearly identify themselves as persons who hold faith perspectives and provide a spiritually and theologically sensitive care and counseling. While listening to the stories and life issues clients bring, pastoral caregivers look at them through "pastoral eyes" (I2) and a "theological lens" (I4). They internally reflect on a religious or spiritual meaning concerning the problems the clients are expressing because the problems are germane to those struggles they have of a spiritual nature (I4). This important aspect of pastoral care-giving—helping people understand a spiritual aspect of their lives relating to behaviors, purposes, and meanings in life—reflects what pastoral caregivers particularly do and why people come to see them.

Many interview participants indicate that looking at and dealing with a spiritual, existential aspect of life and attending to the deeper questions in life in regard to God and the ultimate is what makes pastoral care-giving valuable and unique among other helping professions (I2, I4, I17, I18, I19). Pastoral counselor Walt says that what makes his counseling pastoral is the "inclusion of being open to talk about ultimate, existential God . . . at a primitive level or even a more sophisticated level" (I19).

In dealing with such ultimate concerns in life, pastoral caregivers respect care-seekers while not compromising their own beliefs (S43). As persons of faith, the pastors do not impose their own faith and worldview but are willing to share their personal faith when appropriate (S44, S48). A few research participants mention that they are "flexible and adaptable" in connecting ordinary stories to faith perspectives (I3, I5). Chaplain Bill says that he was "being flexible enough to be able to walk into someone's room and . . . translate the spiritual language of the caregiver into words that are meaningful and make sense to the patient and family who do not use God-language or have a belief in God" (I3).

In the process of caregivers' dealing with the issues and sharing their faith perspectives, theological reflection plays an important role. Many research participants pointed out that theological reflection is a helpful tactic for constructing pastoral identity as well as for helping care-seekers (I1, I5, I14, I15, I19, I20). When the study asked the interviewees what has shaped pastoral identity the most, several participants pointed out theological reflection as a helpful resource, which affirms findings of other studies on theological reflection (O'Connor et al. 2008; Warren et al. 2002). Counselor Rosa says that theological reflection helped her to be able to "see the human condition in theological terms" from her own understanding (I14).

The interview data show several ways by which pastoral practitioners do theological reflection in the pastoral relationship. First of all, theological reflection takes place in the form of a response to care-seekers' explicit theological questions or statements derived from their predicaments (I3, I4, I19). They pose such questions that either are explicitly theological or open the way for a theological response. In such explicit situations, the helpers see the inquirer in demand for theological reflection and conversation. In that sense, pastoral identity is essential for the helper to address the need created by that situation (I4).

Pastoral caregivers are most keenly aware of their pastoral identity when they help people in a quandary through mulling over theological and spiritual issues. Chaplain Bill says,

> the places where I feel I am the most aware of my pastoral identity . . . and the places where I feel my pastoral identity is most realized are the situations where I am with the patient and family and they are really specifically dealing with the religious and spiritual kinds of issues . . . And to me those kind of encounters are the places where I feel my own expertise and identity is most fully realized because those are the encounters where I can make the best use of my skills . . . in care-giving and my pastoral identity. (I3)

Thus, care-seekers' theological struggles call out the helper's pastoral identity, which manifests itself in theological reflection. In such pastoral encounters with those who bring spiritual and theological issues, pastoral counselor Linda hears their calling out of her pastoral identity in their spiritual struggle, which opens her up to theological reflection (as in a block quotation in the beginning of this section).

In particular, pastoral clinicians encounter hard questions, for example, "How could God allow this to happen to our son?" (as a couple whose son was killed in a car accident asks) or "Where was God when this was happening to me?" (as an adult victim in the context of childhood abuse inquires) (I19). Those kinds of questions, according to pastoral counselor Walt, clearly contribute to his pastoral identity because "they are not just asking a therapist that question but they are also asking a pastor that question." They see the helper as a person whom they can trust, and they see that the pastor will also include the spiritual aspects of their life. They may also sense that they can speak to the pastoral theologian confidentially (I19). Thus, those who ask hard questions challenge pastoral identity and open up a necessary theological reflection in response.

Secondly, pastoral caregivers think theologically while listening to sufferers' unfolding stories that are not explicitly religious or theological. Whether or not care-seekers bring spiritual and religious concerns with them, pastoral caregivers look at their issues through a pastoral lens one way or another and deal with where the care-partners are in their spiritual development. In theological reflection, pastoral practitioners often think of some biblical stories or theological themes that arise out of their conscious and "subconscious counter-transferences by association" (S44) with the situation clients are presenting (I2, I4, I11, I17, I18, I20). As the helpers listen more to the story, they become clear about what is going on with the client that leads the caregivers to connect the issue with a biblical image or character.

Depending on care-seekers' levels and degrees of commitment to their faith, the helpers, as pastoral theologians, assist them to reframe their problems in story form or in a way that they can comprehend a meaning. Pastoral caregivers do theological reflection because they believe that human crises are often crises of meaning and purpose, which have a religious and spiritual nature (I4). In the course of pastoral conversations, pastoral theologians will often relate the clients' stories in terms of grace, forgiveness, or reconciliation—concepts that do not necessarily have to be religiously meaningful but do have some meanings to people (I14). Sometimes pastoral professionals further pull material right out of the Scriptures to frame something theologically. They do not hesitate to use biblical materials, not for prescriptive purposes to tell the clients what they ought to do, but rather to "illuminate the situation they are in and help them clarify the ambiguities they are facing as well as the choices that are to be made" (I4).

Furthermore, the pastoral care-providers theologically reflect on the issues with their care-seekers. Reflecting on the story in light of care-seekers' faith positions, the helper may ask them what is the problem about their faith or if the situation they are in says something about their faith (I14). The caregiver may also share his or her theological perspective by way of invitation without directly challenging the care-seekers' perspectives. For instance, pastoral counselor Sage says, "I hear what you're saying, and that seems to be my understanding. I wonder if you've ever thought about it this way" (I11). By introducing a subtle perspective into their stories, pastoral caregivers help care-seekers reframe their stories and sometimes connect them to the larger story of the faith community. Thus, Chaplain Julia maintains that "my job is to hear their story and to make that into a bigger story if they are able to hold it [in order] to see how their narrative fits into the narrative of their God" (I12).

Integration of psychology and theology often takes place in theological reflection. While providing care and counseling that often is psychological and psychotherapeutic, pastoral caregivers integrate the psychological outside with the theological inside by reflecting on human experiences theologically. Pastoral counselor Linda asserts that when counseling a patient who questioned his relationship with God, she saw that experience as a "great opportunity to think about the way [she thinks] of psychology and spirituality and behavior being a kind of braided stream" (I20). By braiding a care-seeker's life issues with spiritual and theological issues and producing theology-embedded pastoral care and counseling, the pastoral professionals find their care-giving integrating theology and psychology (I20).

The inclusion of spiritual and religious aspects of life is a very important quality of pastoral care-giving. The inclusion tells from where pastoral caregivers feel a strong sense of pastoral identity and why people come to pastoral caregivers to help (I17, I18, I19). Since pastoral care and counseling comes down to a question of healing and giving and receiving love and finding peace and reconciliation, which are very important religious terms as well as secular terms, pastoral caregivers bridge the two through theological reflection.

As the study shows, theological reflection is an important element that makes the research participants' ministry pastoral. When they deal with pastoral situations or life stories while attending to the problem a care-seeker brings, they also look internally at some spiritual, existential issues that ask for theological reflection. When appropriate, they share their theological perspectives with the client to illuminate his or her situation. Thus, pastoral clinicians perform theological reflection in their practices, and by doing so, they see themselves as integrating psychological and theological wisdoms.

Meeting Needs through Making Meanings as a Pastoral Facilitator

Since people come to a pastoral clinician with their concerns and needs, the helper tries to meet their needs throughout the care-giving process. Because of the interactive nature of pastoral care-giving, several interviewees set their goals in ministry as serving and meeting whatever the care-seekers' needs are (I6, I8, I11, I13, I16, I19). Chaplain Sam says that his goal in chaplaincy is "to really meet the needs of each patient as best as I can" (I16). Chaplain and spiritual advisor Katherine further describes her sense of vocation:

> It seems to fluctuate with what they need. There may be times where I feel more pastoral; there are times that I feel more like I am a therapist, and that's where we are. Sometimes I feel more like an educator, and it may just keep flowing in and out of those, depending on what conversation comes up, depending on what they need, what they want to talk about, and as they get sicker and sicker, what fears and concerns [they have]. (I16)

Thus, often pastoral clinicians find their goals in meeting people's needs and, thereby, see their sense of vocation depending on their needs.

Meeting people's needs is often a challenging task, requiring the helpers to be open and flexible. To meet care-seekers' needs, pastoral professionals do their best in whatever ways they can with wherever they are at. They can meet care-seekers' needs through presence, through supportive and reflective listening, through responding, and "through how [they] can be compassionate" (I8, I12, I13). Such a challenge offers an opportunity to expand the helper's pastoral identity. Chaplain Gloria maintains that care-seekers help her expand her role and identity. They define her role in a way that she has never had it defined before (I13).

Several caregivers view meaning-making as a central part in the process of meeting one's needs (I11, I12, I14, I20). As they hear what care-seekers' issues are and follow their stories, pastoral practitioners facilitate their meaning-making (I12). They attempt to look for a larger frame of meaning or a larger context that they can put the problem into (I11). Thus, along the line with theological reflection, meaning-making draws a line in pastoral care and counseling.

It is not necessary to use religious language or come from a religious perspective in order to find and make meaning (I14). However, when meeting a care-seeker's needs without making-meaning, pastoral caregivers can fall short of providing "pastoral" care and counseling. For example, interfaith chaplain Sam got a request for a baptism from a female hospice patient in her early nineties who had been lying that she was baptized all these years and felt really bad about it. She was originally a Lutheran and converted to Buddhism at some point in her life, but in her last life stage she wanted to be baptized. Since Sam was ordained to a new small religious group and, as an interfaith chaplain, did not represent any religion or denomination, he tried to find a pastor. However, she wanted Sam to baptize her no matter what religion or denomination she would get into. They created a ritual in her room, she asked forgiveness for her lying, and he baptized her. She felt relieved (I16).

In this pastoral situation, Chaplain Sam met her need for a baptism perfectly. What was missing here, however, is exploring the meaning behind her request. When the interviewer asked the chaplain about the meaning of a baptism to him and to the patient, Sam said, "Well, to the patient I'm not sure what it meant. But, I mean, in this particular case what she told me is she felt a lot better... And so, I just accommodated what she wanted" (I16). Chaplain Sam skipped a meaning-exploration of her baptism and, thereby, missed an important chance to make meaning of the baptism both for her life and for death in the near future.

Accordingly, helping care-seekers and meeting their needs in pastoral care and counseling needs to include the exploration and creation of meaning with them. Pastoral counselor Linda, for instance, counseled a young woman who graduated from college and was willing to do anything but could not find work. While talking about the practical side of her needs, Linda co-created the meaning of work with the counselee by exploring a sense of her purpose in life. Thus, Linda says, "I have really pushed her to become more conscious about her sense of purpose in life and that, you know, moves us into the profound depth areas, and she'll talk about God, and she'll talk about her religious background how it informs her sense of purpose" (I20). As in Linda's case, several pastoral caregivers connect meeting needs with meaning-making and meaning-making with theological reflection (I10, I20).

The helper's theological stance is important in making meaning and reflecting theologically. Talking about her approach to keeping her faith and at the same time being an effective caregiver, chaplain Keri illustrates two kinds of theological stances: theological "fluffiness" and "groundedness." She says:

> I was focusing on spirituality, and I can't remember the author but he talked about how we should not engage in metaphysical marshmallow. That's his expression. Metaphysical marshmallow where, you know, this spirituality, this fluffiness of who knows what . . . What this author said was rather than engaging in metaphysical marshmallow . . . you stay very grounded in your tradition. And it's from the groundedness in your own tradition with an openness, so the boundary is still very fuzzy there, very open, but I am really well centered and grounded that I can engage in the conversation with the other and when they use their language they stay very grounded in who they are and then we communicate and we talk to each other and we try and create shared meaning in that conversation. (I10)

Other than interfaith chaplains (I13, I16), most pastoral care and counseling professionals emphasize the importance of their theological stance in the theological reflection and meaning-making process (I2, I5, I10, I20).

As in Figure 3, the phase of the requested pastoral identity as a compassionate pastor often takes place in a pastoral conversational setting in which a pastoral caregiver listens to care-seekers' calling explicitly and implicitly for a "pastor." This calling happens in a form of verbal conversation in most cases but can at times happen in a hospice setting in which the pastor has to listen internally to what the nonverbal dying patient is calling for. Phenomenologically speaking, as pastoral conversations go on, a pastoral caregiver listens to what care-seekers call him or her to be for them and tries to meet their needs. Beneath the visible process, according to the research participants, pastoral care and counseling professionals have interpersonal dynamics of care-giving and identity construction which deepen the pastoral relationship between the care partners.

While reflectively attending to care-seekers' stories as a fellow listener, learner, and companion, the helper enters, with compassion, into their world as opened in the stories and responds to their calling to be their "pastor." As often implied in the request, becoming their pastor signifies reflecting theologically on their issues and helping them make meaning for their lives. By doing so, pastoral care-giving integrates psychological and theological wisdoms and builds an "identity-embodied" pastoral care and counseling (Park 2005a & b).

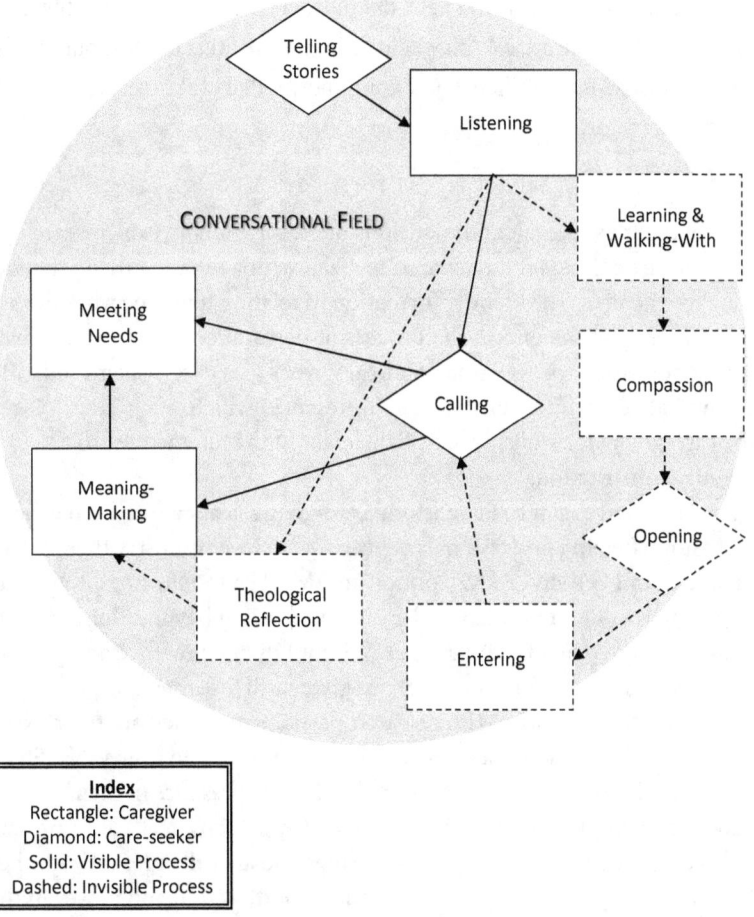

Figure 7. Process of Requested Pastoral Identity as Compassionate Pastor

4. REALIZING A DIVINE PRESENCE AS A PARTAKER OF GOD'S MINISTRY

My strong feeling of pastoral identity comes when I'm with a patient and something unexpected happens in the conversation. It's either something that the patient comes to realize [or] that I've assisted them in realizing, whether it's about themselves or about how God cares for them. I think more my identity is as being a conduit for God's work. I know I'm still who I am and God is using me [as] who I am, but the identity comes up when there is like, "Ah," "Aha," a surprise. Who would have expected this to come out of this conversation? And look, here it is. I don't know if that makes sense.

—Chaplain Shelly

One of the most prevalent dimensions of pastoral identity the research participants articulate is self or shared realization of a divine presence between the care partners. The identity formation in relation to divine work does not occur merely at the end of the process of pastoral care-giving but prevails throughout the process. A pastoral caregiver's and care-seeker's individual or mutual recognition of the divine presence, which often takes place in the care-giving relationship, exists throughout the interactive process of the identity construction.

As we have seen so far, pastoral care-giving is not a solo human activity. Pastoral helping professionals believe that in their ministry there is God's presence and activity. As O'Connor and Meakes (2008) note, theological reflection includes discovering the divine, "moving beyond thinking about God to experiencing God" (p. 121). Without divine presence and power in their pastoral care-giving, pastoral caregivers will lose their spiritual authority and pastoral identity. The research participants articulate their experiences of divine presence and power in their ministry in four ways: First of all, pastoral caregivers are conscious about God's presence in their existence and role as God's representatives. They also actually feel God's presence when they attend to care-seekers' sufferings and are fully present with them. Furthermore, pastoral practitioners realize God's action and power in their care-giving practices with a sense of awe. Finally, care-seekers and others confirm God's presence and action by affirming the care-giving. Thus, pastoral caregivers participate in God's healing ministry as partakers along with their care-partners, rather than as initiators of a subject-object relationship.

Self-Conscious Awareness of God's Presence

As demonstrated in the first section of this chapter, pastoral caregivers see themselves as called by God and endorsed by the faith community and, thereby, understand themselves as divine representatives who suppose God to be in their ministries. They are "aware," "conscious," and "intentional" about God's presence in their ministries and feel a divine presence in that sense. Chaplain Bill says, "My own awareness of and sort of being attuned to the idea [is] that in that moment with [a] patient there is something holy happening that God is there and God is embodied in that . . . So it really has to do with my own intentionality as much as anything that is said or specifically done" (I3). Thus, pastoral caregivers intentionally put themselves in a role of a representative, embodiment, or instrument of God's love and healing.

Pastoral counselor Linda, for instance, speaks of such self-consciousness of God's presence when she talks about what shapes her pastoral identity the most:

> I think it's an internal understanding and sense of myself as a conscious . . . representative of a holy presence. It's hard to get words. When I'm with clients . . . my conscious awareness [is] that we are on holy ground. And if I'm holding that space—I mean the space in which therapy happens—both a geographical space as well as an emotional space where I create with a client, I create an atmosphere of safety and trust, but it's also a spiritual space. And I don't create that, but I invoke it, internally . . . And that, I think I live in that awareness all the time but especially in a counseling session. (I20)

Thus, while Linda is present with her clients, she imagines the encounter as a holy space in which God is present. Likewise, chaplain Bill sits with a girl and is attentive to her while she asks him difficult theological questions. By attending empathically to her, he hopes that his presence communicates to her that if the chaplain can do this then maybe God can also tolerate her without getting angry at her complaints (I3).

As a spiritual figure, a pastoral caregiver is supposed to have this kind of self-consciousness of the divine presence in his or her ministry; but it is not enough. This approach can be a conscious or subconscious manipulation of God's presence if the conscious awareness has no actuality. Pastoral caregivers renew their awareness of themselves as God's representatives by recognizing God's presence in their pastoral relationship and ministries.

Divine Presence Through and Over Pastoral Presence

Pastoral caregivers may be frustrated and reconsider a self-consciousness of the divine presence if care-seekers reject their "pastoral" care-giving or put the helpers in a category of secular caregivers like psychotherapists or social workers. Nonetheless, when the pastoral caregivers are faithfully present with people and walk with them through their sufferings and issues, both care partners, or at least the caregivers, may at times realize God's presence in their care-giving relationships. Pastoral caregivers make possible a connection to divine presence by being "open to multiple experiences of the divine" in their care-giving practices (S17).

The caregivers let God's presence flow through care-seekers by being fully present with them (I13). In other words, God's presence and divine love reveal themselves in the pastoral relationship when the helpers are present with the helped (I2, I3, I5, I13). Entering into an encounter with patients in the name of a religious figure, chaplain Bill hopes to "bring into the room [a] respect of the sacredness of the encounter with them [care-seekers] as well as respect for their own location and their journey, their own experiences of reality and God" (I3). Thus, pastoral counselor Rosa humbly recognizes God's presence in her counseling session:

> The quote I have on my wall says, "Bidden or unbidden God is here". . . it's something that happens between the two of us, that makes things open up, that perhaps I hadn't figured were going to or weren't expecting. So, it's the main driving force of the counseling that I do. (I14)

Thus, divine presence is the driving force in pastoral care and counseling.

Several pastoral practitioners mention that as they approach care-seekers with an open heart and become fully present with them, they see God's presence in that relationship. How could this happen? The sense of God's presence comes across to the care-counterparts through caregivers' listening, through talking, and through the types of conversations they have (I5). In the relationship between the care partners, the caregivers at least feel the third presence, God's presence, in their midst (I2). Pastoral counselor Cale says from his memory of George Buttrick's speech that our presence is small "p" within the larger Presence, capital "P" (I4). Accordingly, pastoral caregivers believe that care-seekers at times feel God's presence through the human presence (I2, I3, I5, I13), which is a transference of divine presence from the caregiver to the care-seeker.

This divine transference takes place uniquely in pastoral care and counseling through pastoral presence and through unconditional caring.

In psychotherapeutic terms, transference means a therapist's conscious and unconscious feelings and thoughts can transmit to the psyche of the client. Likewise, pastoral caregivers' presence and love can penetrate and communicate with care-seekers. Pastoral counselor Linda dares to say that most of her clients would say that she loves them. She goes on to say:

> I believe that I don't do that in my own power, that I am a conduit of the love of God to the folks with whom I work. And some of them have never experienced that in an overt way and I am able to offer that to them. And I am keenly aware that loving them is not enough. It's not sufficient but I do [that]. I think I believe it is necessary and I don't believe I am capable of doing that in my own, under my own steam. So, it's one of the places where I feel very connected to my faith and my spirituality and where I perhaps become somewhat of a bridge for a client. (I20)

Thus, God's presence and love communicate to Linda's counselees through her pastoral presence and unconditional positive regard. Pastoral caregivers' being present and giving unconditional love to care-seekers transfer God's love to them in pastoral care-giving.

In this sense, the ministry of presence is the ministry of divine incarnation. Pastoral caregivers see "God working incarnationally via human encounter with fellow humans" (S38). Pastoral practitioners, like pastoral counselor Neil, refer to the ministry of presence as a "very high calling," defining it with a theological term, "incarnational" (I2). Since God is working in human care-giving, pastoral caregivers are "humbled by the task that [they] can only complete with God's help" (S10). Pastoral practitioners sometimes realize God's presence afterward when they look back on their pastoral encounters, saying, "Wow, God was truly present there" (I10). Thus, the research participants commonly agree that God's presence and love often reveal themselves in their pastoral presence and empathy. Pastoral presence and supportive listening not only communicate to the care-receiver a sense of empathy and understanding but also convey God's presence and love (I11).

In this regard, pastoral caregivers often pray to God to be with them and listen to God's presence in their ministries. They listen "with openness to the Holy Other in the relationship" (S26) and listen "for God's presence and power to unfold" in their work (S41). Accordingly, in pastoral care-giving, pastoral caregivers listen not only to the counselee but also to what is going on in themselves. Moreover, pastoral caregivers listen for the third voice that might speak in or beyond the room (I4).

Moreover, several interviewees report that they feel God's presence more strongly when the care-seekers also open their worlds, allow the caregivers to enter into their lives, and accept pastoral care-giving (I16). Chaplain Shelly says that when a patient is really open to her, she feels much more confident, and that interaction contributes greatly to her identity and ability to give pastoral care (I6). Chaplain Julia also says that she is privileged to walk with patients into a very "sacred territory" (I12). Chaplain Sam further describes his experience of the divine presence:

> P48: I am going to be present with them [patients], just like if my child were sick I would be present with her. So, I know that the patient is sick or suffering in some way and I am going to be present with them. I find that sometimes when patients are very present themselves that sometimes God's grace can come even more strongly between us because it's like that scripture where two or three are gathered together, you know, there I am also. The presence is there. And when more people who are being present are together, there is more presence happening.
>
> I49: Okay. So, it's not like just you and your patient, but there is a third force or third presence and God's grace.
>
> P49: Yeah, there is presence of a mystery or God's presence . . . When I walk into a patient's room it may be stronger because there is a lot of suffering, or there is a lot of anxiety, or there is a lot of grief, or there is a lot of love. And when the patient can open to that and not resist it and I can be open to that and not resist it and be present with it, then what I would call God's mystery, God's grace can come even stronger. (I16)

Thus, pastoral caregivers realize God's presence in their care-giving relationships even more when the relationship goes deeper and makes a full connection between the care partners.

In addition, pastoral practitioners (I8, I12) have a strong sense of the presence of the holiness of God particularly when they are with care-seekers who are very close to extreme human conditions like death. Chaplain Julia realizes how sacred she feels when she gives care to a dying patient. She metaphorically takes off her shoes on the holy ground where a patient is approaching a sacred time in his or her life (I12). Katherine, spiritual advisor in a hospital, also describes God's presence over her pastoral presence with a dying patient:

> It can be an amazing moment. In that moment of death it is like the moment of peace, the moment of truth. It could be the pastoral presence at that moment. It is like a position of honor to be

there. There have been times that I have had nurses say to me, "I feel like you are the presence of God in this room." And I usually don't respond to that because I think in my mind it is so much bigger than me that I feel like it would limit God somehow. (I8)

Thus, Katherine proposes that the moment of death occurs on a "sacred ground," a place where "God draws nearer to people at the end of their life" and where "God is often near enough that God could be touched and felt" (I8). Thus, some pastoral providers witness to God's presence in their ministry to care-receivers who are at the "sacred" moment of dying.

Divine Power in Human Care-Giving

While pastoral caretakers feel a strong sense of a divine presence in a deep relationship and connection with care-seekers, they also realize God's working in their care-giving practices when they listen to God. They are constantly amazed at how God uses them when they remain open to God (S10). Not only is God present with both care partners, but God also acts by (a) guiding them throughout the whole process of care-giving, (b) giving them thoughts and wisdom, and/or (c) making an "aha" moment within them.

First of all, many of the interviewees assert that before, during, and even after pastoral encounters with care-seekers, pastoral caregivers continually ask God for help and guidance. Before the encounter, they practice personal devotions (I17) and meditations (I16) and try to keep connected with God. Interfaith chaplain Sam, for example, does meditations before entering into the room. He says, "I take moments to sit quietly, feel myself, [and] feel my center . . . And I feel connected to what I would call spirit or the mystery of God's grace. I often do that [meditation] . . . before I see somebody so that I can be open and available to what's needed" (I16). Pastoral counselor Joe also sees his own personal devotional life and prayer life as what continues to equip him to stay on top of the best counseling practice he can provide (I17). Chaplain Chris centers himself with spiritual devotion and prayer every day, asking God to guide him throughout his ten-year career (I15).

Moreover, since pastoral caregivers ask God to give them wisdom, strength, and guidance before the encounter, they are conscious of God's working through them during the care-giving (I9). During the care-giving moment, they pursue and pray internally for God's guidance (S41, S32, S24, S62, S24). They seek "God's guidance in the ministry" to which they are called (S41) and listen with openness to be "guided by the Holy Spirit" (S24, S62). Since they "rely on God" (S37), are "connected to God" (S8), and guided by God, they are "not alone in what [they are] doing, working with God to assist clients" (S16). Even as pastoral caregivers give to others, the givers receive from God (S16), who gives caregivers resources to deal with life issues (S18).

Furthermore, pastoral practitioners see themselves as "participating in the liberative activity of God" (S12) and as "co-creator[s] with God in growth and change" not only within clients but also within themselves (S9). Thus, they "witness to God's healing work" in their ministry. Some of the interviewees articulate how they found God's work in their care-giving practices. One of the examples of a divine presence and work in their ministry is what they call an "aha-moment." As noted at the beginning of this section, Chaplain Shelly feels a strong sense of God's presence when she has an "aha" moment. This aha moment comes up when care-seekers realize how God cares for them unexpectedly through the pastoral conversation (I6). They gain "internal insight" and say "Wow!" (I2). Also, when thoughts come up in the minds of pastoral caregivers which they have never thought to say, that makes them express an unexpected "aha." In such situations she feels strongly that God is using her as a "conduit for God's work." And, that realization in turn helps her have a strong feeling of pastoral identity (I6). In such divine encounters, pastoral caregivers confess that God is working in their ministry, and they partake in the divine awe.

Since pastoral practitioners believe that they partake in God's work and wonder, they also rely on God for the outcome of their care-giving. If through the pastoral caregivers' ministry of presence and care-giving people can experience a sense of peace, decreased anxiety, and increased spiritual comfort, then the caregivers feel that they are able to embody for the care-receivers the presence of God who enabled those results to happen in their practices (I3). When the pastoral visit did not go well for some reason, Chaplain Keri remembers that "God was in that room before they [caregivers] got there, and that God was with them [during the visit], and that God stayed in the room once they left" (I10). Thus, Keri sees her ministry as "planting seeds." She may never see her patients again, but then "hopefully God takes those seeds, uses other people to continue fertilizing the seeds and caring for them and something more may happen beyond that" (I10).

Confirmation of Pastoral Identity and God's Presence

According to the research participants' narratives, care-receivers confirm and validate what pastoral caregivers have done for them by interacting with the helpers, affirming their care-giving, and making a referral. First of all, care-seekers help the caregivers' pastoral identity by interacting with them. They ask them all of their spiritual questions they never had anybody to ask before (I7). They give the caregivers a special privilege to access their lives and life stories (I2, I20). Pastoral counselor Linda contends that counselees who have "the courage to be vulnerable" to "share their deepest, darkest truths" have done the most to contribute to her pastoral identity (I20). Thus, pastoral care-seekers allow the caregivers to go underneath their thoughts and explore their feelings and thereby give the helpers a sense of honor to be "pastoral" caregivers (I2).

Moreover, several pastoral helping professionals describe care-seekers' affirmations as important contributions to the construction of pastoral identity (I2, I5, I7, I10, I12, I15, I17, I18). Their affirmations confirm pastoral helpers' vocations (I2) and reinforce their pastoral identity (I14, I15). For example, pastoral counselor Joe recognizes that patients contribute to his identity when they have affirmed that the care-giving was beneficial (I17). Marie, a pastoral counselor, also appreciates counselees' affirmations, saying, "They [are] just affirming that I am serving a very important role in their lives at the time that they seek counseling" (I18). She hears them saying, "I never would have gone to someone else because I needed a person like you just to be here in the midst of what I'm dealing with" (I18). Thus, such a deep trust and relationship embedded in the affirmation contributes to pastoral caregivers' self-understanding. Even if the care-giving is not successful to care-seekers, that still contributes to a pastoral identity by providing an opportunity to rethink and reshape it. Research participants say that both positive and negative feedback contribute to the helpers' construction of pastoral identity (I10, I17).

Care-seekers use various expressions that contribute to the caregivers' self-understanding. In their non-verbals, care-seekers' eyebrows raise, or their facial features change, and more life comes to their body and their body language. Some care-receivers express their appreciation on a card or feedback sheets. Some say things like, "God must have sent you," "You are an angel to me," or "You helped to guide me through this experience to be able to find my own answer with God" (I5, I16). Such feedback reminds pastoral caregivers of God's presence and work in their ministries.

Verbally care-seekers sometimes express their affirmation, saying, "Wow! That is really helpful" (I2). Pastoral counselor Rosa describes this experience:

> I23: In your daily counseling experiences and practices, what gives you a strong feeling or idea of pastoral identity?

P23: The experiences I think that speak to me the most, that they touch me the most are when I can find that I am in touch with whatever it is the client is feeling or trying to express ... Sometimes I can see them light up and say "That's exactly what I was trying to say" or "Gee, that's really a good question." And I may not have even realized that I was particularly empathic with them at that time or that I was asking a particularly wise question. But the fact that something about the way they heard it or something about the timing when I asked [. . .] struck a chord for both of us. That is really exciting. (I14)

In such a case, pastoral counselor Hillary says, "By the grace of God I've hit on a place that is important to them that they think no one ever noticed before" (I9). Thus, care-seekers contribute to pastoral identity by affirming the caregivers' ministry and confirming God's presence and work in their care-giving practices.

Even though care-seekers' affirmations make a contribution to the identity construction of pastoral caregivers, they don't build their identity on this confirmation. They deny a need for affirmation, saying, "I don't need his [or her] affirmation in order for me to feel I have a pastoral identity" (I12) or "I don't need the patient to affirm my pastoral identity" (I16). There is a constant sense of pastoral identity and a sense of being called in a specific situation, and care-receiver's affirmation fits the specific sense of identity (I13). Why, then, is the affirmation important to them? Chaplain Chris says that care-receivers' affirmation gives him a joy, an excitement, a reward, and a sense of fulfillment in his ministry. He joyfully says, "It's just very affirming that I have fulfilled the task, the calling of a fellow pilgrim" (I15).

Finally, referral is another source of the dynamics of constructing a pastoral identity. Referral signals the same affirmation to pastoral caregivers. Care-seekers come to pastoral caregivers by referral and also refer others to their caregivers (I2, I9, I11, I14, I15, I17, I18, I19, I20). People often refer someone to pastoral caregivers for specific reasons like something related to spiritual and religious issues. These reasons also contribute to pastoral care-providers' identity and self-understanding. In addition to care-receivers' referrals, the staff's or other professionals' referral contributes to the identity construction of pastoral caregivers (I5, I7, I9, I17, I19, I20). When the referrers see someone has spiritual needs, they refer him or her to pastoral caregivers whom they see as specialists in that area. Two other professionals, for example, worked with a patient but referred him to Chaplain George because of the spiritual needs the patients had (I5). Also, the staff's affirmation of pastoral care-giving is helpful, as in the case of spiritual advisor Katherine whose hospital nurse says, "I feel like you are the presence of God" (18). And, all of these expressions contribute to an idea of God's representative and/or partaker of God's healing ministry when the pastoral caregiver comes into the next encounter with other care-seekers.

SUMMARY

As we have seen so far, the process of pastoral care-giving is complex and dynamic. Pastoral care-giving takes place in the relational interaction between a caregiver and care-seeker along with God's presence and work. In each phase of the process, pastoral care and counseling practitioners co-construct their pastoral identity with care-seekers, and the seekers contribute to the identity construction in various ways. When we see our clients as our care-partners, we find that they contribute tremendously to our ministry and identity. Pastoral identity is not merely a caregiver's self-awareness, as in a classical viewpoint. Pastoral identity is in full blossom on the way of deepening the pastoral relationship between the care partners and of re-realizing God's presence and power in the inter-relational dynamics of care-giving (see fig. 8).

At any moment within pastoral care and counseling relationships, care-seekers call out a pastoral identity by communicating to the caregiver what kind of persons they need. Care-seekers call out the helper's pastoral identities by accepting or rejecting the pastoral care-giving, by sharing their stories and crises, and by requesting help. In the dialogical interaction with the care-seekers, the helper co-constructs pastoral identities with the seekers by introducing who he or she is and explaining what the pastoral caregiver can do for the care-partners. The caregiver further co-creates identities by being present with, listening to, learning from, and accompanying care-seekers. Moreover, pastoral identity in a specific care-giving context takes a clearer shape, as both care partners go into a deeper relationship by inviting each other to their spaces. The helper responds to care-seekers' calls by making meanings and meeting their needs along the line of theological reflection on the pastoral situations. Pastoral identities continue to take shape to the extent that pastoral caregivers fully understand the God (who is present and works with them and among human care partners) and profoundly set their identities on that discovery about the divine.

96 PASTORAL IDENTITY AS SOCIAL CONSTRUCTION

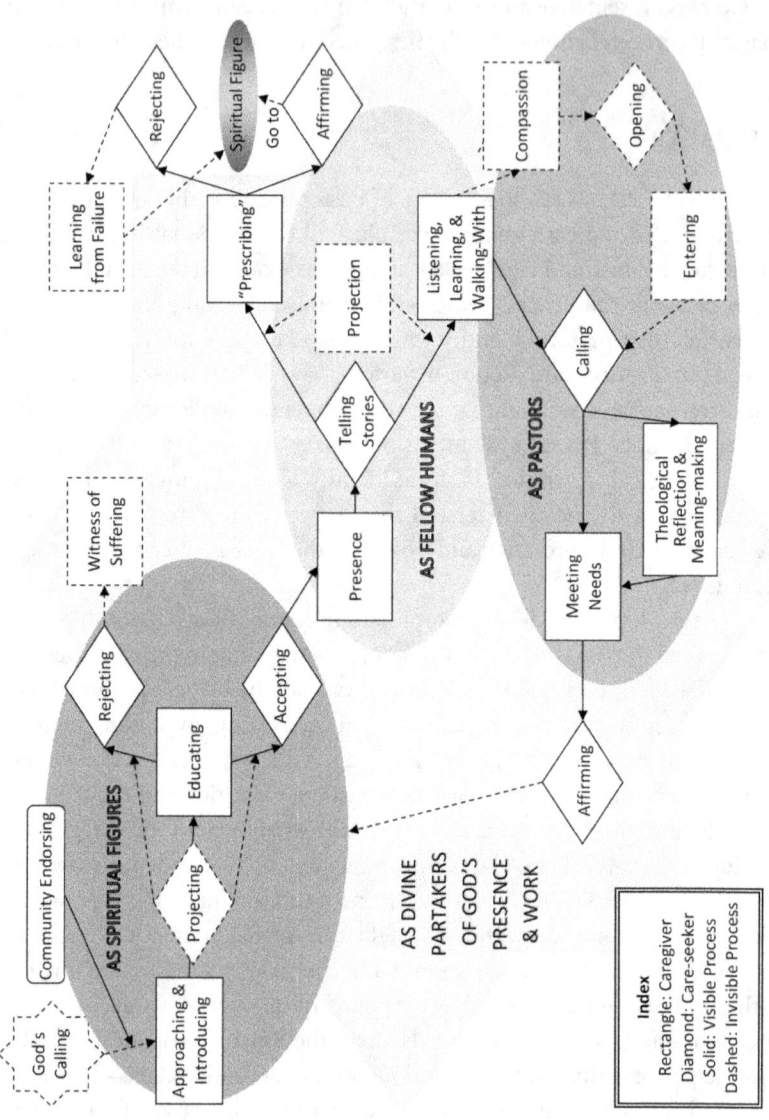

Figure 8. Process of Care-Giving and Constructing Pastoral Identity

4

Pastoral Identity in Postmodern Contexts

PASTORAL IDENTITY FROM MACRO-LEVEL PERSPECTIVES

IN THE PREVIOUS CHAPTERS, I have described my empirical research (in chapter 2) and its findings in narrative form (in chapter 3). The pastoral identity that the research participants narrated and the researcher interpreted through their stories is, in part, interactional, processual, intersubjective, and relationally constructive. The pastoral identity is interactional in the sense that it comes into view through the care partners' interactions. The identity is processual in that it emerges in the midst of an "emergent process" and is never finally established but continually being created and affecting the care-giving interactions (Vryan et al., 2003; Rattansi et al. 1997). The identity described in the previous chapter is also intersubjective and, thereby, relational in that it has "a sharing of understandings and meanings that arises in the 'potential space' of exploration" between the caregiver, care-seekers, and the Divine (Cooper-White 2004, vii). The identity, therefore, is socially and relationally constructive in the sense that the social interactors create their identities by interpreting and making meanings of their interactions. Thus, the emergent concept of pastoral identity supplements, on the one hand, and stands in contrast to, on the other hand, a traditional notion of pastoral identity that is mainly intrinsic, essential, individual, and developmental.

Now that we have explored pastoral identity at the level of everyday interactional practices, this chapter further examines identity from a macro-level point of view. In the following chapters, I deepen my empirical study's findings on pastoral identity by discussing them further in relation to the postmodern structure that shapes pastoral identity (in chapter 4) and by shedding a theological light on the findings (in chapter 5). The issues left over from the previous chapters are contemporary characteristics of pastoral identity explicitly and implicitly depicted in the research participants' narratives. These postmodern features lead us to take into consideration a relationship between pastoral identity and its cultural contexts. In particular, postmodern criticism of, and contribution to, symbolic interactionism furthers our discussion in terms of power and structure that shape identities. In this chapter, I draw upon various resources of empirical, social scientific, and pastoral theological materials relevant to the discussion in order to delineate a residual issue (the relation between identity and cultural structure affecting it).

At first glance, this chapter seems to deconstruct, to some degree, the symbolic interactionist narratives that the previous chapter constructed. However, the chapter helps us reconsider them with a refreshed view of pastoral identity. Sandstrom and Fine (2003) point to three perspectives that criticize and, thereby, contribute to symbolic interactionist approaches to identity. These emerging voices in interactionism are feminism, neo-Marxism, and postmodernism. One can summarize their main critique of SI with the point that "interactionists need to shift the focus of their analysis beyond the situational construction of selves toward the institutional production of selves" (p. 1051). Thus, a main argument against SI is that it has little concern with the power and structure that affect selves. For example, Sandstrom et al. show how feminist scholar Chafetz criticized West and Zimmerman's article "Doing Gender." In the article, they view gender as a product of social interactions and relationships and explain how people carry out and regenerate gender individually and institutionally through micro-level everyday interactions and relations. Chafetz criticizes the article for "placing too much emphasis on conversational practices and focusing too little attention on power" (Sandstrom et al. 1047).

Like feminists who liberate social practice by making gender oppression and inequality visible and deconstructing them, neo-Marxist approaches to SI try to stimulate emancipatory social practices and values by turning their attentions from micro-level everyday interaction strategies to the structure that defines and governs situations and interactions. Moreover, postmodernists, with their critical social and cultural analyses, charge that consumption-oriented capitalist society and its modern technology generate social changes that de-center and erode a sense of selfhood. As a result, identities in postmodern society become multiple, fragmented, and incoherent due to the "social saturation" occasioned by external relationships. Thus, the totally saturated self, according to Gergen (1991), turns out to be no self and, thereby, loses its authentic core-identity.

As these critiques of interactionist approaches to identity indicate, we need to look at some forms of the macro-level power and structure that affect the interactional and processual construction of pastoral identity. In particular, we need to pay more attention to the postmodern assessment of SI. In this sense, we have four issues to address. First of all, we need to explore how structural power and social pressure in (post)modern contexts affect pastoral care-giving practices and identity construction. We also need to consider postmodern marks of (pastoral) identity featured in contemporary everyday life and especially in pastoral care-giving practices. Moreover, we need to examine how pastoral caregivers can face postmodern challenges and come up with an agentic identity in this postmodern milieu. A set of seemingly incompatible dimensions of pastoral identity emerges in identity construction within postmodern and diverse care-giving contexts. These conflicting aspects lead us to consider how to find coherency, authenticity, and agency in multiple identities, which will later (in chapter 5) draw our attention to a theological perspective of identity. Thus, discussions in this chapter need to address the following questions:

- How have contemporary cultures and contexts in our field affected pastoral care-giving practices and identity construction?
- What are remarkable features of postmodern identity with which social psychologists contend? How do contemporary pastoral care-giving and identity construction reflect these characteristics explicitly and implicitly?
- In what way can we address the seemingly conflicting elements of identity construction (e.g., modernity vs. postmodernity)?
- How do contemporary pastoral caregivers survive or overcome their identity fragmentation and erosion in postmodern conditions? How can pastoral caregivers claim integrity, authenticity, and agency in their multicolored identities?

Postmodern cultural power affects and shapes daily interactions and relationships and, thereby, individuals' identity formation. Influenced by (post)modernism, the field of pastoral theology and care-giving and the identities of the practitioners have taken multiple shapes. As psychological, interdisciplinary, institutional, and pluralistic influences impact the field, pastoral practitioners, to a certain degree, adapt to an identity that those (post)modern impacts shape. Nonetheless, the relationship between the human agency (that constructs an identity through everyday interactions) and the structural power (that affects a micro-level interactional construction) is not unidirectional. The research participants indicate and contemporary social psychology alludes to the fact that pastoral care partners adapt to and resist cultural power that affects their identity construction.

Before pursuing a further delineation of this phenomenon, I need to make one point clear. As I mentioned about the boundaries and limitations of the dissertation in chapter 1, it is not my intention or a purpose of the book to do an in-depth critical analysis of pastoral identity. Drawing on the research data and on pastoral theological and social scientific literature, this chapter aims to describe contemporary changes in our care-giving contexts and the resulting practices within them. In this analysis, we look closely at how pastoral practitioners' micro-level everyday practices and interactions with their care receivers interweave with their macro-level social pressure and structural power in constructing pastoral identity.

(POST)MODERN SHIFT IN THE FIELD OF PASTORAL CARE, COUNSELING, AND THEOLOGY

I see the field wrestling with this spiritual marshmallow piece . . . I think there is a fear especially among religious institutions that the pastoral care departments are going to turn to this new age spirituality of metaphysical marshmallow, and they are going to be meaningless. So, I think it is from there that I get to [a] pastoral identity question. We have to figure out who we are as chaplains, individually and as a field, or we are just going to get swallowed up in this fuzziness and the people are going to wonder how [we can] help anybody.
—CHAPLAIN KERI

Around the 1980s, in the midst of the blossom of modernity, people in Christian education and ministry became increasingly aware of the impact of postmodernism on the society and church institutions. Several theologians debated the mission and role of theological education and the need for "practical" theology specifically in a contemporary society (e.g., Chopp 1995; Farley 1983, 1988; Hough et al. 1985; Kelsey 1993). Theology and theological education in a pluralistic society faced a challenge in providing values and norms in which the churches and society could find a moral principle of modern life. In an "age of uncertainty" and its pluralism, theological norms lost authority for guiding social life and actions. Theologians and church leaders felt less relevant and more marginalized in the process of modernization and secularization, including the declination of theological authority and the disrespect for the transcendent reality within a high technology society (Crumpler, 1994). Such a theological dilemma demanded renewed theological methodologies and a suitable position of theology in postmodernity (Park 2005a; see also Browning 1991; E. L. Graham 1996; Mudge et al. 1987; Poling et al. 1985 for a discussion of practical theological methodologies).

In addition to such identity confusion within the larger context of the modern institution of theological education, the field of pastoral care, counseling, and theology encountered another layer of the identity debate. Long discussed in the field, the issue of pastoral theological identity once again faced intensive attentions from pastoral theologians and practitioners. Since its modern burgeoning, the field has evolved in interaction with modern influences, which shape the field theoretically and clinically. Modernity has influenced the field and the concept of pastoral identity in at least four ways. In the following section, I will describe psychological, interdisciplinary, institutional, and pluralistic productions of pastoral identity as modernity has de-structured and re-structured the field and its practices and identity. These modern powers have caused identity confusion, on the one hand, but have also stimulated a renewed sense of pastoral identity within the field of pastoral theology and practice, on the other hand.

Influences of Modern Psychology: Psychological Constructions of Pastoral Identity

One cannot fully understand pastoral theology and practice in a modern era without understanding influences of modern psychologies. In a sense, the field of contemporary pastoral theology, care, and counseling has re-interpreted its form and identity by adapting to and joining with modern psychological discourses. Combining and remodeling a psychological perspective and approach with theological wisdom, the field has developed its education, training, and practice programs, such as clinical pastoral education and pastoral counseling programs. Such a movement of modern pastoral care and counseling has earned its status as a discipline of practical theology in academic institutions with varying names including pastoral psychology, pastoral psychotherapy, psychology of religion, and pastoral care, counseling, and theology. Moreover, professional associations have developed under the influence of psychological/psychotherapeutic institutions. The American Foundation of Religion and Psychiatry, for example, sponsored the formation of the American Association of Pastoral Counselors (AAPC) (Jackson 1964; Stokes 1985).

Thus, psychological influences have produced changes in modern pastoral practices and theology. The psychological power over the field has generated some interesting identity shifts. Some pastoral caregivers have identified themselves closely with a modern psychological identity (e.g., psychotherapists), shifting away from a traditional theological identity (e.g., pastors or theologians) (Houck 1974). Such psychological production of identity of the field and practitioners becomes evident when an adequate balance between theological and psychological perspectives has broken down. Due to the heavy dependency on psychology, several pastoral theologians maintained that the field had lost a pastoral and theological identity (Oden 1980, 1984; Patton 1981; Gerkin 1984, 1997). First, modern approaches to pastoral care-giving came to focus more on individual care and mental health along with the psychotherapeutic paradigm, moving away from the classical ministerial congregational care (Miller-McLemore 1996; Oden 1984). Second, as psychological influences increased and psychotherapeutic methods prevailed in the field, many pastoral clinicians struggled with their identities as psychologists-psychotherapists and/or pastors-theologians (Everett et al. 1983; Houck 1974; Kae-Je 1993; Seaton-Johnson et al. 1980).

As for the second point of the self-concept, pastoral practitioners and theologians traditionally put a strong emphasis on being pastors rather than psychologists (Sanderson 1977; Zimmerman 1953). For instance, Philip Guiles makes the following claim:

> If an explicitly theological approach to clinical pastoral training is to be formulated, those who supervise training must think first, last, and always of themselves as pastors, as clergymen [or women], as ministers, or priests in the Church of Christ . . . If the supervisor views his [or her] pastoral role as incidental and his [or her] psychiatric orientation as primary, then clinical pastoral training will be only incidentally relevant to Christian theological education—no matter how interesting and valuable it may be as a clerical excursion into the world of psychiatry . . . If, on the other hand, the supervisor views his [or her] pastoral role as primary and the insights of psychiatry as valuable adjuncts thereto (but no more), then clinical pastoral training will be profoundly relevant to Christian theological education,

and so to the wider life of the Church. (Quoted from Sanderson, 1977, 122)

In contrast to placing such a strong emphasis on being pastors, Houck (1974), in his research that surveyed 610 pastoral counselors and other clergy, concluded that pastoral counselors show "a greater tendency to identify professionally as psychotherapists, and show a lesser tendency to identify professionally as pastors" (2). Thus, deep involvement in the psychological paradigm of care-giving theories and practices had caused modern pastoral practitioners to view themselves as closely related to psychotherapists.

Even though pastoral theologians have later criticized such psychologically-defined approaches to pastoral care and counseling and psychological construction of pastoral identity of pastoral practitioners (Kae-Je 1993; Miller-McLemore 1996; Stone 1994), the psychological culture and power still remains in the field of pastoral care and counseling and functions as an important dialogue partner in the field. The pastoral caregivers in my empirical study of pastoral identity seem to answer the identity question as to whether they are pastors-theologians or psychologists-psychotherapists by responding "both-and" rather than "either-or." They see themselves not only as theologians but also as therapists, giving primacy to theological perspectives over psychological practices, as the data show (see chapter 2).

Influences of Multiple Relationships: Interdisciplinary Construction of Pastoral Identity

As modern academic enterprises cut across traditional boundaries of their fields, new academic hybrids of interdisciplinary approaches have emerged in academic disciplines. Under such a modern influence, pastoral theology and care-giving from its modern burgeoning consisted in a "hybrid" of theological discourses and behavioral sciences. Later, attempts to combine theological and cultural discourses have become multiplied by a broadened horizon of the field in relation to other various disciplines. As the field utilizes more cultural perspectives, its widened horizon with multiple dialogue partners has blurred the field's boundaries (Ashby 2000). With emerging voices redefining theological education and re-envisioning pastoral theology and "practical" theology since around the 1980s, the field has tried not only to widen its focus by recognizing the importance of communal and cultural contexts shaping individual lives but also to elaborate upon its interdisciplinary methodologies (see Farley 1983, 1988; Gerkin 1984; Hough et al. 1985; Mudge et al. 1987; Patton 1981, 1993).

Chaplaincy, pastoral counseling, and pastoral theology are interdisciplinary in nature and practice. The theologians and practitioners in the field have multiple relationships with other health care professionals (such as doctors, nurses, social workers, and faith community leaders), with various psychotherapeutic and counseling theories, and with varying theological and human and social sciences (including liberation and process theologies, feminism, critical theory, and political sciences). Such multidisciplinary characteristics have evolved through identity turmoil and competitive situations (Park 2007).

A historical survey of pastoral identity shows how the interdisciplinary nature of pastoral care and counseling has often caused identity confusion. Several scholars point out that the field suffered an identity crisis not because the field forgot the tradition but because the field has failed to develop a proper methodology of legitimating the transcendence of theological perspectives in a modern cultural discourse by integrating interdisciplinary dialogues (J. L. Marshall 2004; Park 2007). For example, in his study, Myers (1989) maintains that identity confusion is not a result of a loss of the theological tradition but a loss of its capacity to address the human situation with an appropriate theological methodology. Reviewing an evolution of pastoral theological methodologies in the field, I in my article (2007) have contended that "Adequate methodologies for pastoral theology should include due consideration of how to reflect on pastoral practice and situations where pastoral specialists encounter various human conditions and lived experiences and how to integrate theological and cultural perspectives" (28). Sound methodology undergirds identities of the field and the pastoral caregivers.

Moreover, the interdisciplinary phenomenon of pastoral care-giving not only serves as an "evidence of the process of secularization" that causes identity confusion (Gerkin 1967, 29) but also drives pastoral practitioners into a competitive environment where they often feel that they have to demonstrate their competencies in providing care and counseling. In his conference presentation titled "Identity of the Pastoral Supervisor," pastoral theologian Charles Gerkin (1966) articulates this competitive situation:

> [I]n our increasingly complex culture, the minister has become one among many helping, healing professions. This inevitably raises questions as to what is unique to this identity ... Among other things this creates a competitive climate in which the minister inevitably comes to ask what [her or] his identity has to offer that is more valuable than other helping professions have to give ... we chaplain supervisors often experience that kind of competitive struggle with other helping professions. This

> increasingly complex role value and role expectation situation also create[s] the climate within which the minister experiences increasingly competitive claims as to who he [or she] is to be and the roles he [or she] is expected to fill. (77–78)

Such interdisciplinary settings are indeed challenging to the field and its practitioners and require them to be cooperative with other helping professionals and institutional expectations.

Nonetheless, the interdisciplinary character of pastoral care-giving practices also provides an opportunity for exploring new ways of developing sound pastoral theological methodologies and for reconstructing pastoral identity and the role of the caregivers. This renovated approach has resulted in a contemporary trend toward "public" theology in the field. The discussion of public theology in recent decades has derived from a renewed recognition that pastoral theology and care-giving not only focus on individual care but also include care for a wide communal, cultural, religious, and social context. The public theological approach has become possible as the field engages a broadened methodological approach to multiple resources such as anthropology, sociology, ethics, gender studies, critical analysis, cultural analysis, economic sciences, and political sciences beyond the theological and psychological dialogue. This phenomenon helps pastoral theologians publicly claim their voices on the issues of violence, women, children, poverty, families, and public health care by integrating multiple discourses.

Thus, one can notice pastoral theology has widened its scope as a "practical" theology generated by the discussion of the renewal of theological education since the 1980s and as a "public" theology in the current time, as the field has redefined its scope and broadened interdisciplinary dialogue. However, such a movement toward public theology has challenges to overcome. The first challenge is how to accommodate pastoral counselors and chaplains' clinical obligations to care for individuals and families and pastoral theologians' public claims for ecclesial, social, and cultural contexts. For example, Miller-McLemore (2008) has re-coined a metaphor of objects of care as "the living human document within the web" in an effort to enrich deep engagement between practice and theory of the field. Another challenge the field faces is that we are still peripheral in the multidisciplinary discussion through which we participate in a public forum. Ashby (2000) articulates this dilemma:

> Because we [pastoral theologians] are cross-disciplinary our focus appears to be not so clear. Without the clarity of some specialization, we are not as attractive as a conversational partner.

> Even in the seminary the practical field is not always viewed as having the methodological integrity and rigor as other disciplines within theological education. On the margin our voices are silent. We have been silenced within the academy because the vast bulk of research taking place in the academy does not take seriously the work and insights of pastoral theologians. We are on the margin, on the periphery, invited to participate in the larger conversations at times, but more often than not rarely consulted on an ongoing basis about the critical issues facing society. (pp. 20–21)

Thus, the field has a challenging task to overcome in order to have a full partnership with other disciplines.

Nevertheless, the attempts to engage in dialogue within broader areas of academia and practice have eventually widened our field's horizon to address the transformation of public domains. Interdisciplinary discourses and practices have taken shape in the field of pastoral practices and theology. As Ramsay (2004) points out, "Multiple perspectives are available and needed regarding situations requiring care, and conversations respectful of the value in those differing perspectives are necessary for an adequate response" (160). Such multiple perspectives in pastoral practices can open a new era in which pastoral theology is a more reciprocally interdisciplinary dialogue partner with other disciplines.

Influences of Institutional Power: Institutional Construction of Pastoral Identity

One of the most obvious modern phenomena that impact pastoral care and counseling practices is the church care ministry's outreach to those outside of the faith community. Traditionally, pastors delivered pastoral care and counseling to their congregations and targeted people mainly outside the church for evangelism and mission outreach. However, as pastoral professionals revise their approaches to people by using psychotherapeutic perspectives and techniques, chaplains and pastoral counselors have come to work outside their faith communities and work within (mental) healthcare institutions. On the one hand, a struggle for pastoral identity in a parish setting has derived partly from a "crisis in the exercise of the authority of the ministerial office" (Hardwick 1995, 1). In a specialized setting of pastoral counseling and chaplaincy, on the other hand, the identity struggle results, in part, from a fear of whether "involvement in pastoral counseling [and chaplaincy] is a way of leaving the ministry" (iv).

Modern shifts in pastoral care and counseling have caused its practices to take place under institutional influences rather than faith-communal influences. In the pre-modern era, pastoral care and counseling were held in and by the faith community along with its faith traditions. The faith community was the ultimate and primary contextual community of pastoral care and counseling. According to pastoral theologian Brian Childs (1993), "Pastoral counseling and supervision must belong to the Church and it must be accountable to the Church and if it cannot work within the church building itself it should clearly identify itself as a more than symbolic arm of the Church" (76). Thus, the faith community and church expectations played an important role in establishing an influential context in which pastoral caregivers formed their identities (Moore 1982). In this context, pastoral relationships between caregivers and seekers were usually long term since they had been established before the care-giving encounters and these relationships would continue after the encounters. Thus, the relationships were relatively stable, and the images of the caregivers were comparatively consistent.

However, in many cases pastoral care-giving in a modern context no longer takes place in and by the faith community and has become part of (mental) healthcare institutions such as hospitals and counseling centers. The institutions are now immediate and primary communities of pastoral care-giving. In such modern contexts, connections to and involvement in the faith community and traditions became weak and less influential on some pastoral practitioners who work in an institutional context. Rather, the connection and commitment to the faith community depends heavily on the persons who carry out pastoral care and counseling. Depending on their beliefs in and devotions to the faith community and traditions, pastoral caregivers choose whether to ground pastoral care-giving on theological bases.

Especially, care-giving relationships in institutional contexts are mostly brief and fluid as caregivers have to care for a large number of people in their everyday practices and their religious and cultural backgrounds are diverse. In addition, contemporary therapeutic relationships are likely to be brief and focused on the short-term since many clients have only few sessions (Stone 1994, 2001). Encountering many care-seekers back to back in everyday practices, pastoral caregivers present themselves more inclusively to serve care-seekers who have various religious, cultural, ethnic, and sexual orientations and backgrounds. Thus, pastoral practitioners in an institutional context manage their pastoral images broadly and their pastoral relationships briefly and fluidly. Their practices are short-term and should be effective in such brief and incidental relationships.

Moreover, in today's postmodern milieu, pastoral practitioners' commitment to the faith community does not merely depend on their decision but also on institutional pressure. Chaplaincy in healthcare settings, for example, becomes independent from the faith community and turns into part of a healthcare team that requires chaplains to promote the generic spirituality of care-seekers without a specific religious/denominational ground and orientation (Engelhardt 1998). As a result, chaplains in healthcare settings are supposed to care for patients and their families from a religiously "neutral" perspective and thereby are likely to loosen their connection with, and commitment to, the faith community. Such a postmodern approach is different from the (pre-)modern approach that focuses on the importance of the faith community and tradition.

Likewise, pastoral counselors encounter the same kind of challenges to their pastoral identity. As many pastoral counseling centers locate outside of faith communities and serve ethnically and religiously diverse, and culturally dynamic, local communities, pastoral counselors can reach out to individuals and families, including low-income peoples, in local communities. Some counselors, however, are hesitate to deal with religious or spiritual issues, fearing that they might impose their faith values on care-seekers. Moreover, working in secular counseling centers, some pastoral counselors sometimes suffer supervision that does not recognize religious and faith values. Accordingly, the integration of psychology with theology, a significant category for pastoral identity, is now a challenging precept to some pastoral counselors, as they become more pressed by institutional power.

According to Tristram Engelhardt (1998), institutional power reshapes caregivers' identities. Healthcare institutions hire chaplains to provide spiritual care and counseling, but the nature of that care-giving is unclear and under-defined strategically. Such generic chaplaincy, defined as "religion-non-specific, denominationally-neutral hospital chaplaincy," can lead to role confusions and questions of the "fungibility of spiritual services" (231). Healthcare institutions expect generic caregivers to care for a patient population drawn from all religions and even the unchurched. The author maintains that "Ministers who were once ordained in particular religions are reprofessionalized into trans-denominational roles. Institutional expectations reshape their vocation into the role of generic [caregivers]" (232). Several pastoral clinicians and theologians articulate conflict over the authority, efficacy, and theological soundness of generic spiritual care (e.g., *Christian Bioethics 4* (3), 1998 & 9 (1), 2003).

While church expectations have become less influential, institutions' expectations and financial influences have become primary contexts of pastoral care-giving. Pastoral caregivers formulate stories about their images and practices increasingly in "discursive environments," such as counseling centers and hospitals, which represent "institutional domains characterized by distinctive ways of interpreting and representing everyday realities" (Sandstrom et al. 2003, 1051). Thus, many contemporary pastoral practitioners construct their identities in particular institutional contexts, and the institutions impose the limits on potential language in constructing pastoral identity (cf. Lyotard 1984).

Multi-Religious and -Cultural Influences: Pluralistic Construction of Pastoral Identity

As contemporary clinical settings become increasingly culturally and religiously diverse and pastoral care and counseling have increasingly "globalized," "internationalized," and "indigenized" in Lartey's terms (2004), pastoral practitioners need to equip themselves with a critical intercultural and multifaith perspective in their norms and practices. As pastoral theologian Howard Clinebell (1984) rightly observes, pastoral care and counseling must "become more inclusive in its understanding, concern, and methods ... [and] become transcultural in its perspective ... On a shrinking planet, our circle of consciousness, conscience, and caring must become global" (27). The field of pastoral care and counseling has intensively discussed the issue of spiritual and multicultural competency (e.g., *Journal of Health Care Chaplaincy*, 13 (2), 2004; *Journal of Supervision and Training in Ministry*, 22, 2002). In the discussion, psychologists Mary Fukuyama and Todd Sevig (2004) define spiritual and cultural competency as the capacity "to be self-aware, knowledgeable about different cultural [and religious] traditions, able to understand the client's worldview, and skilled in communicating with and helping diverse clients" (32).

In reality, however, pastoral caregivers and seekers and other religious clinicians have reported their split identities in culturally and religiously diverse contexts. There are some examples of this case, one for care-seekers in postcolonial worlds and the other for caregivers in contemporary Dutch chaplaincy. First, Tapiwa Mucherera (2006) describes experiences of indigenous people in African countries who live in between cultures and religions—the African and the Western—with a sense of "being double" and "being half." Moreover, reflecting on Dutch chaplains called "spiritual caregivers" in the country, Hetty Zock (2008) sees their split identities in healthcare institutions. According to the author, Dutch healthcare institutions increasingly appoint "existential counselors" who do not have an official affiliation with any faith community and focus on making meaning.

As a result, spiritual caregivers as employees of the institutions have come to lose a denominational "mission" and an ecclesiastical office that allows them to carry out religious services and have turned more into existential counselors. Thus, postmodern pluralistic environments of cultures and religions challenge identities of pastoral practitioners, splitting their religious and professional identities (Jacque, 2006).

Contemporary caregivers and seekers are at risk of facing such split identities in this pluralist intercultural and multifaith context. This context demands pastoral practitioners and theologians to respond to our initial question as to how to honor religious and cultural diversity and adequately present wisdom of particular traditions and how to claim caregivers' own religious faith and, at the same time, maintain effective therapy with religious and cultural otherness of clients. In their article "Cultural Diversity in Pastoral Care," Fukuyama et al. partly respond to these questions. To be competent in such a setting of pastoral care and counseling does not have to mean to be fragile in one's own beliefs, values, and traditions. As the authors point out, it implies, for example, that "one can have strong Christian beliefs, values, and cultural identifiers and competently work with someone who is Jewish, Islamic, or from other faith or religious tradition" (ibid. 37). The authors spell out some key points of ethical considerations in being effectively inclusive and multiculturally and spiritually competent in a pluralistic care-giving context in the following way:

> (a) not proselytizing from one's own perspective; (b) being aware of power and privilege issues in how religion has been enacted in this country (e.g., Protestant Christian traditions being seen as the norm); (c) having a pluralistic worldview—no one tradition has the "corner on the truth"; and (d) avoiding an "either/or" dichotomy in viewing these issues, and embracing a "both/and" perspective (e.g., "I can be a strong Christian, and value someone else's experience in being Islamic"). (37)

As noted above, (post)modern influences have generated changes in the field's theorizing and practicing care, counseling, and theology and also in pastoral specialists' senses of who they are as care providers in an epistemologically, culturally, and religiously plural society. Structural and contextual power in the field's disciplinary practices and care-giving environments has become a shaping force that affects identities of pastoral practitioners. In the following sections, I will describe how this structural pressure seems to affect everyday human life and also pastoral care-giving practices and identity production. Before discussing these postmodern features of pastoral identity, I will first describe postmodern characteristics of identity that social psychologists depict.

POSTMODERN CHARACTERISTICS OF SELF AND IDENTITY

According to Gergen's analysis (1991), the ways of understanding the self have changed over time. In the nineteenth century, romanticists viewed the self as located in the deep interior of the person's being, including such aspects as passion, eternal love, deep inspiration, soul, creativity, and moral fiber. A deep commitment to relationships, friendships, and purposes of life formatted the self. By contrast, rationality and observation basically constitute the modernist perspective on self. Modernists characterize the self by having the ability to reason, to form opinions, and to deal with conscious intentions. Thus, both romanticist and modernist perspectives regard the self as stable over time; the self is an entity that one can call either character or personality.

In postmodern thought, however, the idea of multiple selves has challenged the idea of a single and stable self. The self no longer lives in a coherent social world with a consistent set of "truths." Postmodernists see the self as constructed and shaped contextually in social relationships rather than reflecting a fixed inner reality. "Relational reality" now characterizes the self, which was governed by the heart (in romanticism) or by rationality (in modernism). An individual constitutes his or her shifting selves according to the various relationships, conversations, and languages she or he is in. In a postmodern era, the self is an object that is always in relation; postmodernists discover and create their identities within a maelstrom of political, economic, and cultural forces.

Widely accepting such a postmodern perspective on self, identity studies (in social sciences) have articulated postmodern influences on contemporary identity formation and its postmodern characteristics. According to social scientists Ali Rattansi and Ann Phoenix (1997), key features of postmodern conceptualizations of identity are the "de-centering" and "de-essentialization" of identities (127). Under these "twin-headings," the scholars identify six contemporary aspects of identities. Postmodern identities are relational, produced by their socio-historical contexts, opposed to the idea of a core self, always in progress, at times unconsciously operated, and relatively provisional. Postmodern identities thus consist of the "multiplicity, fluidity, and context-dependent operation" of identities (121).

Integrating psychological and sociological approaches to identity, Côté theorizes late modern features in relationships between identity and culture by comparing the features with pre-modern and early-modern types. Among several features, we need to pay special attention to the following ones for our discussion of pastoral identity. First, drawing on cultural anthropologist Margaret Mead's three socialization patterns—postfigurative, cofigurative, and prefigurative— Côté contends that late modern socializing institutions that constitute the bridge between the individual and culture are prefigurative. The prefigurative pattern means that people do not much care about, or employ, traditional norms and guidance and that they become "the primary architects of their own identities" (160). Second, drawing on sociologist David Riesman's three character types—tradition-directedness, inner-directedness, and other-directedness— Côté claims that persons of the postmodern character type are other-directed, have "radar" to trace others' patterns, and conform to the current trends and peer standards of their time in the high consumerist society. Third, people project images and maintain their identities through "impression management," and such image-oriented identities help them gain acceptance from others. Fourth, identities are, as a result, likely to be diffused, rather than achieved, in the late modern society "in response to socialization pressures encouraging other-directedness and . . . impression management" (165). Thus, Côté claims that "[l]ate modern socialization pressures encourage other-directedness, enhanced impression management, and a desire to discover one's identity through image consumption" (166).

Accordingly, the contemporary identity "moves away from signaling a stable core of self, to becoming a strategic, positional concept" (Howard 2000, 386). Identities from a postmodern perspective are unstable, fluid, transitional, and fragmented, to name a few of their characteristics. Such postmodern identities result from a socially "saturated self," which also largely derives from socializing technologies in a highly advanced industrial society (Gergen 1991). Weigert and Gecas (2005) clearly maintain this point by saying "no identities can be experienced as unified, self-same, and continuous because self—the active center of identities—is no longer institutionally supported as such" (166).

These contemporary cultures and features of identity seem to spray a postmodern tint on pastoral care-giving practices and identity. Such postmodern marks may take shape, to some degree, in the caregivers' approaches and responses to the helped. Some contemporary characteristics of pastoral identity are noticeable in narratives of my study participants' perceptions and experiences of pastoral identity. As the following section will show, some of the contemporary features of pastoral identity tend to be immediate, prefigurative, other-directed, inclusive, fluid, relatively provisional, temporal, situational, multiple, and relational.

POSTMODERN CHARACTERISTICS OF PASTORAL IDENTITY

The most challenging thing is *to be with everybody* at the same time. It's really stretching resources more and more. And, there is a very specific reason for this. It seems that pastoral care, the way that we afford it, is much more something which is catered for the individual rather than for the groups. The individual is okay because there is much more a tension, but it consumes an awful lot of time. So, I think that the institutional expectation at this point in time is *to be quicker and to see more people* because they are in direr need of people who need to be listened to.

—Chaplain James (italics added for emphasis)

As noted above, drawing on Gergen's analysis (1991) on romanticist, modernist, and postmodernist approaches to self, one can see a conceptual evolution of pastoral identity in the field of pastoral care-giving and theology. Approaches to pastoral identity in the twentieth century, especially before the 1990s, were mainly limited to romanticist and modernist concepts of identity. Early pastoral practitioners usually located their identity in human beings' inner depths, such as passion, devotion, and deep inspiration, which are romanticist values. These "romanticists" formatted pastoral identity in a deep sense of compassion on immediate lived experiences of care-seekers and belongingness to the faith community and tradition. On the contrary, "modernist" pastoral theologians and practitioners viewed pastoral identity from a rational and scientific perspective. They emphasized critical and theological reflection on their practices along with the behavioral sciences and found pastoral identity in the process of a skillful integration of theological and scientific perspectives on lived experience (Gerkin 1984; Hunsinger 1995). Both romanticists and modernists tended to view pastoral identity as a product of monological self-awareness and as a fixed inner reality of pastoral caregivers.

In this regard, pre-modern and modern approaches to pastoral identity view it as stable over time, intrinsic to the pastoral being, and essential to the pastoral caregivers' personality and ability. Before the postmodern influences on our field, pastoral theologians and specialists in pastoral care and counseling rarely paid attention to the social constructive aspect of pastoral identity. Now, coming to the contemporary features of pastoral identity, as briefly highlighted before, one may find some notable features of everyday pastoral care-giving practices shaped by postmodern cultures. Situated in and influenced by postmodern conditions, pastoral caregivers may tend to negotiate their practices and identities in the following ways.

First, pastoral identity in contemporary contexts is likely to be emergent rather than decisive. This tendency, different from traditional aims of pastoral care-giving based on Christian communities and traditions, is clear when the participants in the empirical study describe their goal of ministry as direct and immediate. They tend to ground their identity less on a traditionally-defined ultimate goal and more on proximate goals for which they co-create meanings within care-receivers' lived experiences.

Traditionally, pastoral theologians have articulated the goals and aims of pastoral care and counseling as "ultimate" and "proximate" goals (Bier 1959) or "total" and "special" aims (Hiltner et al. 1961). According to these pastoral theologians, who kept in mind pastoral counseling in a Christian congregational setting, the primary goal is "nothing less than salvation or redemption in the religious sense" (ibid. 31) and "bringing the individual closer to God and furthering his [or her] eternal salvation" (Bier 10). Proximate goals are "the development of new insight which shows itself in improved behavioral and personal relationships" (ibid.) and to set "self-imposed professional limitations" that should be realistic and modest as to time, skill, and training (Hiltner et al., ibid., 30). According to this tradition, pastoral caregivers should maintain the connection and balance between these two goals to be both pastoral and therapeutic (Jackson 1964).

However, in the empirical study, the contemporary pastoral practitioners do not identify their ultimate goals and proximate goals separately. The caregivers rather co-construct their goals with their care-seekers by meeting spiritual, emotional, social, and/or psychological needs. There are no specific distinctions between ultimate and proximate goals, as spiritual support becomes inclusive, including meeting needs and helping people experience the presence of God. Such a phenomenon can be, in part, a sign of becoming less traditional and authoritative and more "prefigurative" of religious norms in pastoral care-giving. Thus, contemporary pastoral practitioners working in a postmodern culture are likely to find and co-create immediate goals with care-seekers rather than operate on the basis of an ultimate goal preset in mind.

In this regard, pastoral identity in contemporary care-giving contexts, secondly, tends to be other-directed. The pastoral clinicians in the study are very receptive to care-seekers' needs, and their goals focus on meeting these needs. Such other-directed caregivers are "sensitive to others—to their opinions and their approval . . . [and] strive to meet goals, but those goals can shift, and it is staying in tune with the shifts that are of paramount importance to this character type" (Côté 1996, 162). Such sensitivity and adaptation to care-seekers' needs and expectations allow the caregivers to engage in a form of empathy and to care for the seekers on their own terms. This type of pastoral identity culminates when the caregivers feel a sense of calling from their care-seekers. The caregivers seem to have a sensitive "radar" to trace and capture care-seekers' calls for help.

As a result, such an other-directed pastoral identity has a propensity for inclusiveness and fluidity. In pluralistic care-giving contexts, pastoral caregivers encounter many people from different cultures and/or religious orientations from those of the helpers. To gain access to those people, the care providers approach them with more open and inclusive identities. Many pastoral caregivers generalize their ministry with such generic images as "service," "choice," "buffet," and "spiritual support." In particular, the buffet image may reflect what Côté (1996) describes: "postmodern society provides a 'cafeteria' from which identities can be selected and combined with each meal, and then discarded" (41). In particular, those who identify themselves as interfaith caregivers are more likely to be flexible and inclusive in terms of their approaches and identities. By defining themselves inclusively, pluralistic interfaith caregivers try to present as helpful an image as possible so that any care-seeker can accept them. In such an era of the inclusive image orientation, as Côté (1996) sharply points out, (pastoral) identity is likely to be

> reflexively and strategically fitting oneself into, and maintaining oneself in, a community of strangers by meeting their approval through the creation of the right impression . . . [I]dentity displays are employed to gain acceptance from others who often have little knowledge of one's social background or accomplishments . . . and the image-oriented identity is based on a projection of images that meet the approval of a community, gaining one access so long as the images remain acceptable. (163)

Thus, such inclusivity and flexibility are important elements of postmodern pastoral identity.

Accordingly, a fourth pastoral identity in this culture is relatively provisional, meaning that it is temporal and situational. Moments and situations in which care and counseling take place define a specific form of pastoral identity. Pastoral caregivers repeatedly revise identities by constructing, deconstructing, and reconstructing them in their encounters with care-seekers in each specific history and context. Thus, pastoral identities are continually (re-)constructed through relationships and transformed through historicality and locality of what it means to be pastoral (cf. Weigert et al. 2005). In this sense, pastoral identity embodies specific culture and faith between the care partners in their temporal and situational contexts.

Finally, pastoral identity in such contexts is multiple and relational. As chaplain James pointed out in the block quotation, contemporary institutions expect pastoral caregivers to be with more people in a quicker manner. Thus, pastoral clinicians encounter many different people and unique situations with multifaceted "faces" and construct multiple identities, depending on their care-giving situations. According to Gergen (1991), being saturated by superficial relationships, the self loses its inner identifiable core and constructs and situates fragmented and multiple identities. Such a fragmented sense of self reflects multiple relationships that are incoherent and disconnected.

In this postmodern culture, Gergen contends, the emphasis shifts "from self to relationship," and identity is no longer self-centered but relational. Thus, a relational self emerges. Gergen continues to suggest:

> One's own role thus becomes that of participant in a social process that eclipses one's personal being. One's potentials are only realized because there are others to support and sustain them; one has an identity only because it is permitted by the social rituals of which one is part; one is allowed to be a certain kind of person because this sort of person is essential to the broader games of society. (156–57)

By participating in such a social process and playing a role as social actors in that care-giving process—a role that often demands the deconstruction and reconstruction of their images and identities—pastoral specialists become a certain kind of person called "pastoral" or "spiritual" in postmodern contexts. Thus, rather than contending with its core and inner-centeredness, contemporary pastoral identity grows on the basis of relatedness and encounters with others. Thus, pastoral identity is multifaceted in continuously fluid relationships.

As postmodernism produces changes in contemporary contexts of pastoral care-giving, pastoral identity also displays its historicality and locality. Contemporary pastoral identities are often emergent, other-directed, inclusive, provisional, and relational. These postmodern features of pastoral identity grasp important qualities of contemporary changes in care-giving practices and identity construction. Moreover, such postmodern descriptions of pastoral identity help one recognize that postmodern power and conditions influence pastoral care-giving practices and the social actors' identity construction within that context.

Nevertheless, these qualities are not fully substitutable for romanticist and modern values of pastoral identity. Each perspective on pre-modernity, modernity, and post-modernity sheds light on the discussion of pastoral identity; one should not reject one on behalf of another. A romanticist value of emotional attachment, a modernist value of rational scrutiny, and a postmodern value of social construction are all important aspects contributing to pastoral identity (Doehring 2006). As in the interactional construction of pastoral identity described in the previous chapter, the pastoral caregivers in postmodern contexts still hold some form of romanticist and modern values such as integrity, coherence, and authenticity in their identities in spite of their postmodern culture. In other words, postmodern characteristics of pastoral identity do not fully explain how contemporary pastoral practitioners in the study maintain the coherency and agency of pastoral identities that are multiple, emergent, other-directed, and inclusive in the course of their everyday practices. What makes this discrepancy happen? Now, it is time to address this issue.

POSTMODERN INFLUENCES AND LIMITATIONS

Despite the significant changes in modern society and economy that contemporary high technological capitalism brings, scholars (in social psychology) have disagreed about the degrees to which the changes take place (Côté et al. 2002; Furlong et al. 2007). The disagreement is apparent when the scholars use different terms to refer to similar contemporary changes. On the one hand, some scholars (Gergen 1991; Lyotard 1984) use the term *post-modernity*, which signifies a new epochal transition from modernity, as in "the transition from medieval to modern society" (Furlong et al. 2007, 1). On the other hand, other scholars (Giddens 1991; Lash et al. 1992) employ the term *late*, *high*, or *reflexive modernity* "to draw attention to the far-reaching implications of recent socio-economic change, at the same time as expressing the view that, as yet, these changes do not represent an epochal shift" (Furlong et al. 2007, 2).

Likewise, one can find such disagreement within the study of self and identity in the post/late-modern standpoint. To what degree does post/late-modernity generate changes in self and identity in contemporary life? "Whether, and to what extent," Côté (2002) says, "the processes of saturation influence the development of ego identity and a sense of agency" are important questions to ask (30).

Anticipating the future of self and society, some scholars seem to envision two different passages of postmodern identities (Gergen 1991; Côté 2002). The first one is the demise of the concrete entity of self. Hopelessness and despair fill this path. Scholars envision that contemporary environments deprive the self of its coherence, unity, and inner-core. The self loses a basis for authentic and coherent identities. Identities are also diffused as a result of other-directedness and impression management, as James Marcia's research found some evidence of a decrease in identity achievement and an increase in identity diffusion in late modern society. Thus, one can characterize postmodern selves as de-centered, fragmented, illusory, and lacking any core. Gergen sees this path as "final adieu to the concrete entity of self" (ibid. 140).

By contrast, another passage brings us hope for a new self and identity. This path of postmodern identities emerges when a modern autonomous and essential self gives way to the possibility for multiple perspectives on and voices of the self. As essential and authentic selves erode, according to Gergen, the possibility of creating and re-creating personal identity increases in relationships. He anticipates that relationships and immersed intersubjectiveness will construct a relational self as a result of a new consciousness of construction.

For Gergen, these two passages are not separate but evolve from the first one to the second. A question arises: How can the hopeless postmodern passage to the fragmented self change to the hopeful path of the relational self? Gergen postulates the development from a modern centered self to a postmodern relational self through three major phases. Selves in postmodern era reach the final stage of relational selves from the stage of "strategic manipulators" (role-players in social relationships without confirming identity) through the stage of "pastiche personalities" (multiple selves liberating from essence) (see 147–60 for details). For Gergen, the shift from an essential self through a fragmented self to a relational self thus seems developmental and naturally inevitable:

> As belief in essential selves erodes, awareness expands of the ways in which personal identity can be created and re-created in relationships. This consciousness of construction does not strike as a thunderbolt; rather, it eats slowly and irregularly away at the edge of consciousness. And as it increasingly colors our understanding of self and relationships, the character of this consciousness undergoes a qualitative change . . . Where both the romantic and the modernist conceptions of identifiable selves begin to fray, the result may be something more than a void, an absence of self. Instead, if this tracing of the trajectory

is plausible, we may be entering a new era of self-conception. In this era the self is redefined as no longer an essence in itself, but relational. In the postmodern world, selves may become the manifestations of relationship, thus placing relationships in the central position occupied by the individual self for the last several hundred years of Western history. (146–47)

Gergen proposes the self's optimistic evolution, subliming a "reality of immersed interdependence" in which relationship constructs the self (147).

Another question arises: What transforms fragmented selves into relational selves? Gergen (1991) does not explicitly articulate an answer to this question, only alluding to the "consciousness of construction," "consciousness of relational selves," and "postmodern consciousness" (e.g., 138, 157, 170). He does not specify whose consciousness it is. In a sense, Gergen's analysis is highly optimistic. Some scholars criticize his attitude of celebrating postmodernity as "an opportunity for the human species to adopt higher forms of consciousness" (Côté 2002, 25). How can postmodernity destruct an essential self and also construct a relational self? Is not the "relational self" part of a relationally saturated self that is trapped in superficial relationships? By "consciousness," Gergen might want to recognize a form of human agency.

Some scholars seem to respond to the questions of "what transforms" and "whose consciousness" by paying attention to human agency. Côté (2006) summarizes two key differences between the late- and postmodernist approaches to identity: one in view of agency and the other in view of a ground for the agency. He contends that whereas postmodernists decline a possibility of the "stable psychological base" and, thereby, deny human agency anchored to that base at the cost of postmodern forces, late-modernists emphasize human agency for directing their behaviors and lives from a fluid but still reliable psychological base. Late-modernists point to "the potential for individuals to direct their own development by anchoring their ego identity, as opposed to being buffeted about by contradictory societal forces" (13).

From this late-modern perspective, contemporary changes are radical but not exclusively destructive to selves and their agencies since a relational self can emerge—or at least since one can request the intersubjective self—in the postmodern bombardment. Therefore, the central issue that the postmodern self brings to our discussion is *neither* whether the self is fragmented and fully saturated to the extent that it "becomes no self at all" *nor* whether the self loses its agency and authenticity to the degree that it becomes impossible to restore and reconstruct identity. Rather, we need to consider how or in what way fragmented, multiple selves can transform into relational selves and what drives the postmodern selves to become relational.

These questions, in part, reflect what the social sciences have long debated. The questions reflect the disparity in approaches to, and perspectives on, self and identity in the social sciences. The discrepancy takes place in the "individual-society dichotomy" in psychology and the "agency-structure duality" in sociology (Rattansi et al. 1997, 121). This dichotomy can extend itself to the dualism of micro-macro, process-structure, freedom-constraint, stability-change, cause-effect, similarity-difference, singularity-multiplicity, and modernity-postmodernity (Vryan et al. 2003; Sandstrom et al. 2003). In these disparities, the main question is whether human actors are central elements in social structure and social systems are a product of their actions (e.g., interactionism and ethnomethodology) or whether actors are inhabited by social systems that shape the individuals' thoughts and behaviors (e.g., structuralism and functionalism). These divided positions over the primacy of structure and agency now tend to consider the two as complementary forces. In his "structuration theory," for example, Giddens (1991) views identity from a macro perspective and makes a micro and macro connection between the complementary forces. He claims that late-modern social conditions de-structure the interior life of human beings. He, however, clearly points out that people have agentic qualities to adapt to and resist postmodern de-structuring, and such intentional capacities for choice, agency, and reflexivity construct reality and identity in the world.

STRUCTURE, REFLEXIVITY, AND SOCIAL CONSTRUCTION

In their article "Symbolic Interactionist Reflections on Erikson, Identity, and Postmodernism," Weigert and Gecas (2005) explore a symbolic interactionist approach to Erikson's theory of identity that incorporates a postmodernist perspective. They argue for selves that are "embodied agents struggling for meaningful identities by adapting to their social and physical environments and sometimes working to change these environments through individual and collective action" in a postmodern context, which emphasizes "the ephemeral and manipulated aspects of contemporary identity dynamics" (161).

Moreover, in his article, "The Sociology of the Self," Callero (2003) points out three emphases of current sociological approaches to self: power, reflexivity, and social constructionism. He sees an emerging scholarship as "multidisciplinary, methodologically eclectic, and generally postmodern in orientation" (116). He attempts to connect symbolic interactionist and postmodernist approaches to self and identity along with the three concepts. He suggests that Foucault's concept of power offers an important theoretical framework within which to adjust a symbolic interactionist approach to self and identity and that SI's concept of reflexivity opens a door to understand human agency as corrective to the postmodern approach. Callero sees social construction as common ground for bridging symbolic interactionist and postmodern perspectives on self and identity.

Drawing on Michael Foucault, Stuart Hall, Nikolas Rose, and Philip Cushman, Callero (2003) claims that the emerging scholarship contributes to bridging the study of self and identity with the historical deployment of power. The postmodern scholarship demonstrates that "the self is constituted within relations of control and is deeply embedded within systems of knowledge and discourse" (118). According to Callero, Foucault sees the self as the direct consequence of disciplinary power, which not only manipulates a rational self but also imposes disciplinary practices on human behaviors to embody the self. From such a Foucauldian tradition, "the self is forced into existence, *not to become an agent but as a mechanism of control*" (ibid. italics added for emphasis). Even if such a postmodern perspective introduces structural power to the study of identity, Callero maintains, the tradition is problematic in that it eradicated the possibility for an "agentic and problem-solving actor" that can emancipate the self "through organized resistance and political intervention if actors are conceived to be more subjects of discourse" (ibid.).

In de-centering the subject and society and re-centering the social around regimes of power/knowledge, Callero points out that the self is to be an "embodied agent, a knowledgeable, problem solving actor rather than an amorphous 'subject position'" (ibid. 119). For the self to be agentic, it should be reflexive, according to him. Here he draws on a Meadian concept of reflexivity to complement agency that postmodernists miss in their discussion. From a Meadian perspective, the self is "first and foremost a reflexive process of social interaction," and reflexivity refers to "the uniquely human capacity to become an object to one's self, to be both subject and object" (ibid.). Blumer (1969) interprets Mead's concept of reflexivity, saying that human beings are

> an object to [themselves]. The human being[s] may perceive [themselves], have conceptions of [themselves], communicate with [themselves], and act toward [themselves] . . . This gives [them] the means of interacting with [themselves]—addressing

[themselves], responding to the address, and addressing [themselves] anew. (62)

With such a mechanism of self-reflexivity, people cease to be a product of a structure of internalized norms and values but open themselves to "agency, creative action, and the possibility of emancipatory political movements" (Callero, 120). Thus, the symbolic interactionist perspective does not preclude a possibility that forces of structure and domination can colonize self-reflexivity but opens to a possibility of resistance "always on the horizon of the possible" (ibid.).

While Mead sees the self as a (social) process, Foucault views the self as a (consequence of) structure. Despite such an on-going debate of process-structure between symbolic interactionist and postmodernist approaches, Callero finds that a concept of social construction plays an important role in bridging two perspectives:

> Although sharp differences between pragmatists and postmodernists will no doubt remain, and the ontological status and essential origins of self-meanings will continue to be debated, there is today a consensus within the discipline that the self is at some level a social construction. Whether phenomenal or discursive, fragmentary or unitary, stable or transitory, emotional or rational, linguistic or embodied, the self is assumed to be a product of social interaction. It is this fundamental principle that frames most contemporary research on the sociological self. (121)

Thus, current research on self recognizes that self is a social construction shaped both by social process and social structure. In other words, the self is a "bounded, structured object" and, at the same time, a "fluid, agentic, and creative response," both of which mean that social construction is "neither completely determined by the social world nor pregiven at birth" (ibid.).

In *The Self We Live By*, Holstein and Gubrium (2000) pose two options for the postmodern self: either reacting to or transforming a postmodern crisis, which is for the authors, a crisis of confidence. After reviewing affirmative postmodernists Gergen's and Denzin's hopeful reactions to a postmodern self, the authors articulate the second option as "one that resists total capitulation to skepticism and hyperreality" (68). This resistance takes place by tethering "the rampant and ubiquitous 'playfulness' of the hyperreal by returning to the interpretive practice of everyday life, in particular the ordinary work of constructing and reflexively managing who and what we are" (ibid.). Drawing on Lyotard's view, the authors see self as "grounded [not in metanarratives of knowledge but] in the concrete discursive locations of self construction, in various places in everyday life where subjectivity is addressed and its meaning assembled and assigned" (69). Using the notions of subjectivity and discourse, Holstein et al. maintain that it is possible "to spin a new ending that implicates diversely presentational yet grounded selves" (79).

From such a social constructionist perspective, a newly emerging voice proclaims a resurrected self, whereas postmodernists declare the demise of the self. Sociologists Patricia Adler and Peter Adler (1999), for example, conducted a study of resort workers who move around over the span of months, working and living a fragmented lifestyle of transient and superficial relationships. The authors observed that the workers can maintain a core sense of genuine self by adapting to environmental changes. Thus, Adler et al. contend that the "postmodernists' most pessimistic view of the demise of the self has not been borne out; rather, the core self has adapted to contemporary conditions and thrived" (54). Such a view of an agentic and socially-constructive self is a point where one may find a crossroad between process and structure and between groundedness and inclusiveness as the following section discusses.

BALANCING THE PASTORAL THEOLOGICAL DILEMMAS

The discussion of power, reflexivity, and social construction is applicable to pastoral identity, as many parish pastors, pastoral counselors, and chaplains have struggled for their identity construction in a postmodern society. In this situation, one can ask several important questions: How can one ground a pastoral identity in everyday pastoral practices and theological perspectives and also construct it to correspond to postmodern sensibilities? How can one integrate interactional-theological and postmodern-spiritual perspectives in the construction of pastoral identity? How can one find a grounded pastoral identity that adapts to, and is self-reflexive within, a pluralistic and inclusive structural condition? These questions all bring tensions between self and society, between agency and structure, between fluidity and stability, between multiplicity and integrity, between ambiguity and authenticity, between inclusiveness and groundedness, and between modernity and postmodernity. An answer to these inquiries is to make an adequate balance of the tensions along the line of resolving a dilemma between social structure and reflexive agency in the everyday course of identity construction.

When the postmodern impact generates a change in (pastoral) identities, "multiple and sometimes contradictory identities" constructed through interactions between agency and structure rise to the surface (Wiegert et al.

2005, 163). In my empirical study, pastoral caregivers have a set of multiple and seemingly conflicting features of pastoral identity. Speaking from a macro-level perspective, pastoral practitioners, as part of the social systems, conform to institutional disciplines and expectations that influence identity construction and shape pastoral identity to a certain degree. At the macro-level of structural power and cultural influences in a postmodern context, pastoral practitioners experience the religious and professional identity split in an environment in which the institutions and the society require the caregivers to be religiously and denominationally non-specific in their spiritual care and counseling. In addition, the care providers have to deal with the dilemma of being competent and having deeper therapeutic and spiritual relationships with care-seekers in the midst of postmodern brief and superficial encounters. Still, a conflicting situation exists, as pastoral practitioners wonder which community is primary and which is a proximate community in their commitment to faith communities and adaptation to institutional expectations.

From a micro-level viewpoint, pastoral caregivers as social agents work to change social structure, while interacting with care-seekers, by making choices and reflecting on themselves and things around them. In this process, still multiple and somewhat contradictory identities rise to the surface. As described in chapter 3, first of all, pastoral caregivers represent God and faith communities as spiritual figures to provide spiritual support and theological perspectives yet also come to humble and transform themselves into fellow humans to be with care-seekers, listen to them, and learn from them. Second, pastoral practitioners walk along with their care-seekers as companions with compassion and unconditional love yet also guide, admonish, and minister to them as pastors. Moreover, the caregivers want to be neutral and have no agenda to be fully present with care-seekers but also are intentional and theologically conscious to help them realize existential meanings of their life and God's presence in their crises and solutions. Furthermore, pastoral caregivers are humanly present with care receivers by fully attending to them yet also, by doing so, embody the divine presence. Such multiple and complicated identities sum up the dilemma between self and relation and between inclusiveness and groundedness at the micro-level of everyday care-giving relationships and interactions.

In such multiple layers of the paradox of self and relation and inclusiveness and groundedness, many participants in the empirical study of pastoral identity have built a meaningful pastoral identity in the course of everyday practices through which they help others with a clear purpose of providing a holistic care—spiritual, emotional, psychological, physical, and social. Although contemporary postmodern pluralistic contexts lead pastoral caregivers to have a multiple and inclusive sense of pastoral identities, they nonetheless have a less eroded sense of their identities in that context. As embodied and self-reflexive agents, they try to construct their identities with care-seekers in the process of helping them find meaning and identities in their lives, all the while adapting to and attempting to change the cultural power affecting their relationships and interactions. In the following section, I will describe a social construction of identity by both pastoral caregivers and receivers in their pastoral relationships.

SOCIAL CONSTRUCTION OF BOTH IDENTITIES

I think that one of the keys here is to be flexible with, instead of being very rigid in theology . . . I think it is being flexible without losing your theology. . . . [L]osing your theology would be that you don't talk about God at all, that you don't talk about who you are. But I think part of this is emphasizing the common ground that you have with your institution and always looking at those pieces that are going to be theologically applicable with the institution, working with the patient, because there are expectations . . . the patients have . . . But what I find is that if you are able to do that, if you are able to go in and relate your theology appropriately and what is needed—in other words respect for the culture of the clientele of that organization—that you'll get more authority not less.

--CHAPLAIN GEORGE

Multicultural and multi-religious care-giving situations in a secular institutional context set a stage of postmodern challenges in pastoral care-giving and identity construction. Chaplain George is aware of such a situation and finds a way of accommodating his religious call with the needs and expectations of care-seekers and the institution. Although the contemporary care-giving conditions often set a slippery road of superficiality and generality to pastoral practitioners, they resist total surrender to such ephemeral and manipulative role-playing by focusing on meaningful interactions and relationships with care-seekers in everyday practices. Pastoral caregivers are, therefore, grounded in the lived experiences of pastoral practices in which the care partners deal with everyday life where they can address agency and subjectivity and reflect on theological discourse. Accordingly, pastoral identities may be multi-presentational in contemporary conditions yet are grounded in everyday care-giving practices and theological reflection.

In encountering care-seekers with non-religious or different religious/cultural orientations, pastoral practitioners do not give up their identity as pastoral and spiritual caregivers. Pastoral professionals approach each care-seeker with self-awareness of the pastoral nature of their work. They work on their identity construction by being flexible enough to translate their spiritual language into words that are meaningful to their care-seekers. By doing so, the caregivers make sense to their care-seekers, who do not use theological language or have a belief in God. In a setting of religiously and/or culturally different orientations between caregivers and seekers, the caregivers' pastoral and spiritual concerns indicate who they are, which in turn makes (potential) care-seekers explicit about who they are in response to the pastoral approach. Thus, care-giving interactions often define who caregivers and seekers are through their responsive interactions and self-reflexive processes.

Roman Catholic Friar James (I1), for example, describes such an agentic interaction with care-seekers as living human documents. As a stranger, when he crosses the boundaries by getting permission from care-seekers, they become open books through which he listens to their needs and who they are in their stories. While they expose their identities in their lived experiences, they also call for him to be a person pastorally to them. In such an equal and collegial process of care-giving and seeking, both caregiver and seeker construct their identities.

Pastoral counselor Linda (I20) gives a more detailed description of this process. When clients put trust in her and share their stories, they share their deepest, darkest reality about themselves. The reality is who they really are, which is what they are most afraid of telling others. The fear is that their real selves are unredeemable, unlovable, and unacceptable. Thus, when they share their deepest fears, they allow her to see who they think they really are. Entering into their worlds and fears by listening to their stories, the pastoral counselor has an opportunity to reframe, reinterpret, or re-image with care-seekers what that means and who they truly are.

At that point, the caregiver has the privilege of offering them the good and healing news that love, forgiveness, and grace are available. By doing so, the caregiver helps care-seekers discern their true self-images and "illusions," in pastoral counselor Joe's (I17) terms. He continues to say that created in God's image, care-seekers have truths that come from inside (e.g., worthy, valuable) not from what label others gave them (e.g., unlovable, unacceptable). Thus, in the process of helping clients, Linda (I20) says, "when a client exposes their identity . . . both of us enter into those most profound questions about who we really are. So, as they are struggling with their identity, it helps me construct mine."

Thus, in spite of postmodern, pluralistic, and institutional powers, both pastoral caregivers and seekers construct a meaningful sense of their identities by returning to the interpretive practice of everyday lived experiences. Cultural influences make a sense of identity fluid and fragmented. Nonetheless, pastoral caregivers have a clear identity as persons called to God's ministry by constructing their specific identities in each relationship with care-seekers. Such an agentic self-reflection or reflexivity is an important resource for identity construction. Any forces presumed to influence an individual to produce one's behavior cannot fully yield the reflexive agency under the power (Blumer, 1969). With this reflexive agency, pastoral practitioners ground their identities in theological wisdoms rooted in their faith traditions and construct pastoral identities with care-seekers in relationships.

There are three key points that make pastoral identity agentic and authentic in a relatively brief and fluctuating relationship of contemporary pastoral care-giving. These three traits are consciousness, deep encounters, and reflection, which all take place in a reflexive process between pastoral social actors. According to Charles Siewert (2008, online edition) in *The Stanford Encyclopedia of Philosophy*, consciousness consists "in the monitoring of one's own states of mind" or "in the accessability of information to one's capacities for rational control or self-report." Pastoral caregivers are intentionally conscious about their identity as pastoral persons who help care-seekers not only with their immediate concerns but also with their existential and spiritual meanings and values. As chaplain Bill (I3) says, pastoral caregivers are consciously aware of themselves as spiritual nurturers, even if their conversations do not go near religious issues at all. Such an intentional consciousness grounds the pastoral caregivers in theological wisdom and motivates them to construct their identities in the course of everyday practices often embedded in religiously and culturally pluralistic contexts.

Moreover, deep engagement in care-giving relationships helps pastoral caregivers open themselves to diversity and overcome superficial relationships within relatively brief encounters with care-seekers who were once strangers. Brief yet deep encounters are possible in part due to caregivers' pastoral consciousness and compassion and the emotional, existential, and spiritual needs of care-seekers. In a safe space that the caregiver creates, care-seekers have courage to be vulnerable and open their worlds. The care-seekers' openness to their caregivers is a turning point in pastoral care-giving and identity construction. When care receivers also open their worlds, this vulnerability allows caregivers to go into a deeper level of relationship and to have a reflexive moment in which they reflect on their identities as caregivers in that relationship. Chaplain Shelly (I6) notes,

> I think my pastoral care identity is constantly being constructed and evolving through each patient. Because I learn something with each patient, that makes me a better caregiver. And then I'm always who I am at the core of who I am but I come to a deeper understanding of who I am as a pastoral caregiver through the conversation with patients.

Thus, the identity construction process is more reciprocal and dialectic as the care partners provide each other with an inhabitable space and enter into their worlds. As Chaplain Sam points out, pastoral identity is not static or defined, but it is in flux, open, and dynamic. He says, "It is in the process of unfolding, of evolving. But the core of it is being present to myself and being present to what's needed" (I16).

Furthermore, at the core of an authentic and agentic identity of pastoral practitioners is (theological) reflection. Whenever they encounter care-seekers' lived experiences and enter into a care-giving relationship, the care providers reflect on how to respond to and interact with care-seekers' needs. Through such a reflective process, pastoral caregivers find their identities. In pastoral counselor Cale's (I4) words, counselees force him to think about his pastoral identity and call upon him for a pastoral response. Thus, through openness and deep encounters to care-seekers, care-providers receive their partners in their reflection and interweave the seekers' life stories with their own identity construction. Chaplain Julia (I12) thus says, "I hear your story; your story then becomes part of who I am . . . So, each patient has shaped my life, I believe, somehow in the fabric of who I am."

Thus, in pastoral reflection, pastoral caregivers experience a potential space of reflexiveness, the reflecting back of the experience of the person upon him or herself. Through such reflexive processes, pastoral practitioners broaden their understanding of who they are and how they can be of help. As chaplain Gloria (I13) illustrates, care-seekers define and expand pastoral identity in ways caregivers have never before defined it. Pastoral practitioners' identities become interconnected and interweaved with their care-seekers' life stories and identities.

SUMMARY

The participants in the empirical study said that their identities are both stable and fluid and that they have both constant and specific identities. Contemporary postmodern contexts may make pastoral identity fragmented and incoherent. However, pastoral caregivers and receivers can obtain more integrated identities, rather than split identities, by interactionally working toward a shared goal of resolving clients' predicaments. As self-reflexive agents, the caregivers help clients restore more integrated, authentic identities (from fragmented identities) from a perspective that integrates theology with multiple resources of dialogue partners (Jacque, 2006). This helping process, in turn, facilitates caregivers' identity construction

Due to the multiplicity in perspective, pastoral caregivers in a postmodern context may be other-directed. The direction is neither implanted early in religious and spiritual life by the grand narratives of theology and the faith community nor set toward inescapably destined ultimate goals. Rather than claiming an authority from traditional grand narratives of theology or an already implanted inner-directed theology, pastoral caregivers freely choose other-directed approaches by reconstructing a theological perspective on lived experiences of care-seekers through a contextual interpretation of the caregivers' preset theology. Thus, in a postmodern era pastoral caregivers need skillful theological integration rather than no theology at all.

Agency and authenticity can turn strange when we are aware of the multiplicity of pastoral identities in postmodern contexts. However, when we see the multiple identities align into a clear theological perspective in everyday pastoral care-giving practices, they become unified and integrated and achieve authenticity in a processual sense. Here, we need a theological consideration of (pastoral) identity that can offer a theological framework for (pastoral) identity in relation to agency and structure. The next chapter will explore this possibility.

5

Pastoral Identity in Theological Perspectives

A RELATIONAL, AGENTIVE, AND GROUNDED IDENTITY

UP TO THIS POINT, I have articulated my empirical study (in chapter 2), its findings at an interactional level (in chapter 3), and subsequent discussions of the social influences on pastoral identity (in chapter 4) in light of grounded theory, social psychology, and insights gained from pastoral theological resources. While the research findings in chapter 3 have helped to show how pastoral caregivers and receivers construct their identities in their care-giving interactions at a micro level, chapter 4 has explored how such a pastoral identity can adapt to and resist postmodern structural powers at a macro level. The latter chapter has articulated a type of social construction that interweaves cultural structure and reflexive agency as important forces in forming a pastoral identity in a postmodern context. One of the continuous questions that have characterized this book is the relationship among identity and the forces that form it. The chapters have articulated pastoral identity in terms of symbolic interactions between caregivers and seekers (in chapter 3) and in terms of postmodern dilemmas between pastoral agency and structural power (in chapter 4).

Chapter 4 has claimed that there are two cultural forces that affect pastoral caregivers' identity construction. The first force is a postmodern condition in which numerous superficial relationships often saturate the caregiver's sense of a centered self or identity and make it de-centered, fragmented, and lost. In this context, the care practitioners may have to grapple with a paradoxical relationship between personal agency and social structure. Moreover, psychological, interdisciplinary, secular-institutional, and pluralistic care-giving contexts, as the second force, may dismantle, and/or help caregivers restructure, their ecclesial and theological commitment and boundaries by asking them to cooperate with "all people" from a generic spiritual perspective and by requiring caregivers to collaborate with multiple perspectives and discourses. During the dismantlement, caregivers may (temporarily) loosen their theological, ecclesial grounds and, thereby, have trouble finding an appropriate balance between theological groundedness and cultural and religious inclusiveness. To restructure pastoral identity in relation to these cultural powers, pastoral caregivers need to reconcile two paradoxical counterparts: the first reconciliation is between self and relation (or between agency and structure) and the other between theological groundedness and cultural inclusiveness.

Accordingly, we have so far attempted to resolve the following problems: How can contemporary pastoral caregivers in such environments construct their identities (1) without losing their sense of self in multiple relationships and (2) in such a way as to maintain their theological groundedness while being adequately inclusive? We have seen these problems within a larger category of duality between the individual and society, between fluidity and stability, and between process and structure. We have also seen a possible integration of these dichotomies by viewing the two paradoxical counterparts as couplets of both ends of a continuum that can be complementary, as some social psychologists try to balance these paradoxical problems (Giddens 1991; Standstrom et al. 2003; Vryan et al. 2003). As we have observed in previous chapters, pastoral caregivers deal with these paradoxical problems by making reflexive efforts to participate in a social construction between self and relationships and between agency and structure to such a degree that pastoral care partners adapt and sometimes work to change social structure.

Now that we have explored some cultural perspectives of identity that can serve as resources in studying pastoral identity, the current chapter examines theological perspectives on pastoral identity to envision a possible integration among empirical, social psychological, and theological discourses. A contemporary theological discourse of identity influenced, to some degree, by contemporary relational thinking has emphasized the relationality of divine and human identities. However, some theologians challenge such a relational approach in order to move toward an integrative perspective of identity. From a perspective informed by the previous chapters, I thus attempt to delineate a theological perspective of identity that embraces the dichotomy of relationality and substantiality as complementary forces of forming identities. A contemporary trinitarian perspective of identity in light of perichoresis informs this attempt by offering a theoretical and theological framework for capturing paradoxical integrations of self and relationships and of groundedness and openness to diversity.

Drawing on contemporary theological discussions of perichoresis, this chapter thus develops a theological perspective of identity. First of all, the chapter delineates how theological approaches to identity have changed to focus on relationality and what problems this approach has in dealing with the paradoxical dilemmas. Then, the chapter depicts a trinitarian concept of perichoresis as a possible theological metaphor for integrating agency and structure and groundedness and openness to diversity. These theological discourses will help us understand how to construct a relational, agentive, and grounded identity in culturally and religiously inclusive contexts. In this process, we will develop a theological foundation for illuminating the interplay between divine engagement and human participation. As a result, I will illustrate a theological anthropology by integrating a theological perspective into cultural discourses primarily informed by the empirical and social psychological discussions. This theological anthropology will offer a renewed perspective of pastoral practices, as we will see in the final chapter.

A RELATIONAL APPROACH TO IDENTITY IN THEOLOGICAL DISCOURSES

Theological views of identity have changed over time from emphasizing substance to focusing on relationality. Contemporary theologians have often discussed the relatedness of human identity in light of the biblical notion of *imago Dei* and the relationality of divine identity in light of the Trinity (e.g., Grenz 2001; Johnson 1992; McFadyen 1990). Influenced by a postmodern perspective of relationality, contemporary theological perspectives of both divine and human identities take a relation-focused approach. However, some theologians have criticized the relational perspective for its ethical and ontological problems.

In the history of Christianity, the understanding of human identity based on the image of God has changed *from* viewing the *imago Dei* as having human capacities *to* acknowledging it as the human relationship with God and other creatures. According to Grenz (2001), in Christian history there are two major interpretations of the divine likeness. As the dominant view throughout history, the substantial/structural perspective has interpreted the *imago Dei* as possessing certain inner attributes or capabilities inherent within human nature. Later in the reformation, Luther and Calvin articulated a relational interpretation of the *imago Dei* in terms of a fundamental relationship between humans and the Creator. From such a reformed tradition, Horton (2006) points out that the divine image is rightly conceptualized relationally and ethically rather than substantially or ontologically since human beings are created for life in covenant with God. Although the Reformers could not fully substitute their relational understanding of identity for the dominant substantial interpretation, they opened a door to a contemporary relational understanding of human identity.

A contemporary trinitarian theology has reinforced the relational understanding of human identity. The developmental process in history shows that the doctrine of the Trinity started by emphasizing the singleness of the Trinity but moved to focusing on the threeness of the divine Persons. This shift goes beyond the Eastern tendency to view the divine Father as the source of the Trinity or the Western tradition that begins with the single divine nature as a starting point of the Trinity (Grenz, 2004). Rather, contemporary trinitarian theologians approach the doctrine of the Trinity with the conviction that the Trinity reveals three divine Persons in the salvation history. Starting from the threeness of the Trinity, the theologians thus move to the question of the divine unity. Instead of emphasizing the unity or singleness of the Trinity, the theologians focus on the three divine Persons' threeness and relationality.

In this development, Wolfhart Pannenberg has made a special contribution to the relational understanding of the Trinity. According to Peters (1993), Pannenberg has cast a current relational view of the Trinity by determining trinitarian Persons' identity in relation to the others. His relational view holds that relations to the other Persons determine who each trinitarian Person is. In other words, the identity of the triune God depends on the relationships that each Person has with the other Persons in the Trinity. Hence, Pannenberg changes the ancient concept of the Trinity as substance prior to relation into his position that "the concept of substance is subordinated to relation" (p. 136). And this position continues in contemporary trinitarian theology.

Contemporary theologians, like Moltmann, Jenson, and Johnson, thus view the relationality of the Trinity as the key to the unity of the one God. However, this perspective sometimes goes beyond a proper balance to emphasize relationality-inclined position. Elizabeth Johnson (1992), for example, recognizes that trinitarian relationality constitutes the divine Persons. She goes on to interpret this relationality as the ontological priority of relation over substance. She further contends that "there is no absolute divine person. There are only the relative three" (216).

Many contemporary trinitarian theologians agree that human beings created in the image of the triune God are to be understood "relationally rather than in terms of the possession of fixed characteristics such as reason or will" (Gunton 1993, 3). However, we have to be not to claim an "either-or" position, in this case, whether persons are substantial or relational. The trinitarian community does not support only one position but embraces both in a paradoxical integration. As Moltmann (1981) points out, trinitarian Persons and their relations are equally reciprocal and mutually coexistent in the Trinity without priority. At the heart of the relationship of the three divine Persons is reciprocal communion. This perichoretic life that the three divine Persons share constitutes the relationality and identity.

CHALLENGES TO THE RELATIONAL APPROACH AND ITS ALTERNATIVE

A contemporary theological discourse—that presumes human beings are relational—echoes the postmodern social psychological perspective of a relational self (Peters 1993). If we interpret the contemporary relational tendency to mean that we do not need an ontological identity, we then have to face challenges from several directions. First of all, the empirical findings and social psychological discourses articulated in the previous chapters challenge a relationality-only identity. The chapters' challenge to emphasizing relationality involves a concern about a self that may be swallowed up into relationships. This concern points to gender injustice from a feminist perspective (e.g., Grey 2004; Volf 1996), to losing the self from a postmodern perspective (e.g., Gergen 1991; Thiselton 1995), and to dismantling proper grounding in a theological wisdom from a pastoral theological viewpoint (e.g., Ramsay 2004).

The first concern discusses a social system that demands women sacrifice for their relationships, thus causing relational gender injustice, and the second tackles a postmodern consumerist and high-technological milieu in which human relationships are superficial and the self is fragmented. The third concern points to a religiously generic approach by which theologians and practitioners have trouble adequately representing the wisdom of particular theological traditions. Thus, these concerns center on identity that is affected by and in relationships. These challenges and concerns require further discussion of the relationship between persons and relations (and agency and structure). Despite these concerns, the empirical study indicates that pastoral practitioners construct their identities in relationships with others by adapting to and resisting social structures that may dilute a sense of the centered self in numerous relationships. The empirical findings thus challenge theologians to look for an alternative to the relationality-inclined theological understanding of identity.

Moreover, some theologians also challenge the relationality-inclined approach. These challenges can help us think that a concept of identity needs to embrace relationality and substance together so that self and agency can sustain in social relationships. It is also problematic if the pendulum goes from one extreme (substance or oneness) to the other extreme (relationality or threeness). There are two theological challenges to the relational formulation.

First of all, in regard to human identity, several theologians have raised concerns about the relational view of personhood (Harris 1998; Sedgwick 2001; Woodhead 1999). They recognize that "persons are defined by relationships" but reject the notion that humans are to be "defined as relationships" (Sedgwick 2001, 199). The theologians think that "the individual is first established and then becomes liable to influences from outside" (Harris 1998, 215) and that "one could be a complete person and then enter into a relationship" (Sedgwick, 199). According to theologian Harriet Harris, the relational position (proposed by Alistair McFadyen, Elaine Graham, and Vincent *Brümmer*) that personhood is relational and relations precede persons is logically confused, ethically precarious, and ontologically problematic. Harris claims that persons "are ontologically prior to relations" and, thereby, create interpersonal relationships (ibid., 227). She continues to argue that

> [t]he underlying problem in all of the relational accounts considered here is failure to attend to how notions of personal development which have been informed by social science should relate to notions of personhood which are intended to be normative or ontological. Psychologists and sociologists are not in the business of providing normative concepts to inform moral reasoning, nor are they so concerned with finding an ontological basis for their concepts as are theologians and ethicists. If we fail to realize this then we are in danger of collapsing a psychological or even a moral judgment about someone's self-development into an assessment of their ontological status as a person, as though it would make sense to attribute only a limited degree of personhood to someone who has not been properly nurtured in community or who has difficulty in relating to others. (223–24)

Thus, Harris criticizes the relational understanding of personhood not only for its ontological problem but also for its ethical problem: one may see as less than persons those who cannot build or sustain (healthy) relationships or have underdeveloped relationality.

In the same vein, another criticism goes to the concept of "person" that trinitarian theologians employ. Trinitarian theologians have critiqued a modern denotation of persons as individuals and have contended that persons are relational, interdependent, and interactive by nature (LaCugna 1991). Such a relational understanding of personhood overemphasizes the relatedness of the trinitarian Persons over the divine essence, a reversed emphasis from the traditional approach. Whether trinitarian Persons are to be substantial or relational is at the core of the debate between trinitarian theologians and their critics. In "The Use and Abuse of Perichoresis in Recent Theology," for instance, Randall Otto (2001) criticizes Moltmann's trinitarian approach. He asserts that Moltmann appropriates the concept of perichoresis to describe "relationality apart from mutually shared *being*" (366, italics added for emphasis). Otto contends that Moltmann's stance toward perichoresis (from an eschatological perspective that prioritizes potentiality to ontological reality) uproots the notion of perichoresis from its ontological basis in shared essence of the Trinity and renders the term meaningless. In particular, Otto tackles Moltmann's anti-substantialism. For example, Otto critiques Moltmann's position that "the 'trinitarian fellowship and their unique divine Being' require 'no other Being in which it can exist—not even a common divine substance'" (381). Otto asks "What can perichoresis mean if it is divorced from its basis in one divine essence?" (367). He asserts that "Perichoresis demands an ontological basis for relations if there is to be a *real* and not merely *conceptual* relationship" (368).

Thus, a historical pendulum of looking at identity, divine and human, has swung from emphasizing the oneness of God to focusing on the threeness of the Trinity, and from substance to relationality. Some theologians critique the current tilt to relational perspectives of identity. I do not fully agree with the critiques and defer a response to the ethical, ontological, and substantial criticism of relational identity in the final section of this chapter. However, we need to take seriously the theologians' suspicion about the ontology and ethics of relational identity and find a way of making a proper balance between the paradoxical counterparts. Can a person only exist in relation to other persons? Is personal identity only "a compounded sedimentation of a significant history of interaction" (Harris 1998, 218)? Harris maintains that "we need an ethic which distinguishes the identity of individual persons from the sum of their relationships" (232). From these challenges, we need to be more careful in attempting to press the relationality into service as a model of human and divine identities.

Accordingly, a theological perspective of identity needs to balance between substance and relationality and between unity and multiplicity of human and divine identities. Such paradoxical couplets echo the empirical and social scientific request for balancing the paradoxical duality between self and relationships, between agency and structure, and between fluidity and stability. trinitarian theologians have captured the value and significance of perichoresis, but some have bypassed the balance between the two, placing the weight on relationality. In the following sections, I delineate a theological perspective of identity that embraces, in a balanced way, the paradoxical nature of identity in light of perichoresis.

A CRITICAL EXAMINATION OF THE CONCEPT OF PERICHORESIS

Contemporary theologians regard perichoresis as "an old magic word for a new trinitarian theology" (Moltmann 2000b, 111) and "a kind of theological black box" that fills a conceptual gap in theological perspectives of the Trinity and Christology (Crisp 2007, 1). In the doctrine of the Trinity, perichoresis denotes a mutual interpenetration of the three Persons in the one divine Being without commingling them, collapsing them into a third mixture, or separating them. Before proceeding further with the discussion of God's perichoretic identities, it would be beneficial to clarify the meanings of the Greek term *perichoresis* since many authors and theologians assign it diverse meanings.

A verb *choreo* encompasses a broad range of meanings, including both going and containing, in addition to a meaning of making room. Theologians often use the term *choreo* to describe this kind of mixing (Harrison 1991). According to Liddell and Scott's Lexicon (1846), the verb *choreo* first means "to make room for another, give way, draw back, retire, [and] withdraw" (1682). The word also has rich figurative meanings, such as open-heartedness, accepting, grasping, comprehending, permitting, and allowing (Danker 2000, 1094). Thus, when the word *choreo* combines with the prefix *peri*—which means an "extension in all directions as from a centre" or "completion of an orbit and return to the same point" (Liddell et al. 1152)—the term *perichoresis* can have many derived meanings, as we can see in Christian history. Even though *perichoreo* literally means that one goes round or rotates, the meanings of the term include making room in order to contain something or hold someone and making way in order for someone/something to move on or spread among all.

One can more easily grasp the compounded meanings of the word when one imaginatively thinks of the meanings as being derived from a combination of "going" and "containing" along with a bridging meaning of "making room for." Instead of denoting that a thing just moves or advances even if an object lies in front of it, *perichoreo* means that it advances as another makes room for it. When one object makes room, the other can move forward or spread. Such mutual movements mean that the other permeates/penetrates into the one, in one sense, and that the other allows (by entering the room) the one to contain or hold itself, in another sense. Moreover, since the word *perichoreo* can imply aesthetic movements such as moving forward, backward, around, rotating, embracing, and encompassing, one can envision an image of dance from such visual movements (Lawler 1995). The meanings of *perichoresis* expand, implying co-indwelling, co-inherence, and divine dance in the discussion of the Trinity, as we will see later. Thus, *perichoreo* has rich meanings and implications as it involves reciprocal and permeable movements.

From this short linguistic examination, I summarize the meanings of the *perichoresis* in the following manner: The concept of perichoresis implies that A makes room for B so that B can move forward to and spread into it. By such penetration, B can permeate A's room and indwell in it, on the one hand; and A accepts B's penetration and contains B in itself, on the other hand. A also moves forward to and penetrates the space that B has made for A. In turn, by accepting A's permeation, B holds A in itself, and A indwells in B. Through such continuous interpenetration and acceptance, A is in B, and B is in A. Thus, the concept of *perichoresis* comprises movement/dynamism and rest/stability.

Accordingly, the term perichoresis is a brilliant concept that simultaneously describes *both* change, dynamics, and fluid *and* repose, rest, and stability. Two traditional terms delineate dynamic changes and constant fluidity of the world: a Heraclitean concept of flux and a Hegelian notion of dialectic. However, the Heraclitean flux has no purpose or meaning in its constant movement (Gunton 1993). Also, Hegelian dialectic has a dynamic movement to reach synthesis through an interactive process of thesis and antithesis. However, this interactive process is not a constant movement in the sense that one reaches a certain stage or state of synthesis. By contrast, the theological concept of perichoresis contains dynamic movement and mutual engagement and also reciprocal restful indwelling. The concept implies intentional purpose and symbolic meanings of the actors in dynamism and stability and in unity and multiplicity.

Historically, Christian theologians have formulated the doctrine of perichoresis as they deal, first, with the hypostatic union of Jesus Christ and later with the communion of the three divine Persons in the triune God. In developing trinitarian theology, theologians recognize perichoresis as an appropriate concept to preserve each Person's uniqueness while also safeguarding the three Persons' unity without damaging both. Theologians have used the concept not only in the doctrine of the Trinity but also in theological discourses of Christ's two natures and a relationship between God and creatures. Accordingly, perichoresis is an excellent concept to articulate the coexistence and paradoxical integration of stability and fluidity, unity and diversity, substance and relationality, groundedness and openness, and humanity and divinity.

In the following sections, I will deal, first, with the perichoresis of the Trinity and then with Christological perichoresis. I will further explore how the perichoresis can apply to God's relationship with creatures. Before the main sections, it is worthwhile to recall the purpose of this theological excursion. The doctrine of perichoresis will help us find a framework for theological anthropology in which a pastoral caregiver can find an agentive self in relationships while balancing theological groundedness and authentic openness to differences.

TRINITARIAN PERICHORESIS: BALANCING PARTICULARITY AND RELATIONALITY

Do you not believe that I am in the Father and the Father is in me?
The words that I say to you I do not speak on my own;
but the father who dwells in me does his works.
Believe me that I am in the Father
and the Father in me . . .

—JOHN 14:10–11, NRSV[1]

In the doctrine of the Trinity, the concept of perichoresis denotes the complete inner-trinitarian relationships of the three divine Persons in one God (Torrance 1996). As the Father, the Son, and the Holy Spirit, they are one in Being without division or confusion and are distinguished, at the same time, only in their relations to one another. In social psychological terms, one may say that the triune God is one holy Being, fully saturated in relationship, and three divine Persons, fully self-reflexive and agentic. Such paradoxical integration is possible because of the perichoresis the three

---

1. All scriptures are from NRSV unless otherwise indicated.

Persons share with one another in communion. Thus, the doctrine of the perichoresis illustrates more clearly "the identity of the divine Being and the intrinsic unity [and multiplicity] of the three divine Persons" (102).

In this regard, in the Trinity, the social structure that the three Persons form does not harm individual agency; each individual Person does not destroy the community. Rather, the social structure helps each Person thrive in relationship, and the three Persons build community through their unique agency. Such a perichoretic understanding of identity offers a theological lens through which one can look at how pastoral care partners interact with each other. Through their care-giving and receiving interactions, they form a care-giving relationship that helps both partners find their identities by balancing personal agency and social structure.

Perichoresis in Patristic Thoughts of the Trinity

Jesus expressed the idea of perichoresis when he articulated his perichoretic relationship in which, as in the Johannine passage above, one Person (Jesus) in the Trinity is in another Person (the Father) and they dwell in each other. To the Arian question—"How can the one be contained [*chorein*] in the other and the other in the one?"—Athanasius the Great responded, with the concept *homoosion*, that unlike material things, "the whole Being of the Father and the whole Being of the Son mutually indwell, inexist or coexist in one another" (Torrance 1996, 169). Pseudo-Cyril deepened this concept of coexistence in the Trinity by using the noun *perichoresis* to illustrate the unity of the three Persons. He writes in *De Trinitate 10*: "they [the three Persons] are one not so as to be confounded but so as to cleave to one another and they possess coinherence [*perichoresin*] in one another without any coalescence or confusion" (cited in Egan 1994, 87). By the trinitarian perichoresis, Cyril tries to emphasize that the three divine Persons are one triune God not through coalescence but through co-indwelling (for detailed patristic discussions of the trinitarian perichoresis, see Harrison 1991; Stramara 1998).

Thus, patristic theologians identified the triune God in its unique trinitarian perichoresis, the intra-trinitarian relationship that reflects one in essence and three in hypostasis. In Christian history, the concept of perichoresis has deeply engaged the doctrine of the Trinity and has made an important contribution to establishing the complicated doctrine in a balanced way between the Trinity's relational and agentic personhood, between the unity and diversity, between the identity and multiplicity, and between the communality and particularity, to name a few. Moltmann develops his trinitarian theology based on this important concept.

Perichoresis in Moltmann's Trinitarian Theology

In recent theology, many theologians continue to use the concept of perichoresis to express the trinitarian relationship of the Trinity and beyond. Contemporary rediscovery of trinitarian theology leads us to understand that God's way of existence in eternity and God's revelation of salvation in history is not monotheistic but relational in the sense that three trinitarian Persons indwell in each other for eternity and interpenetrate each other in the history of salvation. Moltmann's theology seems to exhibit multiple layers of perichoresis, even if he did not describe them explicitly. The first layer is the primary and inner-trinitarian perichoresis among the divine Persons. Another level of perichoresis is the "christological and pneumatological perichoresis," which is between God and believers. The unity of the believers is a perichoretic community that corresponds to the trinitarian perichoresis in analogy. The third kind of perichoresis is the "eschatological" or "cosmic" perichoresis in which God and the redeemed creation will have mutual indwelling. I call the inner-trinitarian perichoresis the "immanent perichoresis," which is the focus of the current section, and I call God's external perichoresis with redeemed beings the "economic" or "oikonomic" perichoresis, which we will see later in the chapter.

Through Moltmann and his social theory of the Trinity, the concept *perichoresis* has achieved currency in modern theology. In *Experiences in Theology*, Moltmann (1992 2000a) describes two ways of developing a trinitarian doctrine. The first departure point of developing the doctrine is the "metaphysical approach," which presupposes that God is one. From the perspective of singleness, he asserts, "the unity of the Trinity subsists in the shared, homogeneous substance of the three divine Persons" (2000a, 322). In this framework, the divine Persons are a single divine Being and have "one nature, one consciousness, and one will, which then manifest themselves in the three modes of being or subsistence," as in Barth's and Rahner's trinitarian theologies. The first approach thus assumes that the unity of the triune God lies in the sovereignty of the one God and that the unity precedes the threeness of the Trinity.

In the Bible, however, Moltmann finds not one but three "different actors" or subjects—Son, Father, and Holy Spirit—in divine history, as biblical stories describe. Thus, he calls the other departure point the "biblical" approach. He thus asserts that "If we search for a concept of unity corresponding to the biblical testimony of the triune God... then we must dispense with both the concept of the one substance and the concept of the identical subject" (1981, 150). As in the Fourth Gospel, Jesus and the Father relate to each other as Persons, and the Persons' reciprocal indwelling constitutes their unity. Moltmann views this perichoretic form of unity as "the only conceivable trinitarian concept of the unity of the triune God, because it combines threeness and oneness in such a way that they cannot be reduced to each other, so that both the danger of modalism and the danger of 'tritheism' are excluded" (322). Thus, Moltmann clearly delineates the triune God's three agentic Persons and one relational Being as integrated within the perichoretic life of communion. Accordingly, Moltmann views perichoresis as an important concept to integrate oneness and threeness, and relationality and particularity.

Moltmann's formula of three agentic Persons united in one relational Being through perichoresis is obvious in *The Trinity and the Kingdom*. In the book Moltmann (1981) pays attention to the word persona (*prosopon*) and connects its substantial, relational, and historical meanings to the concept of perichoresis. According to Boethius' substantial view of person, trinitarian Persons are individual, unique subjects of the one, common divine substance. According to Augustine's relational understanding of person, the three divine Persons exist in relation to one another: fatherhood, sonship, and the breathing of the Spirit. Moreover, according to Hegal's historical view of person, the three Persons also realize themselves in one another by surrendering themselves to one another in love. Validating all three views, Moltmann believes that the constituents of the triune God mutually subsist in one another to realize themselves in love:

> Each of the Persons possesses the divine nature in a non-interchangeable way; each presents it in his own way... They have the divine nature in common; but their particular individual nature is determined in their relationship to one another... Being a person in this respect means existing-in-relationship... [E]very divine Person exists in the light of the other and in the other. By virtue of the love they have for one another they ex-ist [ek-sist meaning in Greek "stand outside"] totally in the other: the Father ex-ists by virtue of his love, as himself entirely in the Son; the Son, by virtue of his self-surrender, ex-ists as himself totally in the Father; and so on. Each Person finds his existence and his joy in the other Person. Each Person receives the fullness of eternal life from the other. (171–74)

Thus, the triune God consists of three Persons and their relations in one community within which they realize one another through perichoresis among them. The divine Persons do not merely co-inhere in one another, but they also bring one another mutually the eternal divine glory. They glow into perfect form through one another as they make one another shine through the glory.

Moreover, Moltmann (1992) finds that person, relation, and perichoresis in trinitarian theology are "complementary." The perichoresis not only forms the unity of the divine Persons but also leads to the distinctions between the Persons by their different relations. In perichoretic life, for example, the Father is the bond between the two others and also distinguishes among them by different relations with the Son and the Spirit. Perichoresis makes the very thing that divides the divine Persons binds them together. Thus, the unity of the trinitarian Persons lies in the eternal perichoretic communion among them. Accordingly, in Moltmann's theology of perichoresis, the particularity of the divine Persons, their unique relations to one another, and the realization of the Persons in relations are all equally important elements. Thus, the complementary nature among person, relation, and realization will be useful lenses for the later discussion of theological anthropological implications.

How is perichoresis possible in the Trinity? Moltmann asserts that "the trinitarian Persons offer each other *reciprocally the inviting room for movement* in which they can develop their eternal livingness" (318, italics added). For Moltmann, this mutual inviting room and the trinitarian space are possible because of their eternal love. He says,

> It is the power of perfect love which lets each Person go out of himself to the extent that he is wholly present in the other ... In the perichoresis each Person makes himself 'inhabitable' for the two others, and prepares the wide space and the dwelling for the two others. (318–19)

In this sense, Moltmann's understanding of the perichoretic life of the Trinity is not only temporal but also spatial, containing both rest and movement of the trinitarian perichoresis. To make room for one another, the divine Persons "ex-ist" in each other by emptying themselves for the two others. Thus, Moltmann views the Word's incarnation as doing the same thing the Son is doing in eternity with regard to the Father and the Spirit: emptying themselves into one another to give themselves in selfless love (2000b). Thus, Moltmann sees the perichoretic community as a kenotic community. This point leads to his economic perichoresis and "open Trinity," as we will see later.

As we have seen, the perichoresis of the Trinity well illustrates the three divine Persons in one Being without losing each Person's particularity. In the Trinity, God is one in spite of the three Persons because of their perichoresis, which makes them a perfect communion without separating them as individuals or collapsing them into a confused mixture. By making room for and accepting one another and by penetrating and indwelling in each other, three divine Persons make their relationships and interactions the triune identity. Through their perichoretic interactions and relationships, the divine Persons both form one perfect communion of them and distinguish one from the others by their distinct relations as Father, Son, and Holy Spirit.

Balancing Particularity and Relationality

Such trinitarian perichoresis sheds light on how to balance community-building and agency-restoring at the same time. And perichoresis further offers insight concerning how to resolve our paradoxical dilemmas between the self and relationships and between agency and structure. A postmodern discourse of a relational self that derives from recognizing the demise of a modern centered self may end up with self-in-saturating-relationships, as shown in the previous chapter. Several scholars have articulated a problem concerning a self that may be swallowed up into relationships.

The first concern points to the fear of losing the self from a postmodern perspective (e.g., Gergen 1991; Thiselton 1995). A postmodern analysis of identity has construed the self as de-centered, saturated in relationships, and having no agency under the control of cultural powers. From this perspective, one can say that a postmodern relational self that is saturated in relationships and has no agency becomes a passively situated self or self-bound/saturated-in-relationship. In Anthony Thiselton's (1995) terms, the "postmodern self perceives itself as having lost control as [an] active agent, and as having been transformed into a passive victim of competing groups" (12). In a postmodern context, he is thus concerned about a self that loses its reflexive agency within a social structural power.

Another concern addresses gender injustice from a feminist perspective (e.g., Grey 2004; Volf 1996). The feminists discuss a social system that demands that women sacrifice for their relationships, thus causing relational gender injustice. British pastoral theologian Mary Grey (2004), for example, draws attention to a potential danger of gender injustice in emphasizing self-giving sacrifice on behalf of relationality. She argues that "it is not for one gender to sustain the entire burden of caring for society. Rather, both women and men need to develop joint models of caring and mutuality and transform oppressive models" (78).

Such concerns may make pastoral caregivers afraid of losing their agency in numerous and yet often brief relationships with care-seekers in their daily practices. Their work environment often requires pastoral clinicians to be other-directive and inclusive to serve various kinds of needs of care-seekers. Pastoral caregivers may be in danger of losing pastoral identity in the midst of multiple chameleon-like self-images by splitting their consciousness of the pastoral nature of work and their social, institutional expectations. However, the empirical study finds that pastoral caregivers in such a postmodern environment still construct their identities by creatively engaging with care-seekers, or through "perichoretic" interactions with them in theological terms (see chapter 6).

In this regard, one should respond to the dilemmas not by emphasizing relationality only but by balancing particularity and communality, self and relation, and agency and structure. Trinitarian perichoresis offers an alternative to the dilemmas by alluding to a theological model for such balanced integration. In the doctrine of the Trinity, perichoresis denotes a mutual interpenetration of the three Persons in the one divine Being without losing personal agency in favor of relationships (that commingle them or collapse them into a third mixture). Rather, each particular Person thrives in the communal relationships. Thus, perichoresis maintains each person's unique agency while also securing the relationality with others without injuring both. As Gunton (1997) discusses the meaning of the trinitarian theology for anthropology of human identity,

> The person is neither an individual, defined in terms of separateness from others, nor one who is swallowed up into the collective. Just as Father, Son, and Spirit are what they are by virtue of their otherness-in-relation, so that each particular is unique and absolutely necessary to the being of the whole, so it is, in its own way, for our being in society. (13)

Thus, the doctrine of perichoresis offers a theological framework for balancing both oneness and threeness, unity and diversity, relationality and particularity, and personal agency and social structure at the same time. Hence, the contemporary theology of the Trinity and its implications for human identity suggest that God and human beings are both primarily agentive persons-in-relationship, as will be discussed later.

CHRISTOLOGICAL PERICHORESIS: BALANCING GROUNDEDNESS AND OPENNESS

As we have seen above, many theologians have found useful theological metaphors in the rich linguistic implications of the concept *perichoresis*. The theologians use those metaphors not only for describing the triune God's inner-relations but also for illustrating the eternal Logos' hypostatic union. The perichoretic understanding of Christ's hypostatic union has not drawn much attention from contemporary theologians. However, this understanding has affected theologians' explications of Jesus' incarnation and kenosis.

In the following sections concerning Jesus Christ's perichoretic engagement with the humans, we will explore how the Son becomes like other human beings by opening himself to them and embracing the otherness within himself while still remaining a fully divine Being who transforms humans into his divine people. Jesus Christ is fully divine by grounding himself in the trinitarian perichoresis and is fully human by humbling and authentically opening himself to the humans, the otherness, and the difference. This christological understanding of perichoresis will offer a theological lens through which pastoral caregivers see themselves mirroring the divine way of engaging the difference and otherness, while remaining grounded.

Perichoresis in Patristic Thoughts of the Hypostatic Union

Gregory Nazianzen first used the verb *perichoreo* in his discussion of the interchanging between the divine and human properties of Christ. Following Gregory, Maximus the Confessor and Pseudo-Cyril take over the issue of the hypostatic union. Cyril asserts that "each nature interchanges with the other its properties, through the identity of hypostasis and their penetration into one another" (Wolfson 1964, 422). Here, he bases Christ's hypostatic union on two grounds: the unity of person and an asymmetric perichoresis of each nature's properties. Thus, Cyril articulates the way of integrating the two natures in the following manner:

> Through this hypostatic union [accomplished by perichoresis], the flesh is said to have been deified and to have become God, ... and God the Word is said to have become incarnate and to have been made man and to have been spoken of as 'creature' and to have been called 'last.' ... This penetration springs not from the flesh but from the divinity, since it is impossible for the flesh to penetrate through the divinity; still the divine nature,

> having once penetrated through the flesh, bestows on the flesh an ineffable penetration [toward] itself, which in particular we call union. (cited in 423)

From this passage, one can get two important insights into the union of two natures, as Wolfson points out. First, the union does not take place by the two natures' changing into one composite nature but by mutual interpenetration into one another. The hypostatic union in Christ consists of two acts, the penetration of the Word into the flesh (or the deification of the human nature) and the penetration of the human into the divine (or the "humanation"/incarnation of the divine nature). Thus, both the incarnation of the divinity and the divination of the human nature comprise the perichoretic union of Christ's two natures. However, secondly, the christological perichoresis, distinct from the trinitarian perichoresis, is asymmetrical since the divine nature starts the perichoretic movement and empowers human nature to penetrate back. In other words, as the deification starts first, the deified human nature can later penetrate into the divine nature (Harrison 1991) Thus, the divine nature's empowerment of the human nature's participation in the divine life is an important aspect of the transformation of the flesh (perichoretic deification) (for detailed patristic discussions, see Crisp 2005; Harrison 1991; Stead 1953; Wolfson 1964).

Even though trinitarian perichoresis has balanced mutuality and reciprocity of interpenetration and indwelling among the divine Persons, the christological usage of the concept in patristic thought has an asymmetric balance of the divine nature over the human. As Thomas Torrance (1996) points out, the Trinity's perichoresis as complete mutual indwelling and interpenetration of the three divine Persons may not directly apply to the Christ's asymmetric perichoresis in which the divine nature has a priority over the human nature.

Thus, these two similar and yet unique approaches to perichoresis should raise some different implications. It seems to me that whereas perichoresis in the Trinity signifies the principle of how to make complete communion in diversity without losing agentic personhood, the christological perichoresis suggests the principle of how to embrace the otherness by opening to and engaging (deifying and humanating) the difference without losing groundedness. Although the christological perichoresis has not attracted much attention from later theologians, its main idea of perichoresis continues in contemporary discussions of incarnation and kenosis, which is one side of perichoresis ("humanation").

Perichoresis in a Trinitarian Understanding of Kenosis

> Let the same mind be in you that was in Christ Jesus,
> who, though he was in the form of God,
> did not regard equality with God as something to be exploited,
> but emptied himself,
> taking the form of a slave,
> being born in human likeness.
> And being found in human form,
> he humbled himself
> and became obedient to the point of death—
> even death on a cross.
> Therefore God also highly exalted him
> and gave him the name that is above every name,
> so that at the name of Jesus every knee should bend,
> in heaven and on earth and under the earth,
> and every tongue should confess that Jesus Christ is LORD,
> to the glory of God the Father.
>
> --PHILIPPIANS 2:5-11

Along with the advance of trinitarian theology, the evolution of kenotic theology has been one of the most significant breakthroughs in the late-twentieth-century modern theology, especially in Christology (Polkinghorne 2001). In *The Work of Love*, John Polkinghorne and his theological and scientific colleagues see kenosis not only as an expression of Christ's self-emptying in the incarnation and on the cross but also as God's voluntary self-emptying for creatures. According to Sarah Coakley (2001), there are three theological approaches to the kenosis in Christian theology: a "Christological" perspective initiated by the nineteenth century Lutheran theology, a "trinitarian" perspective represented by Hans Urs von Balthasar and Moltmaan, and a "generalized" approach taken by several recent theologians such as Polkinghorne and Gunton. While the next sections focus on the second and third perspectives, S.M. Smith (2001) provides a concise summary of the three positions, asking, "is a kenotic theology to be seen in its uniqueness as the act of divine self-limitation . . . or is it to be seen as either the culminating historical instance of the Trinitarian dialectic . . . and/or the kenotic relation of God to creation in general?" (652).

Examining John Calvin's approach to Jesus Christ's two natures, Carl Mosser (2002) explains a two-level union of the natures. The first and fundamental level is communication of properties between Christ's divinity and humanity. The consequential level is a particular union of Jesus with his believers. Mosser contends that "Christ unites believers to God because in his person God and humanity are already united" (47). While the Lutheran kenotics focus on the first level of union, contemporary theologians seem to emphasize the second level of union in light of kenosis. Balthasar and Moltmann, for example, handle the kenosis as a way of God's uniting with human beings and the world in the context of the doctrine of the Trinity.

As noted above, within the perichoretic relationship, the trinitarian Persons freely give oneself to another to communicate with each other in complete love. Such perichoretic interactions are reflected in the eternal Son's kenotic incarnation. Moltmann (1981) views the incarnation not only as God's necessity for forgiving human sins and reconciling human beings with God but also as God's will to self-communicate with the world out of love. Through self-humiliation, the triune God enters into the limited, finite situation and the sinful, forsaken world to make human beings God's sons and daughters who restore the image of God following Jesus, the primordial image of God. Thus, the kenotic incarnation "intervenes in the inner relations of the Trinity" and is "realized on the cross" (119).

Drawing on Hans Urs von Balthasar, Moltmann (2001) clearly maintains that the Word's incarnation in history reveals what the Trinity does in eternity. He asserts that

> what he does on earth in time is not different from what he does in heaven, and what he does in time is no different from what he does in eternity . . . In his obedience he realizes on earth his eternal relationship to the Father . . . [and] in his obedience to the point of death on the cross he is completely one with the Father. (140)

Such a view of the incarnation and cross as trinitarian events is evident in Moltmann's *The Crucified God* and throughout his works. Looking at the event of the cross from a trinitarian perspective, he (1991) asserts that "In the cross, Father and Son are most deeply separated in forsakenness and at the same time are most inwardly one in their surrender. What proceeds from this event between Father and Son is the Spirit which justifies the godless, fills the forsaken with love and even brings the dead alive" (244). For Moltmann, the death of Jesus Christ on the cross is "an innertrinitarian event" which takes place "in the innermost nature of God himself: the fatherless Son and the sonless Father" before it assumes significance for the deliverance of the world (2000a, 305).

Grenz (2004) summarizes an implication of Moltmann's trinitarian theology of the cross, saying, "As the one who is able freely to take on the suffering of those who suffer, the very heart of God is touched by the world. In fact, the cross marks the entrance of human history with all its pain and evil into God's own life" (78). Through the event of the cross, God in Jesus Christ through the Spirit enters the world, and by doing so they open themselves, let the world come in, and contain it in them. Accordingly, Moltmann views the kenosis of incarnation and cross as a trinitarian event in salvation history and opens a possibility for extending, through the kenotic theology, the Trinity's inner perichoretic relationships to the Trinity's perichoretic interplay between God and the world (see the next section of the chapter).

Therefore, kenosis is a part of perichoresis in which the flesh penetrates into the divine, that is, incarnation or humanation. Moltmann (2000b) thus contends that "The perichoretic community can also be seen as a kenotic community: The persons are 'emptying' themselves into one another. What the Son is doing by becoming human, according to Philippians 2:6, is nothing other than what he is doing in eternity . . . giving oneself" (115). Moreover, such a perichoretic understanding of kenosis is clearer when one looks at the Johannine passage, which says that "the Word became flesh and lived among us" (John 1:14). By humbling himself, the infinite Son "is able to indwell the finite being of creation"; accordingly, "incarnation and indwelling are grounded in the kenosis of God" (Moltmann 2000a, 316). Therefore, through the self-surrender to the Father and by self-humiliation and making room for the humanity, the eternal Son gives himself to the creaturely nature, contains the flesh in himself, and becomes incarnate, while at the same time remaining the trinitarian perichoresis with the Father and the Spirit as a fully divine.

As we have seen, whereas traditional understandings of christological perichoresis and kenosis focus exclusively on the Son's two natures, the contemporary trinitarian discourse of christological perichoresis expands its perspective to the Trinity's perichoretic engagement with human beings. Moreover, trinitarian theologians view the kenosis as the expression of the divine being's perichoretic life. For trinitarian theologians, kenosis is not a new occurrence resulting from the incarnation but an eternal incidence in the reciprocal relationships of the triune God. Consequently, the kenosis, according to the trinitarian perspective, is "the self-realization of the self-surrender of the Son to the Father" as they eternally do in the trinitarian communion (Moltmann 2001, 140). "The inner-trinitarian kenosis," contends Moltmann, "is part of the inner-trinitarian perichoresis" (141). Thus, the trinitarian discourse of kenosis opens a way to express God's perichoretic relationships with the creature.

Balancing Groundedness and Openness

As we have seen, the kenosis as a perichoresis shows how God the Son gives his divinity to the creatures and becomes like humans but still remains as fully divine (and fully human). This christological perichoresis sheds light on our pastoral theological dilemma of balancing theological groundedness and cultural and religious inclusiveness. Jesus Christ's kenotic perichoresis with humanity also provides helpful insight concerning how pastoral caregivers interact with care-seekers who come from different cultural and religious orientations. Moreover, the christological discourse of perichoresis provides pastoral practitioners with the courage and wisdom to adapt to and work to change institutional disciplines and expectations that sometimes demand the caregivers to provide a generic spiritual care.

From a pastoral theological perspective, pastoral theologians and practitioners may have trouble adequately representing the wisdom of particular theological traditions in a postmodern, intercultural, and multifaith society. Especially, working in secular institutions and in culturally and religiously pluralistic contexts, contemporary pastoral caregivers may have to wrestle with their religious calls and pastoral identities. Once endorsed by particular faith traditions and communities, pastoral practitioners are now reshaped into religiously-neutral professionals under such contemporary conditional pressures (Engelhardt 1998). In this situation, pastoral clinicians may encounter two options: grounding themselves with rigid theology or opening themselves with religious fuzziness.

However, the christological perichoresis offers the third option and sheds light on our dilemma of how to be authentically open to care-seekers in cultural and religious pluralistic contexts while still remaining grounded in theological wisdom. Gunton (1992) views kenosis as one "indispensable" concept to present how the Son becomes man while remaining God. By making room for humanity and creation in the divinity and containing/ embracing the otherness in it, the Incarnate unites with the otherness and becomes one person, fully divine and fully human. With the divine agency out of love, the Son freely initiates humbling himself and becomes human, without losing the deity, to redeem creation.

Likewise, pastoral caregivers who participated in the empirical study do not give up the struggle of balancing groundedness in theology and openness to otherness. Pastoral counselor Nate (I2), who was once a navy chaplain, likens such a situation as "render unto Caesar the things that are Caesar's and render unto God the things that are God's." By this metaphor, he means he adapts to institutional expectations and disciplines to serve as a caregiver, but he does not surrender to such pressures by keeping himself grounded in his religious call. As chaplain George (I5) mentioned, one of the keys is "being flexible without losing your theology." Thus, pastoral practitioners humble themselves as fellow humans to be with care-seekers and are flexible in order to meet needs and expectations of the care-partners and institution. And at the same time, pastoral care-providers remain grounded in theological wisdom and reflection by faithfully engaging in reinterpreting and contextualizing their theologies through encounters with the care-seekers' lived experiences.

Such flexible yet grounded identities are possible when we see a theological framework through the Son's kenotic perichoresis. Out of the communicative love of the Trinity with the world, the Son authentically opens himself to the world by humbling himself and becoming a full human being. Nonetheless, Jesus remained fully divine by grounding himself in perichoretic oneness with the other two Persons of the Trinity. Thus, the inter-trinitarian perichoresis extends to include God's perichoresis with the human beings by giving the Son to the world and engaging the difference and otherness. Accordingly, the self-emptying of the eternal Son in the incarnation and on the cross is an expression of the love of the triune God worked out in human history. The following section will explore how this perichoresis from above, or kenotic perichoresis, opens a way to the perichoresis from below, or the deified perichoresis.

COSMIC PERICHORESIS: INTERPLAY BETWEEN ENGAGEMENT AND PARTICIPATION

"... they may all be one.
As you, Father, are in me, and I am in you,
may they also be in us..."

—JOHN 17:21

The triune God's perichoretic engagement with the human beings in the preceding section and their perichoretic participation in the Divine in this section should be two sides of perichoresis. The Trinity's perichoretic engagement with the world through the Son's kenosis is one perichoresis of the divine through the human (incarnation/humanation). The other perichoresis of the human toward the divine (deification) is the world's perichoretic participation in the trinitarian life through the empowerment of the Son's redeeming and Spirit's sanctifying works for the creatures. Thus, kenosis and *theosis* (or deification) form a pair of the Trinity's perichoretic acts. In this regard, pastoral theologians and caregivers may see preliminary perichoretic interplay between God and the redeemed creatures in their daily practices as they partake in God's ministry in which God is present and engages the self.

Perichoresis in Patristic Thought of Creatures' Participation in the Divine

Gregory Nazianzen also uses the verb *perichoreo* in *Theological Oration* 18.42 when he discusses life and death as interchangeable (see Harrison 1991; Lawler 1995). In the text, Gregory associates "perichoresis with issues of anthropology, soteriology, and cosmic redemption" and employs the idea of perichoresis to describe not only Christ's hypostatic union but also the union between Christ and believers (Harrison, 57). Gregory's christological and soteriological concepts of perichoresis influenced St. Maximus, Pseudo-Cyril, and John of Damascus who expands the concepts into the cosmic perichoresis through which creatures, including humans, can participate in the divine.

In a soteriological context, Maximus speaks of the "inexpressible interpenetration [*perichoresis*] of the believers [toward] the object of belief" (57). He sees the deification as believers' finally returning to their origin, an "ever-active repose" in the object of belief, and the participation in mystical divine realities. Such perichoresis between believers and God expands the relationship between God and the world in Maximus' theology. Cyril deepens Maximus' perichoresis (believers' deification) by emphasizing the asymmetry and the divine empowerment to the human nature. According to Cyril, the deification of the saints as perichoresis toward God is only possible by the divine power. Through this divine empowerment, the created penetrate the divine realities, but not completely. Moreover, John of Damascus tries to resolve the paradoxical tension of asymmetry between infinite and finite in Christ. Like Cyril, John also asserts that the deification of the human in Christ arises out of the divine nature, which "grants the flesh participation in its own splendors while remaining impassible" and shares the divine glory with humanity (62).

Thus, the patristic thought indicates and envisages the perichoresis between God and the creatures extended from the perichoretic union of Christ's two natures. However, this perichoresis is asymmetrical in that God's interpenetration through the creation must empower it to penetrate the divine realities by grace. In this sense, when we recognize the creaturely perichoretic participation in the divine realities, we also know that God's perichoretic engagement with us has already started. The participation of the creation in the divine life continues to influence contemporary theologians' thoughts.

Perichoresis as Humans' Participation in the Divine Life

The christological and pneumatological perichoresis occurs when Jesus Christ leads humans into his own perichoretic relationship with God the Father and adapts them as his sisters and brothers. Moltmann makes clear a perichoresis between God and human beings from the Johannine tradition. As in Jesus' prayer for the disciples that "may they also be in us" (John 17:21), human beings indwell in the triune God. Also, the triune God indwells in human beings: "Those who love me will keep my word, and my Father will love them, and we will come to them and make our home with them" (John 14:23). Thus, the mutual indwelling between God and human beings is in love: "those who abide in love abide in God, and God abides in them" (1 John 4:16).

Moltmann acknowledges that the perichoresis of persons in different natures (e.g., God and human beings) is not the same as inner-trinitarian perichoresis by which Persons of the same substance mutually interpenetrate each other. However, he recognizes that the human beings' communion "with God and in God is also a mutual indwelling and perichoretic unity" because they experience God in them and themselves in God in communion with Jesus Christ and in the power of the self-giving Holy Spirit. Moltmann (2008) contends that such communion between God and human beings "mediat[es] between the inner-trinitarian perichoresis and the perichoretic community of human beings" (376). Here, we can see the trinitarian perichoresis extending to the economic perichoresis between God and humans and to the perichoretic community of human beings.

Some studies have articulated the christological and pneumatological perichoresis between God and believers and have emphasized the role of the Holy Spirit in that perichoresis (Crump 2006; M. T. Marshall 2003; McDougall 2002). In his striking analysis of the Johannine Trinity, theologian David Crump (2006) observes that Jesus' disciples replace the Spirit in the trinitarian perichoretic relationship. John's Gospel affirms that God and the Son are in the perichoretic union, but the Gospel offers no evidence about the Spirit in the trinitarian perichoresis. Rather, John depicts the disciples as a "third member of a perichoretic trinity" (395). Crump interprets such Johannine narratives of the Spirit and the disciples in a trinitarian perichoresis as John's having no interest in depicting the Spirit's eternal union within the Trinity and as John's portrait of the Spirit as the Son's alter ego and agent for the disciples. Thus, in the Gospel, the Spirit continues to facilitate Jesus' earthly ministry as the alter ego and deifies the disciples as the agent of the perichoretic union with God. Crump concludes,

> the mutually indwelling Father and Son send the Spirit to indwell disciples as the living presence of the glorified Jesus. In this way, every disciple participates in the divine interpenetration of the Son and the Father, producing the Johannine, perichoretic trio of Father-Son-disciple, a divine bi-unity perichoretically incorporating believers within the Son and the Father through the Spirit. (412)

As Crump has demonstrated through his analysis of the Johannine perichoresis, humans' perichoretic union with God is possible through Christ (the mediator) and the Spirit (the agent) and is at the core of Johannine soteriology, ecclesiology, and pneumatology. Thus, the Johannine Trinity that includes disciples in the trinitarian perichoresis portrays a possibility for humans to have perichoretic union with God and, thereby, to be divinized in Christ through the Spirit. The trinitarian perichoresis invites us to participate in the divine dance of life and fellowship.

Perichoresis in the God-Creation Relationship

Contemporary theologians have explicitly and implicitly articulated a perichoretic relationship between God and creation (e.g., Gunton 1992; Moltmann 1981, 1992; Polkinghorne 2001; Simmons 2006). Even though their perspectives are somewhat different, they look at the creation as God's work of giving the self to and making space for creatures. Such a theological view of the creation as God's self-giving to the creaturely world implies God's perichoretic engagement with the creation.

In *The Trinity and the Kingdom*, Moltmann (1981) delineates his "trinitarian creation" as differing from traditional and the nineteenth century speculative theologies. In distinction from the traditional view of creation as a result of God's absolute liberty and good pleasure, Moltmann sees the creation from a relational perspective: not in accord with God's absolute power but by virtue of the mutual relationship of love. Thus, he contends that "Creation is a fruit of God's longing for 'his Other' and for that Other's free response to the divine love" (106). The inward self-communicating life of the trinitarian Persons initiates their outward communication creatively with the one who is other than themselves. The Trinity creates the finite, temporal, and spatial world by a self-humiliation since the finitude, time, and space cannot coexist with infinity, eternity, and omnipresence.

Even though Moltmann does not explicitly articulate a perichoretic understanding of creation, he clearly describes a kenotic understanding of creation (for more kenotic understandings, see Gunton 1992; Polkinghorne 2001). Moltmann explains a paradox in which the infinite, omnipresent, eternal God creates and co-exists with the Other that, to a certain degree, confines the unlimitedness. "In order to create something 'outside' himself," Moltmann asserts, "the *infinite God must have made room for this finitude* beforehand, 'in himself' . . . Has God not therefore created *the world 'in himself'*, giving it *time in his eternity, finitude in his infinity, space in his omnipresence*, and *freedom in his selfless love*?" (Moltmann 1981, 109, italics added for emphasis).

Moltmann's perichoretic creation starts from his assumption that "the relationship between God and the world has a reciprocal character" (98). Thus, the notion of God's creating the world by making room for it within the triune God is itself perichoretic. This perichoretic understanding of creation becomes clear when Moltmann writes,

> The world process is therefore to be understood as a two-sided one. Every stage in the creation process contains within itself the tension between the light flooding back into God and the light that breaks forth from him. In other words, every act outwards is preceded by an act inwards which makes the 'outwards' possible. God, that is to say, continually creates inwards and outwards simultaneously. He creates by withdrawing himself, and because he withdraws himself. (110)

What Moltmann argues in this passage is that the Trinity, by withdrawing itself and making room for the creation, contains the world in itself, and the world indwells in God. By making room for time in God's eternity, giving space to the world in God's omnipresence, containing finitude in God's infinity, the immanently perichoretic Trinity opens to a cosmic perichoresis of the world toward God. As the Trinity, God the Father creates the world by virtue of the eternal love for the Son and "through him" and "through the operation of the Holy Spirit" (113).

Moltmann's perichoretic understanding of the God-creation relationship becomes clearer in his later works. He asserts that "If the consummation of salvation lies in the reunion with the triune God of creatures who have been separated and torn apart in themselves, then we must understand this unity of the Father, the Son, and the Spirit as an open, inviting, reuniting, integrating unity" (1992, 86). He sees sin as separation from God and salvation as consisting of God's gracious acceptance of the creature into the triune communion. The perichoretic reunion between God and human beings extends to the perichoresis between God and creation. Moltmann (2000a) contends that "Paul formulates the ultimate eschatological vista as God's cosmic She[ch]inah, when God will be 'all in all' (ICor. 15.28)" (323). For Moltmann, such eschatological reunion with God is creation's deification in the eternal presence of the Trinity. All redeemed creatures will find their freedom and living-space in the Trinity by entering into fellowship with God. Thus, Moltmann's trinitarian approach to creation clearly delineates the perichoretic relationship between God and the world.

Baptist theologian Molly Marshall (2003) expands Moltmann's position by emphasizing the Spirit's role of the divine empowerment. In her article on a trinitarian pneumatology, she tries to link trinitarian theology with a renewed theology of the Spirit and interprets the doctrine of perichoresis as a means for humans and all creation to participate in the divine life. She raises the question "Can we expand the image [of the divine dance] so that there is room for humanity—even for the whole of creation—to join in this dance within God's own life?" (145). Drawing on LaCugna's interpretation of perichoresis, Marshall declares that "*Perichoresis* is participation" (ibid.). She sees the Holy Spirit as the mediating power between the divine and creaturely being by making mutual penetration possible. Thus, she views the Spirit "as the means by which the life of the triune God is opened out toward creation and the means by which God 'carries the world back into God's self'" (148). Challenging the view of God as dominative and always triumphing over all that opposes God's way, she proposes that the "work of the Spirit—hidden, nearly imperceptible, humble—is the paradigm of how God works in the world" (149–50). She concludes that

> The Spirit is inviting all creation to join in the dance that characterizes God's life. The Spirit as God's inexhaustible, dancing power creates an ongoing movement between divine and creaturely being. Because the *perichoresis* of God is open for the participation of all creation, all find identity through this overarching rhythm of life. It is by the Spirit that we participate in the life of God and God participates in our life together ... It

> is a Trinitarian virtue to live life opened out in relationality, in the power of the Spirit. (150)

In this passage, Marshall clearly delineates that the Holy Spirit as mediating power between God and creatures deifies creaturely beings to participate in the perichoretic dance with the Trinity. The eternal Son's perichoretic engagement with the otherness of the created opens the way to the creature's participation in the perichoretic life of God through the Spirit's empowerment.

In this regard, Moltmann contends that "the Trinity is an open and inviting and uniting environment for the whole creation redeemed and renewed in God" (2008, 376). In his eschatological and ecological vision, he maintains that "Everything ends with God's being 'all in all' . . . God in the world and the world in God—that is what is meant by the glorifying of the world through the Spirit. That is the home of the Trinity" (1981, 105). Thus, a contemporary trinitarian theology envisages perichoretic interplay and unity between God and the world in an eschatological and ecological sense.

Dynamic Interplay between God's Engagement and Human Participation

As we have seen so far, at the heart of the identity of the triune God is the perichoresis found within the Trinity. This trinitarian perichoresis extends to perichoresis between God and created and redeemed creatures as shown in Christ's hypostatic union and kenotic engagement with the world. The perichoretic dance between God and human beings (and creatures) envisions a theological ground for pastoral caregivers' participation in God's perichoretic engagement in human care-seekers' sufferings and their redemption. Pastoral caregivers who intentionally open themselves to God's engagement in their presence and ministry humbly present themselves to care-seekers. As the care partners deeply open their worlds and share their stories, they mirror the divine perichoresis. They may realize God's engagement in their struggle and lived experiences and partake in God's presence and ministry as a silhouette of eschatological perichoresis.

In the empirical study, pastoral caregivers confirm such dynamic interplay between God and human social actors in their pastoral care-giving relationships. When pastoral caregivers are intentionally aware of themselves as representatives of God yet humbly open themselves to care-seekers, they both may feel God's engagement in their relationships. Chaplain Bill (I3) says, "God becomes real not in my being there for people but in our being there for one another and then the encounter that happens between ... the caregiver and patient." A trinitarian perichoretic God invites human participations in the divine dance by engaging in their ministry and presence as the images of God. Such dynamic reciprocity in pastoral care-giving makes their ministry truly blessing and special.

From the theological discussions, we have learned, first of all, how trinitarian Persons unite as one divine Being without losing each particular Person. Indeed, each person thrives in the perichoretic relationship. Moreover, the trinitarian perichoresis of love fully communicates with and embraces the world by giving the Son to be fully human, but Jesus also remains fully divine by grounding himself in the perichoretic oneness with God the Father and the Holy Spirit. This extended perichoresis culminates in the cosmic perichoresis in which God and the world becomes one through the christological and pneumatological perichoresis in which the divine engagement with the world and the world's participation in the divine can interplay.

THEOLOGICAL ANTHROPOLOGY OF PERSONHOOD

Through the concept of perichoresis, we see God's identity is uniquely revealed in God's communion made of three divine Persons who make room for, reciprocally interpenetrate, mutually contain, and thereby co-indwell one another. Moreover, through a perichoretic union in Jesus Christ, we see that the eternal Son empties and makes room for humanity in order to incarnate himself into the flesh and empowers humanity to contain the divine by deifying the human. Such economic perichoresis extends to cosmic perichoresis through which God embraces the world and dwells in it at the same time in an eschatological sense.

Human identity, as created in the image of God, reflects these perichoretic identities of God. In this sense, the immanent and economic perichoresis set the foundation for illuminating how individuals, as agentive persons, can establish a full relationship with each other, neither blurring one with others nor separating one from others. The agentive persons can also engage the difference and otherness without losing their proper grounds by creating a space in which to open themselves to diversity. Such perichoretic interactions do not merely remain in the human level but also embrace the God-human relationship as God invites us to participate in the divine reality.

While explicating trinitarian theology, contemporary theologians have searched for a possibility of extending trinitarian theology to theological anthropology. As Grenz (2001) points out, "Of the various significant developments in theology over the last hundred years, none has more far-reaching implications for anthropology than the rediscovery of the doctrine of the Trinity" (3–4). He continues to say that "the retrieval of the doctrine of the Trinity has paved the way for a fully theological anthropology" (16). From the empirical, social psychological, and theological perspectives of identity we have discussed, several points are essential to our discussion of (pastoral) identity. The points include the importance of a proper balance between personal agency and social relationality and the concept of perichoresis as a theological metaphor for the balance. In this concluding section, I will summarize who God is and who human beings are in light of perichoresis.

God's Perichoretic Identity as Person and Space

Drawing on the previous discussions of perichoresis, I view God's identity as both Person and Space. According to Moltmann (2008), God is Person and Space, first, within the trinitarian perichoretic communion. The trinitarian Persons as agentive selves make themselves inhabitable for one another and prepare a wide room and hospitable space in themselves. The divine Persons each with unique personality mutually offer "each other the inviting, open room for movements to develop their eternal livingness" (374). By virtue of perichoresis, the divine Persons voluntarily offer a self-giving space to one another and receive one another in themselves. Thus, the triune God consists in a wide room and open space for the penetration and the indwelling of thee divine Persons. In this sense, Moltmann sees the Trinity as kenotic Person and Space because the divine Persons make space in themselves and are constituted of their reciprocal indwelling.

Moreover, the Trinity is also Person and Space for the creation. Moltmann boldly asserts that "the triune God is not only the three-personal God, but much more the threefold divine Space for the indwelling of all the creatures" (375). Thus, he asserts that the perichoretic unity of the Trinity as Person and Space is open enough that the whole creation can find room and the fullness of eternal life within it. In the cosmic perichoresis of the Trinity with the creation, the triune God extends the inviting room for the creation to participate in the divine perichoretic dance in that trinitarian Space.

Moltmann's theology of the "open Trinity" especially delineates the relationship between the creation and God as Person and Space. In distinction from "the closed Trinity," whose images are a circle or triangle, Moltmann (2000a) contends that the Trinity is open "not out of deficiency and imperfection, but in the superfluity and overflow of the love which gives created beings the living space for their livingness, and the free scope for their development" (323). Thus, the trinitarian perichoretic life makes a wide and habitable space for human beings and other creatures. The open Trinity is "the inviting encompassing reality of the whole, redeemed and renewed creation, which, for its part, then becomes the encompassing world for the divine indwelling" (ibid.). Hence, Moltmann (2008) contends that "The trinitarian God is the redeeming 'broad room' for all creatures and the life-space for all living beings: 'May they also be in us'" (375). Thus, the perichoretic trinitarian God and the kenotic life-giving God meet at one point where the Trinity is open, inviting, and integrating to the renewed beings.

From such a perspective of divine identity as person and space, we may have a sense that the divine Persons are in relation to one another by creating within themselves the inhabitable Space in which they can penetrate and indwell one another. Likewise, the triune Persons have relationships with the creation by making in themselves an inviting Space in which the creatures can indwell while opening themselves to receive Personal God in their welcoming spaces. In this sense, space becomes a phenomenological field in which relationships can develop and persons can thrive in these relationships.

PERICHORETIC HUMAN IDENTITY AS PERSON AND RELATION

A perichoretic understanding of identity does not simply adapt and conform to contemporary philosophical and social psychological understandings of relationality. Going back to the debate regarding whether persons are to be substantial and relational, we find that the perichoretic understanding offers an alternative perspective from which we can see identity as fundamentally relational and, at the same time, as essentially substantial in making oneself available and agentive in relation to others. What trinitarian theology implies for our discussion of human identity is that identity comprises relationality and substantiality together to make personhood.

The first theological anthropological point is that persons, divine and human, are not only relations but also subjects. From a trinitarian perspective, one can contend that the divine Persons are both active agents and communal relations without losing their own particularities in relational saturation or putting their relationships in jeopardy on behalf of particularity. We do not have to struggle with whether persons are ontologically substantial or relational. Rather, we can assert that humans are subjective relations and relational subjects, or what we have currently called persons-in-relationship.

In this regard, Torrance (1996) uses a concept of "onto-relations" or "substantive relations" and asserts that "Person is an onto-relational concept" (157). By onto-relation, he (1982) means a "being-constituting relation" that is "the kind of relation subsisting between things which is an essential constituent of their being, and without which they would not be what they are" (42–43). In this sense, Torrance contends that the triune God is "not only a fullness of personal Being in himself, but is also [a] person-constituting [relation]" (43). Perichoresis makes a perfect communion, preserving such a balance between fullness of personal being and person-constituting relation. By maintaining that person is an onto-relation rather than saying "person is relation," Torrance thus means to recognize the person-as-relation that subsists in an ontological substance, instead of seeing person-as-vacuum-relation. Thus, we need to avoid building a theological construction of perichoresis that has no ontological ground of relations.

Moltmann's (1981) early theory of persons clearly states the point that trinitarian persons are "subjects of the one, common divine substance, with consciousness and will" (171) and should not be reduced to relations. Rather, one has to understand that persons and relations are in a "reciprocal relationship . . . [T]here are no persons without relations; but there are no relations without persons either" (172). As Peters (1993) points out, the idea of relationships prior to persons is the "product of our modern and emerging postmodern Western mind" (185).

In the perichoretic relationship, each Person of the triune God participates in the communion with the others while distinguishing one from the others. In the Trinity, immanent or economic, there are three subjects, and the subjects equally participate in life-sharing perichoresis, thus making one perfect communion. The three divine Persons are what they are by virtue of their otherness-in-relation, and each particular Person, thereby, is unique and absolutely necessary to the being of the whole. Thus, particularity and relationality both go together to what it means to be personhood.

Such relational and particular humanity based on trinitarian theology of perichoresis can offer a resolution to the postmodern dilemma of human identity in relationships. As noted above, the dilemma is that human identity is relational often at the cost of losing a centered self (from a postmodern perspective), at the expense of disconnection from a self-affirming personhood (from a feminist standpoint), or at the price of exchanging adequate grounding with pluralistic inclusivity (from a pastoral theological perspective). One may find a balance between personal agency and social structure as a common key for resolving these paradoxical problems of identities in both secular and theological disciplines.

There are two theological responses to the postmodern self that has lost its center in relationships: one favors relationality at the expense of agency, and the other is in harmony between both. The first theological response to a postmodernism is Stanley Hauerwas's (1998) appreciation of the postmodern conception of the loss of the self and agency. According to him, the modern emphasis on the self as the center of human life puts the human in the place of God. Postmodernists deny, Hauerwas asserts, the modern centered self that is "created by the displacement of God" (99). They construct a de-centered self, which has some affinities with what Christian saints pursued. From this perspective, he claims that postmodernism offers "some extremely helpful ways for a display of holiness without a loss of the Catholic character of the church" (78). Christian sanctification, he contends, does not require a self. Rather, the postmodern emphasis on the loss of the self can help Christians "rediscover holiness not as an individual achievement but as the work of the Holy Spirit building up the body of Christ" (ibid.). Hauerwas, therefore, envisages a Christian community neglecting the self and agency. In this regard, his position to the postmodern self "goes overboard in his description of the body of Christ as the annihilation of the self," as Charles Marsh (2002) points out (259).

Fully aware of a postmodern fragmented self and its discontinuity with the pre-modern stable self, Linda Woodhead (1999), from a different theological perspective, recognizes that stable and agentic identities still co-exist with fragmented identities in the modern society. She asks a theological question about contemporary identities that consist of both relationality and agency: "How is it possible to maintain belief in human agency whilst insisting that the self is constituted by relationality?" (70). In his theological search for a postmodern identity, Marsh (2002) seems to answer the question. From Dietrich Bonhoeffer's christological and Eberhard Jüngel's trinitarian perspectives, he contends that

> The promise of a trinitarian account of the self lies in its capacity to illustrate a conception of life with others that embraces both the distinctive identity of persons (God the Father and the Son and the Holy Spirit) and yet requires the movement of and to the other in the perfect communion of the one triune God. (278)

As he rightly pointed out, a trinitarian way of subjects-in-relationship helps the constituents form their communion and, at the same time, preserves their distinctive particularity through actively offering inhabitable space for others and sharing life with them. This theological understanding offers a helpful way of validating both relationality and agency of human life.

Just as focusing heavily on the singleness of the Trinity harms the perichoretic communion of the three Persons, an exclusive emphasis on their relatedness also damages the dynamic communion. Miroslav Volf (1996) has rightly pointed to this problem and used the doctrine of perichoresis to balance personality and relationality. He sees perichoresis as affirming the three Persons' relationality without losing each Person's particularity and agency and also as holding on to the presence of the others in one's personality without slipping into inequality and oppression.

From the second approach to personal agency and social structure, the theological understanding of human identity based on trinitarian theology and communitarian anthropology can provide a resolution to the postmodern dilemma of attaining a relational community at the cost of losing agentive self. Grenz (2001) summarizes theological implications of innertrinitarian perichoresis for human identity:

> The ingenious use of perichoresis to describe the manner in which the trinitarian persons are constituted by the mutuality of relationships within the life of the triune God opened the way for the development of a dynamic ontology of persons-in-relationship or persons-in-communion. This ontology characterizes the essential nature of personhood as consisting of mutuality and interdependence . . . By offering the impetus toward a thoroughgoing relational ontology, the concept of perichoresis opens the way as well for an ontology that takes seriously and in fact ensures the integrity of both the 'one' and the 'many,' preserving both within the dynamic interrelations. (317)

It is evident in this passage that perichoresis plays an important role in articulating not only the unity but also diversity. The constitution of the triune God comprises oneness and threeness, relatedness and distinctness, and relational community and personal agency. Thus, from the trinitarian approach to person and relations, one can contend that an agentive self and relational community can coexist and that humans can attain a relational self without losing self-reflexive agency. Accordingly, the trinitarian understanding of identity nurtures a relational self that is an actively agentic self-in-relationship or self-agentive-in-relationship.

Perichoretic Human Identity as Agentive Self-In-Relationship

By rendering self-agentive-in-relationship possible, the perichoretic understanding of identity offers a theological framework for resolving the paradox between self and relation. Dynamic perichoretic interactions and interrelationships that make persons one community are at the heart of the theological solution based on trinitarian theology. This perichoretic identity not only affirms that a person is a self-in-relation but also goes beyond that affirmation. LaCugna (1991) points out that the doctrine of perichoresis "avoids the pitfalls of locating the divine unity either in the divine substance (Latin) or exclusively in the person of the Father (Greek), and locates unity instead in diversity, in a true *communion* of persons" (271). In my estimation, this passage should read that the doctrine locates unity instead in a true perichoretic communion of Persons, not in communion as affirming only relationality. In this regard, we need to differentiate the perichoretic communion (that constitutes both the unity and diversity of the three trinitarian Persons) from relationality (that discounts personality or particularity).

The trinitarian perspective of identity explicates a model of a perichoretic identity in which three Persons freely give themselves to one another in eternal love and act as agents in relation to one another in salvation history. The contemporary theological perspective of identity in light of trinitarian theology and the *imago Dei* indicates that human beings are agentive self-in-relationships with others, self, and God. As liberation theologian Leonardo Boff points out,

> In the light of the Trinity, being a person in the image and likeness of the divine Persons means acting as a permanently active web of relationships: relating backwards and upwards to one's origin in the unfathomable mystery of the Father, relating outwards to one's fellow human beings by revealing oneself to them and welcoming the revelation of them in the mystery of the Son, relating inwards to the depths of one's own personality in the mystery of the Spirit. (cited in Grenz 2001, 53)

God's inner-relationship within the Trinity overflows to God's interrelationship with creatures in creation and providence, and thus divine relatedness creates relational humankind in the image of God. Imaging or mirroring the divine relationality, human beings act as a "permanently active web of relationships" with God, self, and others. In this sense, the self-giving perichoretic acts of each Person serve to make one perfect communion; and the very communion-making acts, at the same time, make each Person agentive and enhance each Person's particularity as the Son, Father, or Spirit. Accordingly, the perichoretic identity affirms both communion-forming-selves and self-thriving-community, which make life-sharing-selves-in-relationship.

Such a perichoretic understanding of identity derives not only from self-consciousness but also from agapeic love. Grenz (2001) clearly makes this point. A postmodern perspective says that we are relational because of our social interactions. As the postmodern maxim suggests, "to be an individual person is to be in relationship" and our identity "grows continually through interaction with other individuals and with the wider world around us" (Peters 1993, 15). In a Meadian perspective, as self-reflexive beings, we are who we are by reflecting ourselves through social interactions. This notion can mean, however, that one might say that we are not self-reflexive and, thereby, not relational if we are not interacting socially. In other words, we interact socially; therefore, we are relational but not necessarily vice versa. In this regard, we are defined *by* relationships but not necessarily defined *as* relational beings. Thus, the social psychological perspective of relationality based on the conception of self-reflexive interactions has a limit in scope.

Overcoming the Meadian tradition's limitation, the trinitarian perspective of identity helps us understand that the divine perichoretic relationality derives primarily from agapeic love that motivates perichoretic movements and communion of the Trinity. Grenz (2001) maintains that the mutual agapeic love comprises the divine unity of three self-giving Persons who compose one perichoretic communion of God. Thus, through the self-giving agape, each divine Person makes room for one another, embraces the others in the self, and establishes joyful communion of love. Likewise, by pouring the self-giving agape, the Trinity willingly opens an inhabitable Space for the creation, contains it, and indwells in it.

Thus, a nuanced difference between Meadian and trinitarian perspectives of identity is that the Meadian person gives the self to him or herself reflexively through interactions, but the trinitarian person gives the self to others and reflects him or herself in relation to others. The Meadian perspective of identity focuses on self-reflexivity as a means of serving the self, by which persons construct their own identities by reflecting themselves through interactions and relationships with other social actors. The trinitarian theological perspective of perichoretic identity emphasizes self-giving agape through which each person mutually serves one another, builds the community with others, and thereby constructs his or her identity with them.

Communal life requires love not only in a Christian sense but also in a general sense. Personalist philosopher John Macmurray makes this point clear. Viewing community as the context in which true personhood emerges, he asserts that community exists "for the sake of friendship and presupposes relationships built on love," whereas a society "might organize around a common purpose" (LaCugna 1991, 258). According to him, community results from free agentive persons who relate not out of fear of the other or fear for self but out of love—like the family as the original human community. Even though humans often fail to live out such a love-sharing community, what Macmurray argues conveys an important point regarding personhood and community. Summarizing this point, LaCugna contends that a "person is a heterocentric, inclusive, free, relational agent" (259).

Gergen states that we have no language yet to articulate socially constructed agency (Rathbun, 2005). Through a theological lens of perichoresis, one can contend that persons are relational beings with agency who contribute to the community building, which, in turn, is a foundation for nurturing personal agency in a perichoretic interplay. We have called such a relational person a reflexive/agentive self-in-relationship. This term has derived from combined efforts of social psychology and trinitarian theology in searching for an adequate metaphor of balancing between identity and relationality and between theological commitment and cultural inclusion. From this trinitarian perspective, persons are not selves-trapped-in-relationship but selves-agentive/reflexive-in-relationship through agapeic love and perichoretic communion. The contemporary theological perspective of the *imago Dei* makes a connection between trinitarian relationality and human relationality by viewing the image of God as humanity's essential/ontological relationality-in-love.

In this sense, perichoresis sheds light on the relation between persons and a community of individuals. Perichoresis does not unify the differences under one single powerful person by whom differences are to be cut off. Also, perichoretic identity does not unify the otherness under one common universal principle by which differences are void. Rather, a perichoretic unity leads us to a community in which we make space for one another and mutually share a life of communion-forming and self-thriving with one another by engaging differences and being united with the otherness. In this perichoretic community, persons open themselves to one another, giving and receiving love that unites them. By doing so, the perichoretic community validates both the unity and diversity of the persons and nurtures a self-thriving and community-forming relationship.

SUMMARY

From our empirical findings and a social psychological perspective, we have viewed pastoral identity as a social and relational construction mutually created through dynamic care-giving and receiving interactions between pastoral caregivers and seekers within a specific social context. Pastoral identity is socially constituted and constructed through caregivers' agentive interplay with (adapting to and resisting) a structural power in a macro-level context and through their self-reflexive interactions with care receivers in micro-level everyday practices. Such a construct of pastoral identity is possible when the self can co-exist with and thrive in relationships. The agency and reflexivity of the self thus work—despite the postmodern structure that may cause de-centeredness and fragmentation of the self—by adapting to and attempting to change the social structure.

Such a perspective of identity challenges contemporary theology to embrace personal agency and social structure together as complementary constituents of identity. Fortunately, such conceptualization of identity is theologically compatible with a contemporary trinitarian perspective of perichoresis. In Christian theology, the concept of perichoresis derives not only from depicting the Trinity's inner-trinitarian relationship but also from articulating dynamic relationships between God and creation envisioned by the union of the Son's divine and human natures. From this theological excursion, this chapter has opened a door to apply perichoresis to a human personhood and community.

Especially, God's perichoretic interplays within the Trinity and with the creation shed light on our discussion of pastoral identity and help us delineate ways of constructing pastoral identity in care-giving interactions and in relation to the structural power. The theological perspective of identity in light of perichoresis sets the foundation for integrating self and relation, unity and multiplicity, stability and fluidity, and groundedness and inclusiveness. Thus, this perichoretic understanding of identity has provided us with a new theological framework through which we can see care-giving practices and pastoral identity construction in a renewed way. Pastoral care-giving is kind of perichoretic interplay through which care partners build a community that nurtures personal agency. Thus, pastoral care and counseling nurture both community-building and self-thriving relationships through perichoretic interplay, as will be seen in the final chapter.

6

Perichoretic Pastoral Identity in Caregiving Practices

PERICHORESIS IS AN EXCELLENT theological concept and metaphor for our whole discussion of pastoral identity. First of all, perichoresis gives us a lens through which we can describe how pastoral care partners interact in their care-giving relationships by opening their worlds and accepting each other in their spaces. This perichoretic process of care-giving and receiving allows the partners to become a sustaining community without losing each person's identities. Moreover, through perichoresis, we can find a way of articulating how pastoral caregivers authentically open themselves to the otherness of care-seekers, especially those who come from diverse cultural and religious contexts, while at the same time faithfully positioning themselves in their theological wisdom. Furthermore, perichoresis offers a sound theological metaphor by which we can delineate how God engages our care-giving ministry with God's presence and work and how we can participate in the Divine reality.

Thus, perichoresis extends its application to pastoral care-giving relationships in which caregivers hold an agency of self-reflexivity and other-embracement in relationship by making room for others (and God) and containing the otherness. Using perichoresis as a major metaphor, I sum up the book in this final chapter. The chapter is comprised of three main sections. In the first section, I summarize the process and main theses of the volume. I then develop principles for pastoral care and counseling and envision a way of pastoral identity construction within daily care-giving practices. In the last main section, I redefine pastoral identity, wrapping up the previous discussions. Concluding this project, I will articulate implications of this study and note future areas of study.

IS PASTORAL IDENTITY SOCIALLY CONSTRUCTED?

Throughout the book, we have mainly inquired whether pastoral identity is socially constructed. The question derives partly from my research on historical understandings of pastoral identity and contemporary work environments of pastoral care-giving. Traditional understandings of pastoral identity often rest in the interiority of the persons who work in the name of God and their faith communities. However, contemporary care-giving environments have changed, and the caregivers need to find a way of constructing their identities along the shifting environments. Such recognition was the starting point of my research question and set the context for looking at pastoral identity from a renewed perspective.

In the field of pastoral care-giving and theology, pastoral identity is of tremendous importance, not only providing pastoral persons with values, meanings, and boundaries of their ministries but also helping them maintain proper relationships with their care-partners, faith communities, the Divine, institutions, and other professionals. Nonetheless, pastoral care practitioners and theologians have often articulated their pastoral identity based mainly on how they perceive themselves in relation to their faith communities. They have claimed their denominational endorsement, belongingness, and commitment to the community of faith as the basis of their pastoral identity. Accordingly, traditional approaches to pastoral identity have often conceptualized it as the inner depth of the persons, connected it with theological and ecclesial commitment, and handled the concept from a developmental perspective. This approach has earned credit for emphasizing the importance of theology and faith communities and the inner integrity of pastoral persons.

Such a traditional and community-based construction of pastoral identity, however, becomes less relevant to contemporary work environments of chaplains and pastoral counselors. Pastoral care and counseling in healthcare settings become independent from the faith community, and secular institutional work situations often require the caregivers to promote a generic spirituality irrespective of their theological and faith traditions. As a result, in these work environments, emphasizing the integration of mental healthcare with theology becomes a challenging precept to some pastoral caregivers. Thus, contemporary intercultural and multifaith contexts require a new way of looking at pastoral identity.

As the field has encountered postmodern, multicultural, and international contexts of pastoral theology and practices since the 1990s, new perspectives and paradigms become available. Thus, the field has evolved via a new frame of perspectives, methods, and contexts. In this sense, the field has a task of establishing a renewed framework of reference for pastoral identity. As a way of responding to that task, we have explored social construction of pastoral identity as one of the new frameworks.

From such a point of view, the initial inquiry we had pursued was to look closely at what pastoral caregivers actually do in their everyday practices in order to form their unique identities. The study, as a whole, has thus tried to find an answer to the following question: "In postmodern, intercultural, and multifaith contexts, how do contemporary pastoral caregivers establish pastoral identity within their daily care-giving practices?"

To investigate the question, I have first attempted to find out how contemporary chaplains and pastoral counselors form their pastoral identities in their care-giving ministry. The question has helped me understand how pastoral practitioners interact with care-seekers and construct their identities while providing care and counseling to them. The inquiry has also led me to another question about a relationship between personal agency and social structure. When the care partners interact with each other and construct their identities, how do social structure and cultural contexts that govern their interactions and practices influence their identity construction? This question has further led me to a theological inquiry. How can we theologically respond to the relationships between care-giving partners and between agency and structure?

Thus, to investigate the initial question, we have raised three main questions:

1. How do contemporary pastoral caregivers form pastoral identity in their daily care-giving practices?

2. How do postmodern cultures and contexts influence and shape pastoral care-giving practices and identity construction? How do caregivers respond to such contemporary environments?

3. How do these empirical and social scientific discourses inform a theological discourse of identity, and how can theology respond to them? What theological model can provide pastoral caregivers with a framework for constructing their identities in postmodern, intercultural, and multifaith contexts?

The first question has taken us directly to discuss a pastoral identity that is socially constructed between caregivers and seekers. The next question involves a pastoral identity culturally constructed between human agency and social structure. And the final question embraces the two questions from a theological perspective.

SOCIAL CONSTRUCTION OF PASTORAL IDENTITY

After examining the three questions, we can summarize three important points of pastoral identity. First of all, from the empirical study, we have found that pastoral identity is constructed socially through interactions and relationships between caregivers and seekers in their efforts to reach a shared goal of care and counseling. In responding to the second question, we have found from a social psychological discourse and the empirical study that postmodern contexts influence pastoral caregivers' daily practices and identity construction, but the caregivers also work to change cultural contexts by creatively performing their religious calls. Thus, social structure and personal agency come together in the construction of identity. Finally, from a trinitarian perspective, pastoral care partners construct their identities through the dynamic interplay between agency and structure, between groundedness and openness to diversity, and between human partners and the Divine.

Pastoral Identity Constructed in Care-Giving Relationships

To address the first question, I employed a qualitative study. The study combined surveys and interviews based on a grounded theory method. Grounded theory was a helpful resource for the study, offering a useful tool for collecting and analyzing data and a framework to generate a theory. The empirical study set the context for addressing the question by providing a description of lived experiences of the caregivers and concrete data of their perceptions and practices. Participants in the study indicated that pastoral care-giving situations sparked them to think of their identities. The pastoral clinicians also articulated that care-seekers contributed to constructing a pastoral identity through various care-giving interactions and pastoral relationships.

Accordingly, guided by grounded theory, the study has theorized an interactional, intersubjective, and constructive model of pastoral identity in the following way:

> Pastoral caregivers construct pastoral identity through care-giving interactions and relationships with care-seekers. In pastoral

encounters, the care partners interact in mutual efforts to find alternatives to the seeker's predicaments and, in this course of care-giving, construct their identities. In this process, the pastoral caregiver and seeker mutually allow the other to enter his or her world to find existential (and theological) meanings. In addition, the care partners at times realize that God is present and acts with them and that the caregiver has been a partaker of the divine presence and work.

The findings are compatible with a contemporary symbolic interactionist approach to identity that social psychologists widely accept. Thus, symbolic interactionism supports the findings and offers an explanation of them in a micro-level interactional analysis.

Pastoral Identity in Negotiation with Cultural and Institutional Powers

Such a constructive model explains how contemporary pastoral caregivers construct their identities in their everyday practices. However, the study of identity needs to combine the analysis of micro-level interactions into a macro-level analysis of postmodern social structure that affects daily interactions. Thus, the micro-level analysis of everyday interactions between caregivers and seekers leaves a new question about the roles culture and structure play on individual interactions. One should not discuss identity without considering systematic powers and disciplines that govern everyday life and practices. Thus, a challenge from postmodern scholars sets another context for our discussion of pastoral identity. How do structural powers and cultures influence personal agency? How does agency respond to that influence? These issues relate to what the second question asks: "How do postmodern cultures and contexts influence and shape pastoral caregiving practices and identity construction? How do caregivers respond to such contemporary environments?"

From a macro-level perspective, a postmodernist analysis of self and identity and a social constructionist perspective of identity are helpful resources. I have drawn on these discourses of identity and discussed a postmodern perspective on identities and its limitations. These perspectives indicate that contemporary understandings of identity have shifted their approaches to relational and constructive aspects of identity formation. From postmodern and late-modern perspectives, I have articulated that there are two paradoxical dilemmas of constructing identities in postmodern, intercultural, and multifaith contexts. The first one is a paradoxical relationship between self and social structure. Postmodern social relationships often prevent people from having a centered self and cause a diluted sense of identities. Likewise, another dilemma relates to a paradox between groundedness and openness to diversity. How can pastoral identities be grounded in existential and theological life experiences and also be responsive to diverse situations and meanings?

From a social constructionist approach to those paradoxes, self and relation (agency and structure) should not be contradictory but complementary. Thus, we have explored how a recent social psychological perspective provides a framework for resolving the paradoxical dilemmas. The participants in the empirical study also indicate that they construct their pastoral identities with care-seekers by creatively responding to cultural influences. Through these explorations, we have reached a point where pastoral caregivers can construct their identities despite postmodern structure and conditions. The following is the summery of the discussion:

> Postmodern, intercultural, and multifaith contexts impact the care partners' interactions and their identity construction. These postmodern structural powers may often prevent pastoral professionals from claiming a pastoral authority in light of their ecclesial commitment and traditional grand narratives of theology or their already implanted inner-directed theologies. Pastoral practitioners need to (re)construct a theological perspective on lived experiences of the clients by empathically understanding their situations and contextualizing caregivers' own theology while remaining grounded. Thus, by using agency, pastoral caregivers interactionally construct their identity with care-seekers, both conforming to and working to change the contemporary cultural structure. In the process of constructing their identities, the care practitioners ground themselves in care-giving practices and relationships with care-seekers from a theological perspective and at the same time open themselves to the otherness of care-seekers and institutional expectations.

Pastoral caregivers have to adapt to institutional and cultural disciplines in many ways. However, the caregivers, as reflexive agents, do not merely accept a passively imposed identity but actively construct their identities by finding a way of embodying their vertical and horizontal calls. Thus, pastoral identity is socially constructed in negotiation with structural and cultural powers.

Pastoral Identity in Dynamic Interplay

The empirical study and the social psychological discussions of identity show how pastoral identity dynamically interplays with personal agency, social structure, centrality, and diversity. Interactions between the care partners are a basic layer of the interplay, on top of which is an invisible interplay with the Divine. Structural powers and disciplines may interrupt and facilitate the first interplay by interacting with the human agency of the care partners. The caregivers employ their agency in a dynamic relationship to care-seekers and institutional culture by helping the seeker and creatively positioning themselves on the theological ground along with openness to diversity. This discussion has led us to the third question, a theological one: How do these empirical and social scientific discourses inform a theological discourse of identity, and how can theology respond to them? What theological model can provide pastoral caregivers with a framework for constructing their identities in postmodern, intercultural, and multi-faith contexts?

Balancing the paradoxical nature of pastoral identity challenges a theological discourse of identity. To handle the paradoxical problems, I have drawn a theological perspective of identity based on the trinitarian understanding of perichoresis. The trinitarian perspective of identity provides an excellent theological model for resolving the dilemmas of balancing the paradox. A renewed perspective of the triune God within the Trinity and with the creation has changed the traditional view of identity by embracing personal agency and social structure together and holding a grounded identity with openness to diversity. In light of the trinitarian understanding of perichoresis, we can articulate the following theological perspective of identity:

> The triune God's perichoretic identity interplays in and out among the three divine Persons while making them one perfect social Being without swallowing up each distinct agentic Personhood. And the Trinity's perichoretic life of love overflows to a perichoretic engagement and participation between God and the creaturely beings (as in the Incarnate Jesus Christ's two natures). The divine perichoresis invites the finite and limited beings into the perichoretic divine dance and embraces their otherness in the divine inhabitable space without losing the grounded holiness.

The trinitarian concept of perichoresis offers a theological framework for a dynamic interplay of pastoral identity. The perichoretic understanding of personhood serves as a foundation for describing how pastoral caregivers and receivers can construct their identities. The caregivers construct identities by interacting with care-seekers (and God) and by grounding themselves theologically while at the same time being authentically open to the other and creatively interacting with culture.

Pastoral identity interplays between the care partners while making them a caring community without gulping down each particular personhood and agency. Rather, pastoral identity develops as the partners open their worlds by creating inhabitable spaces for each other. Thus, the perichoretic perspective of identity creates a dynamic integration between self and relation, between agency and structure, and between groundedness and inclusiveness. Perichoretic construction of identity offers a theological framework for human (and pastoral) identity and has profound implications for constructing identities in contemporary pluralistic contexts.

By responding to these paradoxical problems discussed in the previous chapters, I have articulated the ways pastoral caregivers can construct their pastoral identities in daily care-giving practices. From empirical, scientific, and theological perspectives, one can summarize that reflexive and agentic pastoral care partners socially construct their identities within their perichoretic community of love, compassion, and liberation. In the perichoretic community, the pastoral caregivers negotiate their therapeutic and theological positions with care-seekers by adapting to and resisting social structural powers and through creative embodiment of their vertical and horizontal calls.

PASTORAL CARE-GIVING AS PERICHORETIC INTERPLAY

Perichoresis has profound implications not only for theological and ethical constructions but also for pastoral theology building and care-giving practices. In this section, I will articulate principles for pastoral care and counseling that derive from our previous discussions. I hope this section will shed light on how a pastoral caregiver, as a person-reflexive/agentive-in-relationship, can build a life-sharing perichoretic communion with care-seekers.

As we have seen, perichoresis is a concept for articulating not only inner-trinitarian relationships of the three divine Persons but also God's relationships with human beings and the world. This perichoretic community is "the ground of every other type of communion" (LaCugna 1991, 259). In the Philippians' kenotic passage, Paul uses the Son's kenotic engagement as a model for an earthly ecclesial community: "Let the same mind be in you that was in Christ Jesus" (Phil 2:5). Thus, the perichoresis extends its application to human relationships in which persons hold an agency of the self-reflexivity and other-embracement in relationship by making room for others and containing the otherness (e.g., Lawler 1995). In such a perichoretic community, people are not trapped in a web interwoven by superficial relationships; instead, they proactively build relationships by embracing others in themselves and meaningfully interacting with them.

I believe that counseling relationships, especially pastoral care-giving relationships, are one of the outstanding spaces in which the care partners can build such kind of perichoretic community. There are four key themes in such a perichoretic view of pastoral care-giving: agentive community-building, reciprocal self-giving interactions, perichoretic space-creation, and a perichoretic dance out of compassion/love.

Pastoral Care-Giving as Promoting Agency by Building Community

Care-giving is establishing a relationship and, thereby, fostering healing and liberation by empowering care-seekers to find meanings in and alternatives to their predicaments. In this process, caregivers do two important things: build rapport and support the care-seeker's agency. Both acts must take place in care-giving. On the one hand, without establishing a relational community, caregivers cannot empower the self of the care-seeker. On the other hand, without fostering the self-agency, the therapeutic relationship often engenders the seeker's dependency on his or her caregiver and can trap the self in the relationship. Accordingly, social actors in a care-giving community should build a self-nurturing relationship in which caregivers empower the partners to find and use self-agency.

Pastoral care-giving furthers this process by attending to existential and spiritual aspects of life and offering a holistic approach to care-seekers' problems. Pastoral caregivers empower clients' agency and connect it with a spiritual power on which the seekers (can) rely. As chaplain Bill (I3) contends, God's empowerment involves care-giving situations in which caregivers and/or seekers find human powerlessness. Accordingly, pastoral care-giving often tries to build not only a caregiver-receiver relationship but also God-human rapport. Through building rapport, pastoral care-giving enhances not only a human agentive self but also cherishes a divinely empowered self. Therefore, pastoral care-giving consists in nurturing agentive self-in-community by community-building social actors (caregiver, seekers, and God).

In social psychology, contemporary social psychologists see the self as a product of social interaction of reflexive individuals who hold "agency, creative action, and the possibility of emancipatory political movements" (Callero 2003, 120). In this sense, the interacting community of individuals constructs an identity that is reflexive and agentic in relation to the others. From a trinitarian perspective, the Trinity constructs divine identities by forming a perichoretic interaction and communion made by three agentic Persons in which each divine Person has a distinctive relationship with one another. Thus, trinitarian Persons' formation of a divine community nurtures agentic personal selves of the Persons and vice versa.

The empirical research findings show such a pastoral care-giving phenomenon. Building a connection to and relationship with potential care-seekers and actual care-receivers is a crucial task for the pastoral caregivers who have participated in the research. As they establish rapport, they are also interested in finding the care-seekers' connection to and relationship with God and try to help clients strengthen the relationship. They seek to help care-seekers have "a sense of spiritual connection" and "a sense of the presence and reality of God in the midst of their struggles" (I3) while building a rapport with the clients. Also, the caregivers foster the self-agency of the seekers who walk "in the valley of pain, fear, or anxiety" by accompanying them as friends (I15). By doing so, the caregivers may help care-receivers see God, who quietly approaches, walks with them, and encourages them, as Jesus did with two disciples going to Emmaus (Luke 24). In such a process, pastoral professionals not only nurture the clients' agentive selves but also promote the agency by bridging it with their senses of the divine empowerment.

Pastoral Care-Giving as a Reciprocal Self-Giving Interaction

Pastoral care-giving that focuses on promoting agency and building a community is not unidirectional but mutual. Rapport-building in a care-giving community cannot take place through a monologue (one giving and another receiving). Rather, the care-giving process ought to be interactional and reciprocal. Contemporary care-giving relationships focus on reciprocity and mutuality between the care partners. Thus, mutual efforts and intersubjective interactions constitute building a relational community that engenders agency. The community-formation and agency-enhancement start and result from reciprocal care-giving interactions.

The view of community as a construction made by social actors is evident in Mead's philosophy. Mead views a human community or society as constitutive of social interactions between parts of the community. Mead's scheme sees society not as a social structure or system, but rather as "a process of building up joint actions" and "a vast number of occurring joint actions" (Blumer 1969, 75). Moreover, perichoretically agentive relationships within the trinitarian community consist of reciprocal interaction and indwelling of relational subjects. As a trinitarian theology has shown, perichoresis is "an interplay of self-giving that calls forth reciprocal sharing of life" (M. T. Marshall 2003, 145).

In this sense, to be in a care-giving relationship is to interact in a dynamic of mutual giving and receiving. Mutually giving oneself by sharing life stories with the partner, which in turn constructs a renewed self, is what pastoral care-giving is about. In distinction from one's monological self-giving that carries on the entire burden of sustaining the relationship, the mutual self-giving builds a community that achieves a shared goal of healing and liberation. Through such interplay of sharing and receiving, the care partners participate in each other's life.

The research participants clearly state how care-seekers act in care-giving relationships. Care-seekers are not just recipients of care and counseling but also contributors of care-giving. When pastoral practitioners open their eyes to the care-seekers' parts in care-giving relationships, they may see a mutual enterprise emerging. The research findings show how care-giving partners interact by their agentic initiatives in forming a healing community in which the actors construct their identities. While caregivers introduce their pastoral ministry and are present, listen to, and accompany care-seekers, the counterparts accept (or reject) care-giving ministry and open their world of pain and predicaments by telling their life stories and requesting for help. Such reciprocal interactions help the care partners form a deep community and sustain care-seekers' self-agency.

Pastoral Care-Giving as Perichoretic Space-Creating

At the heart of pastoral care-giving as a reciprocal self-giving interaction is perichoretic space-making. In (pastoral) care-giving, the care partners make a space for one another in order to interact and have a deep relationship with each other. For pastoral caregivers, this space-creating in care-giving means *inviting* the seeker to their hospitable care, *providing* him or her with an inhabitable space in which the seeker can share his or her life stories, and *opening* the door to a spiritual space in which the care-receiver may find God's presence. Care-seekers also create a space for their caregiver by accepting him or her, sharing their lived experiences, and opening the "deepest, darkest world," in one interviewee's (I20) terms. In such opened spaces, pastoral care partners deepen their relationship, find a shared sense of rapport, make meanings of predicaments and human encounters, and envision a spiritual encounter.

From a trinitarian perspective, the kenotic Persons mutually offer one another an inviting, open space in their eternal perichoresis. By making themselves inhabitable to one another and preparing a wide space and inhabitable room in themselves, the trinitarian Persons interact with one another and make a life-sharing community. The mutually dynamic interplay among the three Persons deepens their divine fellowships within that embracing space, making threeness oneness and vice versa. Such kenotic and perichoretic interactions envision a divine dance. To put it in Lawler's (1995) words, "God is triune freely and dynamically, because the three Thous joyfully dance and interweave hand in hand, making room for one another in intricate relatedness and communion" (53). This mutual interplay of the perichoretic Trinity is what makes the Trinity equalitarian and reciprocal.

Our empirical research findings have clearly delineated such spacing-creating interactions between pastoral caregivers and receivers. Pastoral caregivers, as hospitable-space creators, humble themselves as fellow humans, are present with care-seekers, and listen to their stories and needs. By attentively listening to lived experiences of the care-seekers, pastoral practitioners open their safe spaces to embrace the clients' pains and sufferings. Such safe spaces allow the care-seekers to go into a deeper relationship with the caregivers in which the seekers also create their own spaces where the helpers can enter. The care-receivers' created spaces become a door to hope, healing, and divine mystery, as pastoral care-giving proceeds.

Metaphorically speaking, a pastoral listener offers an open space in which the story-teller shares a story of pain and predicament. By listening, the hearer can enter deeply into the story-teller's spacious worlds. Thereby, the inhabitable room created by listening becomes a space for potential healing and meaning-making. Accordingly, pastoral care and counseling offer a hospitable space in which the care-seeker can make meaning (S31), create a story for the mystery to unfold (S6), and manage a safe holding environment (S9).

The creating of space is especially important in a postmodern, diverse cultural and religious context. In pastoral care and counseling, when spiritual powers that the clients rely on and the caregivers represent are different, pastoral practitioners need to be careful in making an inhabitable space in which the care-seekers can enter and build a relationship with caregivers. Instead of offering a space from traditional grand narratives of theology or an already implanted fixed theology, pastoral caregivers should

> possess a critical or prophetic or reforming or apophatic element in their religious belief. One must be able to stand back from one's own religious claims, explore where they came from, what moral and religious idolatries they foster, what emotional and political needs they serve, and how they have evolved as one has developed from child to adult, laity to clergy, and insider to one willing to engage one's tradition with outsiders. (Miller-McLemore 2008, 13)

Thus, instead of seeking to convince, convert, and transform the "strangers," pastoral professionals need to offer a space, allow care-seekers to enter it, embrace their predicaments and otherness, and, thereby, find a way of constructing a shared religious value for liberating the care-seekers from the predicaments.

Christ's kenosis refers to God's voluntary openness toward the creation in order to allow inhabitable room in which finite creatures become truly free to be themselves in relation to God. In this sense, a kind of kenosis that creates a pastoral space allows room for the care-seekers to find true liberation in God. Thus, pastoral care-giving advocates authentic openness to diversity in building a care-giving community with care-seekers and at the same time respects pastoral care providers' uniqueness and groundedness in relation to God.

Pastoral Care-Giving as a Perichoretic Dance out of Love and Compassion

The reciprocal self-giving interactions in the perichoretic trinitarian community are possible because of the love that the Trinity is and shares. According to Zizioulas (1985), love is constitutive of God's being and causes God to be who God is since it produces communion among divine Persons. Grenz (2001) contends that "God is love . . . not only because the first trinitarian person loves but also in that the divine essence is the agape that characterizes the life of the triune God" (314). For the dynamic trinitarian perichoresis, Stramara (1998) further articulates a divine love among the Persons. He argues that trinitarian Persons share "mutual admiration, each Person 'falling all over' the other, glorying in the other. In a sense, the Persons are continually 'falling in love.' Authentic love disposes persons to be 'mutually inclusive'" (261). Thus, in the communion of love, each divine Person comes to be by making room for the others and pouring him/herself into them. Thus, the love found at the heart of the triune God is constitutive of God's trinity and unity.

Love and compassion are core essences in pastoral care-giving. One of the most common emotional reactions that the research participants feel toward the helped is compassion and empathy. Because of these empathic qualities of love, pastoral caregivers are able to be with the care-seekers (by being willing to open emotional, psychological, spiritual, and social spaces to embrace their pains) and accompany the care-seekers in their journey to grief and hope, and even as they face death. The more comfortable room a pastoral caregiver can offer with greater compassion, the more deeply the care-seeker opens his or her inner world and the greater the honor the caregiver has in accessing the world. Thus, the love and compassion that underlie pastoral care and counseling penetrate the space of the care-receiver and introduce healing and liberation into that space.

Accordingly, what makes pastoral care-giving an instrument of God's healing is not merely the caregivers' self-reflexive agency through which they can reflect on themselves in relation to care-seekers and interact with them. Rather, the power of pastoral care and counseling comes from the pastoral relationship in which God's love and compassion (and those of the caregiver) overflow to the oppressed and marginalized. As pastoral counselor Linda (I20) believes, pastoral care-providers do not minister to people in their own power; rather, they are aware that they are conduits of the love of God to the people with whom they work. As compassionate agents of God and the embodiment of God's love, pastoral clinicians thus reflect God's love, healing, and liberation. Pastoral healing and care-giving is not merely based on what humans might do but rather on what God does for humans and how they accept God's gifts of loving, healing, and liberating presence. The pastoral relationship out of love and compassion that reflects God's engagement with humans leads to a perichoretic community of enhancing the agency and healing.

In that community, one may find a perichoretic dance between the care partners. At first, as a divine representative, a pastoral caregiver makes room for potential care-seekers by humbling him or herself like them in suffering. In turn, the care-seekers make (or close) room for the humble visitor by welcoming (or rejecting) him or her to (or from) their places. The visitor also opens his or her heartfelt space by being present with care-seekers and listening to their stories. The care-seekers enter the space and dwell in it, sharing their lived experiences and suffering. The indwelling place where the storytellers share their lives and crises becomes an opening space where the listener penetrates their world. In their world-space, the caregiver has a companionship with them, which makes him or her deeply compassionate and attentive to care-seekers' sufferings and calls for help. Calling to be their caregiver and pastor is an invitation to the empathic listener to come in the care-seekers' deepest and darkest world. In the co-indwelling communion, the perichoretic partners share (theological) reflection and make theological and existential meanings with each other.

Mysteriously, the very communion made by the agentive partners is a holy space where God is present. In the communion, God has been with them, silently listening to their conversations and being present in the suffering and in their encounters. The care partners may recognize God's perichoretic engagement in their communion in which God allows their participation in the divine communion. And such perichoretic engagement and participation becomes a shadow of eschatological perichoresis that God and the redeemed beings will share eternally.

REDEFINING PASTORAL IDENTITY

From this renewed perspective of pastoral care and counseling, we can now redefine pastoral identity. In the beginning of the study, we preliminarily defined pastoral identity from a sociological-cultural perspective that supplements a psychological-developmental perspective. From this perspective, we have seen pastoral identity as a social and relational construction mutually created by pastoral caregivers and seekers through a dynamic interplay of care-giving interactions within a specific social context. Since we have examined empirical, social psychological, and theological perspectives of identity, we can re-describe pastoral identity as follows:

> Pastoral identity refers to, but is not limited to, a social construction of pastoral relationships created in the process of dynamic interactions among the care partners, culture, and the Divine in a specific care-giving context. Pastoral identity is constructed in the process of care-giving in which the care partners enhance personal agency in a community-building relationship through a perichoretic interaction of love, healing, and liberation. Such a constructed pastoral identity pays attention to calls from care-seekers as well as God and, thereby, opens the way to creative transformation through mutual interactions between the care partners. This renewed definition includes three important aspects of pastoral identity: pastoral identity as identity-in-pastoral-relationships, as a twofold calling, and as pastoral trans-formation.

Pastoral Identity is an Identity-in-Pastoral-Relationship

Identities do not appear in a vacuum but in relationships with others. However, identities do not occur automatically in relationships but in reflexive interactions in which the agentive self reflects her or himself in relation to others. This maxim is what contemporary social psychology and trinitarian theology try to formulate as a core of their theories. The trinitarian Persons form the identity of the Trinity through their reflexive interactions or perichoretic self-giving communications. In the perichoretic communion, the Persons both establish a perfect community and support particular selves. Such identities do not change as they interact with the otherness of human beings or other creatures. Through perichoretic interactions, the trinitarian Persons include that otherness while remaining grounded in the eternal divinity.

Likewise, pastoral identity is an identity-in-pastoral-relationship and an embodiment of pastoral relationships. It does not automatically appear in a pastor's mind as an inner-directed phenomenon. Pastoral identity is socially constructed in a pastoral relationship in which the pastoral partners find who they are through mutually reflexive interactions and perichoretic communications. In the pastoral relationship, a pastoral caregiver experiences a potential space of reflexiveness, the reflecting back of his or her experiences (in relation to care-seekers) upon him or herself. Pastoral identity is embedded in reflexivity of one's self in relation to those needing help. Through such reflexive processes, pastoral practitioners broaden their understanding of who they are and how they can be of help. In this regard, pastoral care-seekers are not only recipients of care-giving but also contributors to the pastoral identity construction (as well as co-creators of their own identities). Thus, pastoral caregivers not only create hospitable room for the clients in need but also receive their invitations to their spacious worlds.

This identity-in-pastoral-relationship expands pastoral identity to identity-in-perichoretic-relationships with care-seekers and with God. If pastoral identity is only born in pastoral relationships with the helped, then the identity is likely to be shaky as well as fluid, and inclusive but not grounded. A clear relationship with God and connection to the theological community and tradition is an important aspect of what it means to be pastoral. Thus, pastoral identity consists of pastoral self-in-perichoretic-relationships with care-seekers and God, the relationship embedded in and embodied by the perichoretic community. In this framework, pastoral caregivers can find a resolution to a paradox between self and relation (or agency and structure) and between grounding in a theological view and inclusiveness in cultural relationships. Therefore, pastoral identity is an embodiment of perichoretic pastoral relationships with care-seekers and God.

Pastoral Identity is a Dynamic Call not only from God but also from the Seekers

A socially-constructed pastoral identity is, accordingly, a call from the care-seekers who ask for help from the pastoral person. As the research participants have indicated, finding and responding to "what is being called for" is a core of their pastoral identity. Sensing this horizontal call often requires the helper to listen carefully to care-seekers' lived experiences. The calling from care-seekers derives from sensing and realizing their deepest needs and participating in their lived experiences. Thus, pastoral caregivers listen to the request for help from care-seekers, and this call for help often provokes pastoral caregivers' identity. Thus, pastoral identity derives not only from the primary, vertical call from God but also from specific, horizontal calls from the care-seekers.

H. Richard Niebuhr (1956) proposes a fourfold typology of the call to Christian ministry. The four calls to ministry are a call to be a Christian, a secret call that directs one into a special form of ministry, a providential call that describes one's gifts and graces and marks one as an apparent candidate for carrying out the ministry, and an ecclesiastical call by means of which a congregation or other ecclesial institution certifies a person for ministry in a particular setting. Although denominations endorse pastoral practitioners to work outside their own faith communities and congregations, the professionals also have another call that confirms these four calls. Many research participants have confirmed their calling through their (often "unchurched") care-seekers' call for help.

These calls are both supplementary and paradoxical. The horizontal calling that comes from care-seekers' request for help is a confirmation for their divine calling. Some others also see the calling from the horizon leading them to specific care-giving ministries. When a pastoral person is not sure about his or her call from God, specific calls from others can help the person to find a right direction. However, particular calls do not legitimate the primary call. Without a clear call from God, the pastoral caregiver may be confused by the many different callings from the care-seekers in particular needs and situations. Moreover, when the care-seekers react negatively to the care-provider's ministry, these negative reactions (or calls, if you will) might shake the primary call. Nonetheless, pastoral identity consists of a primary vertical call and a specific horizontal call. To echo Chaplain Julia's remarks, the vocation for pastoral care-giving is bestowed on the pastoral caregivers by the grace of God and given to them by those with whom they walk, who bless them in their ministry.

Pastoral Identity is Pastoral Transformation

Traditionally, theologians have viewed pastoral identity as part of pastoral formation. Thus, they believe that persons can achieve pastoral identity as they grow and develop over time in a formative process or training program. Supplementing this view of pastoral identity, this study proposes pastoral identity to be pastoral trans-formation across space in an interactive process. The latter view emphasizes an accidental, interactional aspect of identity construction among different social actors. This type of identity is not formed and sedimented over time but deconstructed and restructured over time as the interactions impact at a different level. Accordingly, this kind of pastoral identity is deconstructed, re-formed, and transformed within daily care-giving interactions and communications.

This transformative pastoral identity takes place when a pastoral caregiver invites care-seekers to full partnership in their perichoretic interactions. As Townsend (2002) points out, such a partnership leads not only the helped toward their own healing and liberation but also moves the caregiver toward a more challenging and renewed knowledge and awareness of who he or she is and who God is. This renewed perspective also allows the pastoral person new directions for empowering the clients. Accordingly, through such a perichoretic pastoral relationship, which makes possible a mutual transforming community, pastoral care partners socially construct a transformative pastoral identity.

In the same vein, socially constructing a pastoral identity is like a "hermeneutical experience" between a caregiver and a care-receiver (Gadamer 1975). When the otherness of the care-seeker who comes from a different cultural and faith tradition encounters the horizon of understanding of the pastoral caregiver, a hermeneutical experience takes place between both dialogue partners. Both the pastoral caregiver and seeker bring their own pre-understanding into the hermeneutical experience. The caregiver, on the one hand, should have critical self-awareness of his or her biases and interests. On the other hand, the helper can claim his or her own life of faith, which is part of who he or she is in a socio-historical location. Thus, a pastoral identity emerges from such a hermeneutical experience, which derives from a socio-historically embedded encounter.

Accordingly, in intercultural, pluralistic, and religiously diverse contexts, pastoral caregivers may approach the religious and cultural otherness of care-seekers by opening a hermeneutic space in which the horizons of understanding can fuse as each care-seeker brings to the encounter different cultural and religious experiences. In other words, a pastoral caregiver who upholds his or her own life of faith creates in an inclusive space a co-understanding of different lived experiences with each new care-seeker who has a different cultural and religious tradition from the caregiver.

Therefore, pastoral identity is not merely a pastoral formation in which a pastoral person grows and takes shape as a person called by God. Rather, pastoral identity is also a pastoral transformation in which the pastoral person interacts with his or her care-partners, gets challenged by their lived experiences, and enters into a mutually transforming relationship by hearing and learning from the marginalized. In this sense, pastoral identity is more than a sense of being a representative of a particular authority on the caregiver's side (e.g., his or her faith community and tradition). Pastoral identity connotes an image of a care-giving relationship in perichoretic interactions between care-seeker and giver who mutually reflect on and transform human predicaments (e.g., nurturer, co-sufferer, liberator, healer, sustainer, and/or empowerer).

IMPLICATIONS OF A SOCIALLY CONSTRUCTED PASTORAL IDENTITY

Throughout the review of contemporary theological, postmodern, and social psychological discourses, we have seen that they all agree that human identity is embedded in and embodied by relationships that the self adapts to and constructs. From this perspective, we have envisaged pastoral care-giving and pastoral identity. In a renewed view of pastoral care and counseling and pastoral identity, we can now draw implications not only for practices of care-giving, training, and supervision, but also for seminary education.

Practical Implications in Clinical Pastoral Contexts

Perichoretic pastoral identity delineated in this study sheds light on our clinical practices as pastoral caregivers and supervisors. We need to pay more attention to our care-partners as we develop a more mutual and egalitarian relationship with them, not only in terms of how we approach them but also in light of how they interact with us in that relationship. Through this interactive and intersubjective lens, pastoral clinicians can learn new insights into how to better care for and counsel people in need and how care-seekers will better see us as their partners and "pastors."

Such a relational perspective helps us formulate a renewed way of training and supervising our trainees and students. The traditional focus on developmental and formational aspects of training pastoral practitioners is still necessary for their pastoral formation. From this perspective, one sees supervision as a process of formation. In their colloquial symposium on "supervision and formation in Christian ministry," Herbert Anderson and his colleague (1994) examined the relationship between supervision and formation, thinking that formation occurs through supervision that prepares trainees and supervisees for ministry.

From a renewed perspective of pastoral formation, clinical supervisors further need to focus more on helping students to see their ministry to and interactions with care-seekers as a process of transformation. Supervisors should pay more attention to interactive and transformational dimensions of pastoral relationships with care-seekers. This study has determined that pastoral formation and identity construction take place through care-giving relationships. We not only see the supervisory relationship as forming pastoral identity, but we should also look at the care-giving partnership as de-forming, re-forming, and trans-forming pastoral identity (Townsend 2002).

Such a care-giving perspective and practice allows us an authentic pastoral relationship in which caregivers and receivers mutually and reciprocally interact in pastoral care and counseling. Perichoretic pastoral identity and care-giving practices open a possibility for establishing an equalitarian community via pastoral relationships based on the idea that God mutually indwells in the other equal Persons of the Trinity. As LaCugna (1991) asserts, a perichoretic relationship, "embodied in inclusiveness, community, and freedom, is thus the 'form of life' for God and the ideal of human beings whose communion with each other reflect the life of the Trinity" (273). Through such a pastoral relationship, we help our care-partners transform their oppressed and marginalized lives and stories by transforming our preset theological lenses of lived experiences.

Practical Implications for Theological Education

Bridging the gap between seminary education and practical ministry in a postmodern era has been one of the greatest challenges in practical theology (Chopp 1995; Farley 1983, 1988; Hough et al. 1985; Kelsey 1993; Scalise

2003). To connect the gap, those who work in ministry are concerned with connecting what they learned in seminary to what they find in ministry; those who educate students in seminary are primarily concerned about how well seminary education prepares students with proper curricula, hoping that the graduates can apply their learning to the practice of ministry. A problem regarding this approach to seminary education is an applicative model by which students learn first from seminary and apply what they have learned from school to practical ministry.

Viewing pastoral identity in this way, theological schools try to educate and train students to form their pastoral identity during the education so that when they are in the ministry they can perform wonderfully. Such an application model is likely to fail because, in this model, the identity formation is closely connected with education/training and is loosely applied to ministerial contexts. Addressing the concern about seminary education, Drew University professors Janet Fishburn and Neill Hamilton (1984) have reported interesting findings from their empirical study with their 22 graduates (three years after graduation) who were ministering to congregations. No participants could mention a single theology course that best integrated theology of ministry with their practices of ministry. The theologians assert that "the habit of connecting theology and practice was never formed in seminary" (111). The application model does not adequately integrate the knowledge of theological disciplines needed for ministry with the everyday practices of ministry. The schools thus need to train students to construct pastoral identity in their ministerial contexts rather than assume that education will help them establish a conclusive pastoral identity.

Informed by the renewed perspective of pastoral identity, we can now revisit the education model and reconstruct it into a relational and interactive model. Rightly observing the reality, the Fishburn and Hamilton pointed out that identity formation of beginning clergypersons depends on satisfying the expectations of the first parish they serve and that they need to "acquire the self-image of being a professional capable of providing the services a congregation declares it needs from its minister" (108). However, the theologians did not this kind of formation and separate ministers' sense of vocation from their responding to the parishioners' needs. The researchers saw the needs as "the incessant, manifold demands" that overshadow the pastors' sense of calling (ibid.). Thus, instead of exploring more how seminary education helps students respond to and interact with the needs and expectations of their ministry "partners," the theologians request that denominations supervise the fledging pastors carefully.

We have learned so far that pastoral identity is an identity embedded in and embodied by relationships and is an identity that emerges in pastoral relationships with and calls from parishioners and care-seekers. We now need to assist seminarians to better minister to and interact with parishioners by helping the students look at them as "partners" in ministry and create a hospitable and interactive space for them. Just as we cannot separate a pastoral identity from relationships with God and the ministry "partners," theological education should not disconnect the students' pastoral identities from their ministry contexts in which they encounter and interact with their "partners."

Moreover, this perspective goes beyond a formation-first model and moves toward a formation-practice-together model. The practice-theory-practice model proposed by many practical theologians is still a valid paradigm for practical theology (Browning 1991; Poling et al. 1985). The practice-theory-practice model is not sequentially ordered, however. One should mold theory and practice together like praxis (or theory-laden practice and practice-informing theory). Likewise, one does not first form pastoral identity and then perform pastoral practices accordingly. Rather, one forms and performs pastoral identity in practice at the same time. Thus, pastoral practitioners form their pastoral identities in the midst of their pastoral practices, and pastoral identity informs pastoral practices.

FUTURE STUDY AREAS

This research project is a small contribution to a large pool of scholarship on pastoral identity. From a social and contextual perspective, the project points out that pastoral identity is, in part, interactional, relational, and constructional. By shifting a paradigm of looking at pastoral identity, the study naturally suggests further areas of inquiry and scrutiny. These areas include a more in-depth micro-macro analysis of pastoral identity, an interactive model of pastoral identity for parish ministers, a multidimensional approach to pastoral identity, a theology of a horizontal vocation, and perichoresis as a therapeutic mode.

First of all, the overall framework of the research project has been concerned with a social and contextual dimension of pastoral identity. In particular, the project has focused on a micro-level social/interactional dimension and a macro-level postmodern contextual aspect of pastoral identity. More areas to explore in a future study include, at a micro-level, care-receivers' perceptions of their caregivers' identities and practices and the recipients' interpretations of pastoral care-giving relationships and interactions. For this purpose, a researcher needs a field observation of care-giving and receiving interactions and in-depth interview with care-seekers as well as care-providers.

From a macro-level perspective, future studies need to examine the influence of institutions on pastoral identity. Previously, pastoral theologians have focused on influences of a particular faith tradition and church expectations on pastoral identity (J. L. Marshall 1994; Moore 1982). Concerning contemporary clinical contexts, future studies need to look closely at how secular institutional policies and expectations impact a pastoral caregiver's identities and practices. The studies should also determine how these institutional practices and powers impose limits on potential language in pastoral care-giving and constructing pastoral identity. Furthermore, the future studies ultimately need to employ a comprehensive approach to pastoral practices and identity by looking at how both faith and secular institutional powers interplay in pastoral care-giving within religiously and culturally diverse contexts.

In a related vein, secondly, this research project exclusively focused on clinical pastoral contexts. For the study's purpose, the targeted population of the empirical study was chaplains and pastoral counselors. Future studies may need to cross-check in order to apply the findings of this study to parish ministers' pastoral identity construction. In parish settings, ministers have better potential language and protected authorities for ministry than do pastoral clinicians. Despite ecclesial and denominational endorsement of pastoral authorities, parish ministers also have trouble with their pastoral identities as transcendental values and authorities fade in postmodern environments and as parishioners' faith and theological wisdom compete with scientific knowledge. In that situation, clergypersons can easily experience burnout because of a "blurred pastoral identity" more than of overwork (Trull et al. 2004, 24). Questions to be examined include how parish ministers interact with their parishioners in this postmodern context and whether and how the ministers recognize these interactions as a valuable contribution that calls out their pastoral identities. What if, for instance, the Drew theologians look at personal and congregational needs and expectations placed on parish ministers as a challenge for and contribution to a social construction of pastoral identity, instead of seeing the needs as overshadowing the pastors' sense of calling? Future studies need to explore a possible relational model of pastoral identity for parish ministers.

Third, a more comprehensive future research project is needed from a multidimensional perspective. Identity forms and develops in its psycho-developmental and socio-cultural dimensions (Côté 1996). In the same sense, a more comprehensive approach to pastoral identity should integrate psycho-developmental approaches with a renewed socio-cultural approach.

Such an approach to pastoral identity will surely bring a rich conversation to varying forces influencing pastoral identity, including the faith community and traditions, institutional disciplines, ministerial and therapeutic methods, theological reflection, and multi-perspectives of personal and social issues. Also, an influence of public and prophetic participation in communal issues such as social, ethic, and gender injustice is another area to explore for pastoral identity construction.

Furthermore, I believe that this study has opened a path to develop a renewed theology of vocation that pays attention to a horizontal call. Theologians have rarely addressed this dimension of vocation. In *Called by God*, for instance, Frances Nemeck and Marie Coombs (1992) construct a theology of vocation from a relational and trinitarian perspective. However, their theological construction of vocation is vertical, viewing it as chosen, called, and consecrated by God. There is no place where calls from people who need our ministry can be accommodated.

The empirical research participants clearly expressed that their calls derive not only from God but also from human partners of ministry. The participants depicted how much the horizontal calls impact their pastoral identity and care-giving practices. In the Bible, when God called humans as God's co-workers, they also heard calls from those whom they would serve. For example, St. Paul had a vision in which a Macedonian was calling him (Acts 16:9–10). Constructing a theology of vocation that recognizes callings from the afflicted, oppressed, and marginalized will reshape a ground of Christian ministry as well as pastoral identity.

Finally, perichoresis as a dynamic interplay, out of love, between building a community and honoring the self is a crucial element of this study of pastoral identity. As we have seen, perichoresis is an excellent concept for bridging self and relation, person and community, agency and structure, identity and sociality, unity and multiplicity, and stability and fluidity to name a few. Thus, the concept of perichoresis has rich implications for Christian theology and ministry (e.g., Lawler 1995). In particular, perichoresis sheds light on pastoral practices and relationships and theory building of pastoral care, counseling, and theology. Future studies need to articulate how perichoresis can work as a central therapeutic mode in pastoral care and counseling.

FINAL REMARKS

To conclude, pastoral counselor Linda captures what we have discussed:

> When they [care-seekers] have the courage to be vulnerable, it allows me to minister to their deepest need, which I think is the good news that they can't be excluded from God's love ... When they allow me to know their deepest fears I think what they are telling me is who they really are. And, they are afraid that who they really are is unredeemable, unlovable, [and] unacceptable. And, when they can be that vulnerable to let me see who they really are ... that gives me the opportunity to reframe or reinterpret or re-image with them what that means and who they really are ... When a client exposes [his or her] identity ... I think both of us enter into those most profound questions about who we really are. So, as they are struggling with their identity it helps me construct mine. (I20)

Pastoral identity is a central theme of Christian scholarship and ministry. Based on calls from God and from those who need help and on the relationships and interactions with the callers in a specific care-giving context, pastoral caregivers construct their pastoral identities. Pastoral identity is embedded in a dynamic interplay of fluidity and stability of perichoretic pastoral relationships. Pastoral identity is an embodiment of mutually transforming relationships (between the partners of ministry) of divine love, care, healing, and liberation.

Bibliography

Adler, P. A., & Adler, P. (1999). Transience and the postmodern self: The geographic mobility of resort workers. *Sociological Quarterly, 40*(1), 31–58.
Anderson, H. (1998). Pastoral theology after Christendom. *Journal of Pastoral Theology, 8* 29–41.
Anderson, H., & Scanlon, J. (1994). Symposium: Supervision and formation in Christian ministry. *Journal of Supervision and Training in Ministry, 15*, 116–242.
Ashby, H. U. J. (2000). Pastoral theology as public theology: Participating in the healing of damaged and damaging cultures and institutions. *Journal of Pastoral Theology, 10*, 18–27.
Berzonsky, M. D. A (1993). Constructivist view of identity development: People as postpositivist self-theorists. In J. Kroger (Ed.) *Discussions on ego identity* (pp. 169–203). Hillsdale, NJ: L. Erlbaum.
Bidwell, D. R., & Marshall, J. L. (2006). *The formation of pastoral counselors: Challenges and opportunities.* Binghamton, NY: Haworth Pastoral.
Bier, W. C. (1959). Goals in pastoral counseling. *Pastoral Psychology, 10*(91), 7–13.
Blumer, H. (1969). *Symbolic interactionism: Perspective and method.* Englewood Cliffs, NJ: Prentice-Hall.
Blumer, H., & Morrione, T. J. (2004). *George Herbert Mead and human conduct.* Walnut Creek, CA: AltaMira.
Browning, D. S. (1991). *A fundamental practical theology: Descriptive and strategic proposals.* Minneapolis: Fortress.
———. (2000). *From culture wars to common ground: Religion and the American family debate.* Louisville: Westminster John Knox.
Burke, P. J. (2003). *Advances in identity and research.* New York: Kluwer Academic/Plenum.
Burton, A. L., & Weinrich, C. A. (1990). So great a cloud of witnesses: The use of family systems process in forming pastoral identity and facilitating pastoral functioning. *Journal of Pastoral Care, 44*(4), 331–41.
Callero, P. L. (2003). The sociology of the self. *Annual Review of Sociology, 29*(1), 115–33.
Childs, B. H. (1993). Community service setting. In Robert Wicks, Richard Parsons, and Donald Capps (Eds.) *Clinical handbook of pastoral counseling vol. 2* (pp. 425–39). New York: Paulist.
Chopp, R. S. (1995). *Saving work: Feminist practices of theological education.* Louisville: Westminster John Knox.

Clinebell, H. J. (1984). *Basic types of pastoral care and counseling: Resources for the ministry of healing and growth* (Rev. and enl. ed.). Nashville: Abingdon.

Coakley, S. (2001). Kenosis: Theological meanings and gender connotations. In J. Polkinghorne (Ed.), *The work of love: Creation as kenosis* (pp. 192–210). Grand Rapids: Eerdmans.

Coombs, M. T., & Nemeck, F. K. (1992). *Called by God: A theology of vocation and lifelong commitment*. Collegeville, MN: Liturgical.

Cooper-White, P. (2004). *Shared wisdom: Use of the self in pastoral care and counseling*. Minneapolis: Fortress.

Côté, J. (1996). Identity: A multidimensional analysis. In G. R. Adams, R. Montemayor & T. P. Gullotta (Eds.), *Psychosocial development during adolescence* (pp. 130–80). Thousand Oaks, CA: SAGE.

———. (2005). Editor's introduction. *Identity: An International Journal of Theory and Research*, 5(2), 95–96.

———. (2006). Identity studies: How close are we to developing a social science of identity?—An appraisal of the field. *Identity: An International Journal of Theory and Research*, 6(1), 3–25.

Côté, J. E., & Levine, C. (2002). *Identity formation, agency, and culture: A social psychological synthesis*. Mahwah, NJ: L. Erlbaum.

Couture, P. D. (1991). *Blessed are the poor? Women's poverty, family policy, and practical theology*. Nashville: Abingdon.

———. (1996). Weaving the web: Pastoral care in an individualistic society. In J. Stevenson-Moessner (Ed.), *Through the eyes of women: Insights for pastoral care* (pp. 94–106). Minneapolis: Fortress.

———. (2000). *Seeing children, seeing God: A practical theology of children and poverty*. Nashville: Abingdon.

———. (2003). The effect of the postmodern on pastoral/practical theology and care and counseling. *Journal of Pastoral Theology*, 13(1), 85–104.

Creswell, J. W. (2002). *Educational research: Planning, conducting, and evaluating quantitative and qualitative research*. Upper Saddle River, NJ: Merrill.

Crisp, O. D. (2005). Problems with perichoresis. *Tyndale Bulletin*, 56(1), 119–40.

———. (2007). *Divinity and humanity: The incarnation reconsidered*. Cambridge: Cambridge University Press.

Crump, D. (2006). Re-examining the Johannine trinity: Perichoresis or deification? *Scottish Journal of Theology*, 59(4), 395–412.

Danker, F. W. (2000). *A Greek-English lexicon of the New Testament and other early Christian literature* (3rd ed.). Chicago: University of Chicago Press.

Davis, J. J. (2012). Practicing ministry in the presence of God in partnership with God: The ontology of ministry and pastoral identity: A trinitarian-ecclesial model. *Evangelical Review of Theology*, 36(2), 115–136.

Dittes, J. E. (1999). *Pastoral counseling: The basics* (1st ed.). Louisville: Westminster John Knox.

Doehring, C. (1995). *Taking care: Monitoring power dynamics and relational boundaries in pastoral care and counseling*. Nashville: Abingdon.

Doehring, C. (2006). *The practice of pastoral care: A postmodern approach*. Louisville: Westminster John Knox.

Egan, J. P. (1994). Toward trinitarian perichoresis: Saint Gregory the theologian, (oration) 31.41. *Greek Orthodox Theological Review*, 39(12), 83–93.

Engelhardt, T. H. J. (1998). Generic chaplaincy: Providing spiritual care in a post-Christian age. *Christian Bioethics (Routledge), 4*(3), 231–38.
Everett, C. A., & Seaton-Johnson, A. W. (1983). An analysis of pastoral counseling supervisors: Their identities, roles and resources. *Journal of Pastoral Care, 37*(1), 50–59.
Farley, E. (1983). *Theologia: The fragmentation and unity of theological education*. Philadelphia: Fortress.
———. (1988). *The fragility of knowledge: Theological education in the church and the university*. Philadelphia: Fortress.
Fishburn, J. F., & Hamilton, N. Q. (1984). Seminary education tested by praxis. *Christian Century, 101*(4), 108–12.
Franks, D. D. (2003). Emotions. In L. T. Reynolds, & N. J. Herman-Kinney (Eds.), *Handbook of symbolic interactionism* (pp. 787–809). Walnut Creek, CA: AltaMira.
Fukuyama, M. A., & Sevig, T. D. (2004). Cultural diversity in pastoral care. *Journal of Health Care Chaplaincy, 13*(2), 25–42.
Furlong, A., & Cartmel, F. (2007). *Young people and social change: New perspectives* (2nd ed.). Maidenhead: McGraw-Hill/Open University Press.
Gadamer, H. (1975). *Truth and method*. New York: Seabury.
Gergen, K. J. (1991). *The saturated self: Dilemmas of identity in contemporary life*. New York: Basic Books.
Gerkin, C. V. (1966). Identity of the pastoral supervisor. In Institute of Pastoral Care (Ed.), *Pastoral supervisor and his identity: Fall conference of chaplain supervisors* (73–99). Atlantic City, NJ: Council for Clinical Training.
———. (1967). Interprofessional healing and pastoral identity. *Saint Luke's Journal of Theology, 11*(1), 25–31.
———. (1984). *The living human document: Re-visioning pastoral counseling in a hermeneutical mode*. Nashville: Abingdon.
———. (1997). *An introduction to pastoral care*. Nashville: Abingdon.
Giddens, A. (1991). *Modernity and self-identity: Self and society in the late modern age*. Stanford, CA: Stanford University Press.
Gill-Austern, B. L. (2003). Pastoral counseling: The art of ascetic witnessing. *Pastoral Psychology, 52*(12), 81–96.
Glaser, B. G. (1992). *Emergence vs forcing: Basics of grounded theory analysis*. Mill Valley, CA: Sociology.
Glaser, B. G., & Strauss, A. L. (1967). *The discovery of grounded theory: Strategies for qualitative research*. Chicago: Aldine.
Goodliff, P. (1998). *Care in a confused climate: Pastoral care and postmodern culture*. London: Darton, Longman and Todd.
Graham, L. K. (1996). *Transforming practice: Pastoral theology in an age of uncertainty*. London: Mowbray.
Greenwald, C. A., Greer, J. M., Gillespie, C. K., & Greer, T. V. (2004). A study of the identity of pastoral counselors. *American Journal of Pastoral Counseling 7*(4), 51–69. doi:10.1300/J062v7n04•04
Grenz, S. J. (2001). *The social God and the relational self: A trinitarian theology of the imago Dei* (1st ed.). Louisville: Westminster John Knox.
———. (2004). *Rediscovering the triune God: The trinity in contemporary theology*. Minneapolis: Fortress.

Grey, M. C. (2004). *Sacred longings: The ecological spirit and global culture*. Minneapolis: Fortress.
Gunton, C. E. (1992). *Christ and creation*. Grand Rapids: Eerdmans.
———. (1993). *The one, the three, and the many: God, creation, and the culture of modernity*. Cambridge: Cambridge University Press.
———. (1997). *The promise of trinitarian theology* (2nd ed.). Edinburgh: T. & T. Clark.
Hardwick, G. L. (1995). The development of pastoral identity in parish ministers and pastoral counselors of the United Methodist Church (doctoral dissertation). Garrett-Evangelical Theological Seminary.
Harris, H. A. (1998). Should we say that personhood is relational. *Scottish Journal of Theology*, 51(2), 214–34.
Harrison, V. E. F. (1991). Perichoresis in the Greek fathers. *St Vladimir's Theological Quarterly*, 35(1), 53–65.
Hauerwas, S. (1998). *Sanctify them in the truth: Holiness exemplified*. Nashville: Abingdon.
Hermans, C. A. M., Immink, G., Jong, A. d., & Lans, J. v. d. (2002). *Social constructionism and theology*. Leiden: Brill.
Hiltner, S., & Colston, L. G. (1961). *The context of pastoral counseling*. New York: Abingdon.
Holstein, J. A., & Gubrium, J. F. (2000). *The self we live by: Narrative identity in a postmodern world*. New York: Oxford University Press.
———. (2003). *Inside interviewing: New lenses, new concerns*. Thousand Oaks, CA: SAGE.
Horton, M. S. (2006). Post-reformation reformed anthropology. In R. Lints, M. S. Horton, & M. R. Talbot, *Personal Identity in Theological Perspective* (pp. 45–69). Grand Rapids: Eerdmans.
Houck, J. B. (1974). The professional role identity of pastoral counselors (doctoral dissertation). Illinois Institute of Technology.
Hough, J. C., & Cobb, J. B. (1985). *Christian identity and theological education*. Chico, CA: Scholars.
Howard, J. A. (2000). Social psychology of identities. *Annual Review of Sociology*, 26(1), 367–93.
Hughes, E. (1998). Two contemporary examples of Christian love. *Christian Bioethics (Routledge)*, 4(3), 279–83.
Huh, John Joon-Young. (2011). Embracing your bicultural identity: Implications for pastoral theologians from an Asian American perspective. *Pastoral Psychology*, 60(3), 355–62.
Hunsinger, D. v. D. (1995). *Theology and pastoral counseling: A new interdisciplinary approach*. Grand Rapids: Eerdmans.
Hunter, G. I. (1982). *Supervision and education—formation for ministry*. Cambridge, MA: Episcopal Divinity School.
Hunter, R. J. (1997). A bird's eye view: Postmodernism and the future of pastoral care. *Journal of Pastoral Care*, 51(4), 373–75.
———. (1998). Religious caregiving and pedagogy in a postmodern context. *Journal of Pastoral Theology*, 8, 15–27.
Institute of Pastoral Care. (1966). *Pastoral supervisor and his identity: Fall conference of chaplain supervisors*. Atlantic City, NJ: Council for Clinical Training.

Jackson, G. E. (1964). Pastoral counselor: His identity and work. *Journal of Religion and Health*, 3(3), 250–70.

Jacque, Z. (2006). Formation in the context of economic disparity. *American Journal of Pastoral Counseling*, 8(3), 125–41. doi:10.1300/J062v08n03☒09

Jennings, J. T. W. (2005). Pastoral theological methodology. In R. J. Hunter, & N. J. Ramsay (Eds.), *Dictionary of pastoral care and counseling* (Expanded ed. with CD-ROM, 862–64). Nashville: Abingdon.

Jernigan, H. L. (1961). Pastoral counseling and the identity of the pastor. *Journal of Pastoral Care*, 15(4), 193–203.

Johnson, E. A. (1992). *She who is: The mystery of God in feminist theological discourse*. New York: Crossroad.

Joseph, T. (1998). Secular vs. orthodox chaplaincy: Taking the kingdom of heaven seriously. *Christian Bioethics (Routledge)*, 4(3), 276–78.

Kae-Jé, B. (1993). Psychologist or theologian: Pastoral counseling, supervision, and professional identity. *Journal of Pastoral Care*, 47(1), 65–72.

Kelsey, D. H. (1993). *Between Athens and Berlin: The theological education debate*. Grand Rapids: Eerdmans.

Kuhn, M. H., & McPartland, T. S. (1954). An empirical investigation of self-attitudes. *American Sociological Review*, (19), 68–76. doi:10.2307/2088175

LaCugna, C. M. (1991). *God for us: The trinity and Christian life* (1st ed.). San Francisco: HarperSanFrancisco.

Lartey, E. Y. (2002). Embracing the collage: Pastoral theology in an era of "post-phenomena." *Journal of Pastoral Theology*, 12(2), 110.

———. (2003). *In living color: An intercultural approach to pastoral care and counseling* (2nd ed.). London: Jessica Kingsley.

———. (2004). Globalization, internationalization, and indigenization of pastoral care and counseling. In N. J. Ramsay (Ed.), *Pastoral care and counseling: Redefining the paradigms* (pp. 87–108). Nashville: Abingdon.

Lash, S., & Friedman, J. (1992). *Modernity and identity*. Cambridge, MA: Blackwell.

Lashley, M. E. (1994). *Being called to care*. Albany: State University of New York Press.

Lawler, M. G. (1995). Perichoresis: New theological wine in an old theological wineskin. *Horizons*, 22(1), 49–66.

Liddell, H. G., & Scott, R. (1846). *A Greek-English lexicon, based on the German work of Francis Passow*. New York: Harper.

Lints, R., Horton, M. S., & Talbot, M. R. (2006). *Personal identity in theological perspective*. Grand Rapids: Eerdmans.

Lyotard, J. (1984). *The postmodern condition: A report on knowledge*. Minneapolis: University of Minnesota Press.

Mann, C., & Stewart, F. (2003). Internet interviewing. In J. A. Holstein, & J. F. Gubrium (Eds.), *Inside interviewing* (pp. 241–65). Thousand Oaks, CA: SAGE.

Marsh, C. (2002). In defense of a self: The theological search for a postmodern identity. *Scottish Journal of Theology*, 55(3), 253–82.

Marshall, J. L. (1992). Internal pastoral authority in an ecclesial tradition: Psychological and theological dynamics (doctoral dissertation). Vanderbilt University.

———. (1994). Toward the development of a pastoral soul: Reflections on identity and theological education. *Pastoral Psychology*, 43(1), 11–28.

———. (2004). Methods in pastoral theology, care, and counseling. In N. J. Ramsay (Ed.), *Pastoral care and counseling: Redefining the paradigms* (pp. 133-54). Nashville: Abingdon.

Marshall, M. T. (2003). Participating in the life of God: A trinitarian pneumatology. *Perspectives in Religious Studies, 30*(2), 139-50.

McDougall, J. A. (2002). Room of one's own? Trinitarian perichoresis as analogy for the God-human relationship. In J. Moltmann, & C. Rivuzumwami (Eds.), *Wo ist gott? Gottesräume, lebensräume* (pp. 133-41). Neukirchen-Vluyn: Neukirchener.

———. (2005). *Pilgrimage of love: Moltmann on the trinity and christian life.* Oxford: Oxford University Press.

McFayden, K. J. (1994). Threats to the formation of pastoral identity in theological education: Insights from the Tavistock model of group relations (doctoral dissertation). Southern Baptist Theological Seminary.

McGrath-Merkle, C. (2011). Gregory the Great's metaphor of the physician of the heart as a model for pastoral identity. *Journal of Religion and Health, 50*(2), 374-88.

Mead, G. H., & Morris, C. W. (1934). *Mind, self and society from the standpoint of a social behaviorist.* Chicago: University of Chicago Press.

Mellon, B. F. (2003). Faith-to faith at the bedside: Theological and ethical issues in ecumenical clinical chaplaincy. *Christian Bioethics (Routledge), 9*(1), 57-67.

Miller-McLemore, B. J. (1993). The human web: Reflections on the state of pastoral theology. *Christian Century, 110*(11), 36-69.

———. (2003). *Let the children come: Reimagining childhood from a christian perspective.* San Francisco: Jossey-Bass.

———. (2004). Pastoral theology as public theology: Revolutions in the "fourth area." In N. J. Ramsay (Ed.), *Pastoral care and counseling: Redefining the paradigms* (pp. 45-64). Nashville: Abingdon.

———. (2008). Revisiting the living human web: Theological education and the role of clinical pastoral education. *The Journal of Pastoral Care and Counseling: JPCC, 62*(12), 3-18.

Moltmann, J. (1981). *The trinity and the kingdom: The doctrine of God.* San Francisco: Harper & Row.

———. (1991). *The crucified God: The cross of Christ as the foundation and criticism of Christian theology.* San Francisco: HarperSanFrancisco.

———. (1992). *History and the triune God: Contributions to trinitarian theology.* New York: Crossroad.

———. (2000a). *Experiences in theology: Ways and forms of Christian theology.* Minneapolis: Fortress.

———. (2000b). Perichoresis: An old magic word for a new trinitarian theology. In D. M. Meeks (Ed.), *Trinity, community, and power: Mapping trajectories in Wesleyan theology* (pp. 111-25). Nashville: Kingswood.

———. (2001). God's kenosis in the creation and consummation of the world. In J. C. Polkinghorne (Ed.), *Work of love: Creation as kenosis* (pp. 137-51). Grand Rapids: Eerdmans.

———. (2008). God in the world—the world in God: Perichoresis in trinity and eschatology. *Gospel of John and Christian theology* (pp. 369-81). Grand Rapids: Eerdmans.

Moore, R. P. (1982). Identity formation of psychotherapy supervisors: An exploratory study of Anne Alonso's theory (doctoral dissertation). Boston University.

Moss, D. M., III. (1981). Pastoral identity and the fee-for-service contract. *Organization and administration of pastoral counseling centers* (pp. 115–22). Nashville: Abingdon.
Mosser, C. (2002). The greatest possible blessing: Calvin and deification. *Scottish Journal of Theology, 55*(1), 36–57.
Mucherera, T. N. (2006). Pastoral formation of counselors in intercultural societies. *American Journal of Pastoral Counseling, 8*(3), 99–111.
Mudge, L. S., & Poling, J. N. (1987). *Formation and reflection: The promise of practical theology*. Philadelphia: Fortress.
Narramore, B. (1973). Therapist identification and role identity as a barrier to integrative Christian counseling. *Journal of Psychology and Theology, 1*(4), 39.
Nauta, R. (1993). Pastoral identity and communication. *Journal of Empirical Theology, 6*(2), 5–31.
–––. (1996). Psychological dynamics of pastoral identity: The different faces of empathy. *Journal of Empirical Theology, 9*(1), 51–68.
–––. (2003). The performance of authenticity: Ordination and profession in pastoral care. *Pastoral Psychology, 51*(5), 425–31.
Neuger, C. C. (1998). Religious belief in a postmodern era: Framing the issues. *Journal of Pastoral Theology, 8*, 114.
–––. (1999). Women and relationality. *Feminist and womanist pastoral theology* (pp. 113–32). Nashville: Abingdon.
–––. (2000). Narratives of harm: Setting the developmental context for intimate violence. In J. Stevenson-Moessner (Ed.), *In her own time: Women and developmental issues in pastoral care* (pp. 65–86). Minneapolis: Fortress.
–––. (2004). Power and difference in pastoral theology. In N. J. Ramsay (Ed.), *Pastoral care and counseling: Redefining the paradigms* (pp. 65–85). Nashville: Abingdon.
Niebuhr, H. R. (1956). *The purpose of the church and its ministry: Reflections on the aims of theological education* (1st ed. ed.). New York: Harper.
Oates, W. E. (1982). *The Christian pastor* (3rd ed., rev ed.). Philadelphia: Westminster.
O'Brien, M. R. (2007). A study of ministerial identity and theological reflection among lay ecclesial ministers. *International Journal of Practical Theology, 11*(2), 212–33. doi:10.1515/IJPT.2007.14
O'Connor, T. J., & Meakes, E. (2008). A Canadian qualitative study on theological reflection in pastoral care and counseling. *Journal of Spirituality in Mental Health, 10*(1), 19–34.
Oden, T. C. (1980). Recovering lost identity. *Journal of Pastoral Care, 34*(1), 4–23.
–––. (1988). Recovering pastoral care's lost identity. In L. Aden, & J. H. Ellens (Eds.), *The church and pastoral care* (pp. 17–31). Grand Rapids: Baker.
O'Hanlon, W. H., & Beadle, S. (1999). *A guide to possibility land: Fifty-one methods for doing brief, respectful therapy*. New York: Norton.
Otto, R. E. (2001). The use and abuse of perichoresis in recent theology. *Scottish Journal of Theology, 54*(3), 366–84.
Palmer, R. E. (1969). *Hermeneutics; interpretation theory in Schleiermacher, Dilthey, Heidegger, and Gadamer*. Evanston, IL: Northwestern University Press.
Pannenberg, W. (1977). *Jesus, God and man* (2nd ed.). Philadelphia: Westminster.
Park, S. (2005a). History and method of Charles V. Gerkin's pastoral theology: Toward an identity-embodied and community-embedded pastoral theology. part I, history. *Pastoral Psychology, 54*(1), 47–60.

———. (2005b). History and method of Charles V. Gerkin's pastoral theology: Toward an identity-embodied and community-embedded pastoral theology. part II, method. *Pastoral Psychology,* 54(1), 61–72.

———. (2007). An evolving history and methodology of pastoral theology, care, and counseling. *Journal of Spirituality in Mental Health,* 9(1), 5–33.

Patton, J. (1981). The pastoral counselor as specialist within ministry. *Pastoral Psychology,* 29(3), 159–68.

———. (1983). *Pastoral counseling: A ministry of the church.* Nashville: Abingdon.

———. (1993). *Pastoral care in context: An introduction to pastoral care* (1st ed.). Louisville: Westminster/John Knox.

Peters, T. (1993). *God as trinity: Relationality and temporality in divine life* (1st ed.). Louisville: Westminster/John Knox.

Poling, J. N. (1991). *The abuse of power: A theological problem.* Nashville: Abingdon.

Poling, J. N., & Miller, D. E. (1985). *Foundations for a practical theology of ministry.* Nashville: Abingdon.

Polkinghorne, J. C. (2001). *The work of love: Creation as kenosis.* Grand Rapids: Eerdmans.

Pruett, J. W. (2004). Pastoral counseling and supervision competence: A formation process. *Journal of Supervision and Training in Ministry,* 24, 33–43.

Rathbun, R. J. (2005). A pastoral theology of the self that focuses on relationality (doctoral dissertation). Brite Divinity School, Texas Christian University.

Rattansi, A., & Phoenix, A. (1997). Rethinking youth identities: Modernist and postmodernist frameworks. In J. M. Bynner, L. Chisholm & A. Furlong (Eds.), *Youth, citizenship and social change in a European context* (pp. 121–50). Brookfield, VT: Ashgate. doi:10.1207/s15327060xid0502_2

Reynolds, L. T., & Herman-Kinney, N. J. (2003). *Handbook of symbolic interactionism.* Walnut Creek, CA: AltaMira.

Rollins, E. C. (1987). Facilitating the process and development of personal and professional identity: Through the use of autobiographical story within the context of clinical pastoral education (doctoral dissertation). Drew University.

Ryan, G. W., & Bernard, R. H. (2000). Data management and analysis methods. In N. K. Denzin, & Y. S. Lincoln (Eds.), *Handbook of qualitative research* (2nd ed., pp. 769–802). Thousand Oaks, CA: SAGE.

Sager, A. H. (1994). Why not try this on as a metaphor for ministry: Pastoral identity revisited. *Trinity Seminary Review,* 16(1), 17–20.

Sanderson, P. D. (1977). A descriptive analysis of supervision in clinical pastoral education (doctoral dissertation). Boston University.

Sandstrom, K. L., & Fine, G. A. (2003). Triumphs, emerging voices, and the future. In L. T. Reynolds, & N. J. Herman-Kinney (Eds.), *Handbook of symbolic interactionism* (pp. 104–57). Walnut Creek, CA: AltaMira.

Scalise, C. J. (2003). *Bridging the gap: Connecting what you learned in seminary with what you find in the congregation.* Nashville: Abingdon.

Schilling-Estes, N. (2004). Constructing ethnicity in interaction. *Journal of Sociolinguistics,* 8(2), 163–95. doi:10.1111/j.1467–9841.2004.00257.x

Schmidt, K. W., & Egler, G. (1998). A Christian for the Christians, a Muslim for the Muslims? Reflections on a Protestant view of pastoral care for all religions. *Christian Bioethics (Routledge),* 4(3), 239–56.

Schneider-Harpprecht, C. (2003). Hospital chaplaincy across denominational, cultural and religious borders: Observations from the German context. *Christian Bioethics (Routledge), 9*(1), 91–107.
Schwandt, T. A. (2007). *The SAGE dictionary of qualitative inquiry* (3rd ed.). Los Angeles: SAGE.
Seale, C. F. (2003). Computer-assisted analysis of qualitative interview data. In J. A. Holstein, & J. F. Gubrium (Eds.), *Inside interviewing* (pp. 289–308). Thousand Oaks, CA: SAGE.
Seaton-Johnson, A. W., & Everett, C. A. (1980). An analysis of clinical pastoral education supervisors: Their identities, roles and resources. *Journal of Pastoral Care, 34*(3), 148–58.
Sedgwick, P. H. (2001). Who am I now? Theology and self-identity. *Theology, 104*(819), 196–203.
Shostrom, F. L. (1985). The definition and assessment of professional identity in clergy (doctoral dissertation). Kansas State University.
Sievernich, S. J. M. (2003). Pastoral care for the sick in a post-secular age: An Ignatian perspective. *Christian Bioethics (Routledge), 9*(1), 23–37.
Siewert, C. (2006). Consciousness and intentionality. In E. N. Zalta (Ed.), *The Stanford Encyclopedia of Philosophy* (fall 2008 ed., online).
Simmons, E. L. (2006). Quantum *perichoresis*: Quantum field theory and the trinity. *Theology and Science, 4*(2), 137–50.
Smith, H. L. (1972). Language, belief, authority: Crises for Christian ministry and professional identity. *Pastoral Psychology, 23*(223), 15–21.
Smith, S. M. (2001). Kenosis, kenotic theology. In W. A. Elwell (Ed.), *Evangelical dictionary of theology* (2nd ed. ed., pp. 651–53). Grand Rapids: Baker Academic.
Sophocles, E. A. (1957). *Greek lexicon of the Roman and Byzantine periods (from B.C. 146 to A.D. 1100)*. New York: F. Ungar.
Stead, J. (1953). Perichoresis in the christological chapters of the *de tritate* of pseudo-Cyril of Alexandria. *Dominican Studies, 6*, 12–20.
Stokes, A. (1985). *Ministry after Freud*. New York: Pilgrim.
Stone, H. W. (1994). *Brief pastoral counseling*. Minneapolis: Fortress.
———. (2001). *Strategies for brief pastoral counseling*. Minneapolis: Fortress.
Stramara, D. F. J. (1998). Gregory of Nyssa's terminology for trinitarian perichoresis. *Vigiliae Christianae, 52*(3), 257–63.
Strauss, A. L., & Corbin, J. M. (1990). *Basics of qualitative research: Grounded theory procedures and techniques*. Newbury Park, CA: SAGE.
———. (1997). *Grounded theory in practice*. Thousand Oaks, CA: SAGE.
———. (1998). *Basics of qualitative research: Techniques and procedures for developing grounded theory* (2nd ed.). Thousand Oaks, CA: SAGE.
Thiselton, A. C. (1995). *Interpreting God and the postmodern self: On meaning, manipulation, and promise*. Grand Rapids: Eerdmans.
Thornton, E. E. (2005). Identity, pastoral. In R. J. Hunter, & N. J. Ramsay (Eds.), *Dictionary of pastoral care and counseling* (Expanded ed. with CD-ROM ed., pp. 56–78). Nashville: Abingdon.
Torrance, T. F. (1982). *Reality and evangelical theology* (1st ed.). Philadelphia: Westminster.
———. (1996). *The Christian doctrine of God: One being three persons*. Edinburgh: T. & T. Clark.

Townsend, L. L. (2002). Theological reflection, pastoral counseling and supervision. *Journal of Pastoral Theology*, 12(1), 63–74.

———. (2006). Theological reflection and the formation of pastoral counselors. *American Journal of Pastoral Counseling*, 8(3), 29–46. doi:10.1300/J062v08n03⊠03

Trull, J. E., & Carter, J. E.,. (2004). *Ministerial ethics: Moral formation for church leaders*. Grand Rapids: Baker Academic.

VandeCreek, L., & Burton, L. (2001). Professional chaplaincy: Its role and importance in healthcare. *Journal of Pastoral Care*, (1), 81–97.

Volf, M. (1996). *Exclusion and embrace: A theological exploration of identity, otherness, and reconciliation*. Nashville: Abingdon.

Vryan, K. D., Adler, P. A., & Adler, P. (2003). Identity. In L. T. Reynolds, & N. J. Herman-Kinney (Eds.), *Handbook of symbolic interactionism* (pp. 367–90). Walnut Creek, CA: AltaMira.

Ward, K. (2001). Cosmos and kenosis. In J. Polkinghorne (Ed.), *The work of love: Creation as kenosis* (pp. 152–66). Grand Rapids: Eerdmans.

Warren, H. A., Murray, J. L., & Best, M. M. (2002). The discipline and habit of theological reflection. *Journal of Religion & Health*, 41(4), 323–31.

Webb, K. S. (1990). Pastoral identity and the ministry of presence. *Journal of Pastoral Care*, 44(1), 76–79.

Weigert, A. J., & Gecas, V. (2005). Symbolic interactionist reflections on Erikson, identity, and postmodernism. *Identity: An International Journal of Theory and Research*, 5(2), 161–74. doi:10.1207/s1532706xid0502_5

Wenger, E. (1998). *Communities of practice: Learning, meaning, and identity*. Cambridge: Cambridge University Press.

Wimberly, E. P. (1980). The pastor's theological identity formation. *Journal of the Interdenominational Theological Center*, 7(2), 145–56.

———. (2003). Pastoral theological method and post-nihilism. *Journal of Pastoral Theology*, 13(1), 25–35.

Wittwer, T. (2006). Pastoral formation: Storying professional identity. *Lutheran Theological Journal*, 40(1), 20–27.

Wolfson, H. A. (1964). *The philosophy of the church fathers* (2nd ed., rev ed.). Cambridge, MA: Harvard University Press.

Woodhead, L. (1999). Theology and the fragmentation of the self. *International Journal of Systematic Theology*, 1(1), 53–72.

Yang, B. (2002). A study of pastoral identity in light of the works of Henri J. M. Nouwen and its implication for the Korean pastoral context (doctoral dissertation). Southwestern Baptist Theological Seminary.

Yim, R. J. R. (2001). The discipline: Its impact on my theological perspective, pastoral identity and practice. *Journal of Health Care Chaplaincy*, 10(2), 69–81.

Young, J. H. (1997). Seeking pastoral identity for those in ordained ministry. *Touchstone*, 15, 415.

Zierenberg, M. (2003). The word's eternal silence: A commentary on Schneider-Harpprecht's essay. *Christian Bioethics (Routledge)*, 9(1), 109–22.

Zimmerman, J. S. (1953). Christian theological approach to clinical pastoral training. *Journal of Pastoral Care*, 7(2), 59–76.

Zizioulas, J. (1985). *Being as communion: Studies in personhood and the church*. Crestwood, NY: St. Vladimir's Seminary Press.

Zock, H. (2008). The split professional identity of the chaplain as a spiritual caregiver in contemporary Dutch health care: Are there implications for the United States? *Journal of Pastoral Care and Counseling, 62*(1–2), 13–79.

www.ingramcontent.com/pod-product-compliance
Lightning Source LLC
Chambersburg PA
CBHW070256230426

43664CB00014B/2551